Heads in the Sand

Heads in the Sand

How the Republicans Screw Up Foreign Policy and Foreign Policy Screws Up the Democrats

MATTHEW YGLESIAS

WILEY

John Wiley & Sons, Inc.

Published by John Wiley & Sons, Inc., Hoboken, New Jersey
Published simultaneously in Canada

For general information about our other products and services, please contact our
Customer Care Department within the United States at (800) 762-2974, outside
the United States at (317) 572-3993 or fax (317) 572-4002.

Wiley also publishes its books in a variety of electronic formats. Some content that
appears in print may not be available in electronic books. For more information
about Wiley products, visit our web site at www.wiley.com.

Library of Congress Cataloging-in-Publication Data:

Yglesias, Matthew, date.
    Heads in the sand: how the Republicans screw up foreign policy and foreign policy
screws up the Democrats/Matthew Yglesias.
        p. cm.
    Includes bibliographical references and index.
    ISBN 978-0-470-08622-3 (cloth)
    1. United States—Foreign relations–2001– 2. Political parties—United States.
    3. Democratic Party (U.S.) 4. Republican Party (U.S.: 1854–) I. Title.
    JZ1480.Y45 2008
    327.73—dc22

                                                                    2007044574

Printed in the United States of America

10 9 8 7 6 5 4 3 2 1

To the memory of my mother,
Margaret Karen Joskow

CONTENTS

PREFACE

THE ETERNAL RECURRENCE
OF TOM FRIEDMAN

Writing in the November 20, 2003, issue of the *New York Times*, the columnist Thomas Friedman, probably the most influential foreign affairs commentator in the country, opined that "the next six months in Iraq—which will determine the prospects for democracy-building there—are the most important six months in U.S. foreign policy in a long, long time."[1] This was a bold proclamation, and the world waited with bated breath for the outcome. But on the June 3, 2004, episode of NPR's *Fresh Air*, Friedman expressed impatience with anti-war liberals who wanted to see the war brought to an end. "What I absolutely don't understand," he said, "is just at the moment when we finally have a UN-approved Iraqi-caretaker government made up of—I know a lot of these guys—reasonably decent people and more than reasonably decent people, everyone wants to declare it's over. I don't get it. It might be over in a week, it might be over in a month, it might be over in six months, but what's the rush? Can we let this play out, please?"

Obviously, it did play out. Just as obviously, it wasn't over one month later and it wasn't over six months later. Instead, on the October 3, 2004, edition of *Face the Nation*, Friedman told host Bob Schieffer that "what we're gonna find out, Bob, in the next six to nine months is whether we have liberated a country or uncorked a civil war." Two months later, Friedman's patience with the war was running thin, as he wrote in his *Times* column that "Improve time is over. This is crunch time. Iraq will be won or lost in the next few months. But it won't be won with high rhetoric. It will be won on the ground in a war over the last mile."[2]

Thus a full year after Friedman first proclaimed the next six months to be decisive, he determined that the next few months were going to be decisive. Were they? Well, no. On the September 25, 2005, edition of *Meet the Press*, Friedman announced to Tim Russert that "we're in the end game now." In particular, "I think we're in a six-month window where it's going to become very clear and this is all going to preempt, I think, the next congressional election—that's my own feeling—let alone the presidential one." Three days later in his *Times* column he mused "Maybe the cynical Europeans were right. Maybe this neighborhood is just beyond transformation. That will become clear in the next few months as we see just what kind of minority the Sunnis in Iraq intend to be. If they come around, a decent outcome in Iraq is still possible, and we should stay to help build it. If they won't, then we are wasting our time."[3] Back on *Face the Nation* on December 18, 2005, he said "We've teed up this situation for Iraqis, and I think the next six months really are going to determine whether this country is going to collapse into three parts or more or whether it's going to come together." Two days later, he repeated the point on PBS's *Charlie Rose*: "We're at the beginning of, I think, the decisive, I would say, six months in

Iraq, OK, because I feel like this election—You know, I felt from the beginning Iraq was going to be ultimately, Charlie, what Iraqis make of it." Then, on the January 23, 2006, edition of *The Oprah Winfrey Show*, Friedman said, "I think we're going to know after six to nine months whether this project has any chance of succeeding—in which case, I think the American people as a whole will want to play it out—or whether it really is a fool's errand."

But two months after he appeared on *Face the Nation*, on the February 2 edition of NBC's *Today*, Friedman hadn't changed the time frame. Instead, he argued that "the next six to nine months are going to tell whether we can produce a decent outcome in Iraq." And on the May 11, 2006, edition of *Hardball*, Friedman extended the window, telling Chris Matthews that "I think that we're going to find out, Chris, in the next year to six months—probably sooner—whether a decent outcome is possible there, and I think we're going to have to just let this play out."

Two and a half years after Friedman first told the American people that they were facing a decisive six-month period in Iraq, the columnist still thought we were six to twelve months away from knowing for sure. The columnist's habit of ever-shifting goalposts then became the subject of a report by the lefty media watchdog group Fairness and Accuracy in Reporting (FAIR).[4] The FAIR account gave birth to the term *Friedman Unit* (FU), in the blogosphere, meaning a six-month window of opportunity in Iraq with the implication that, like Friedman, the speaker would never actually pull the plug. Thus when Zalmay Khalilzad, then the U.S. ambassador to Baghdad, told NPR's *All Things Considered*, that "the next nine months are critical" back on June 29, 2005, he was predicting that we were 1.5 FUs away from having a better grasp on the Iraq situation. I dubbed the phenomenon "The Eternal Recurrence of Tom Friedman," referencing a passage from Nietzsche:

What, if some day or night a demon were to steal after you into your loneliest loneliness and say to you: "This life as you now live it and have lived it, you will have to live once more and innumerable times more; and there will be nothing new in it, but every pain and every joy and every thought and sigh and everything unutterably small or great in your life will have to return to you, all in the same succession and sequence—even this spider and this moonlight between the trees, and even this moment and I myself. The eternal hourglass of existence is turned upside down again and again, and you with it, speck of dust!" Would you not throw yourself down and gnash your teeth and curse the demon who spoke thus? Or have you once experienced a tremendous moment when you would have answered him: "You are a god and never have I heard anything more divine."

For the past five or six years, American liberals have been in the first of Nietzsche's scenarios, gnashing our teeth and cursing at demons as we watch the same mistakes get made over and over again.

On September 11, 2001, the country was attacked by terrorists who murdered thousands of innocent people. Shortly—indeed, almost immediately—after that, George W. Bush and his allies in and out of government began an effort to use the sense of crisis created by the attacks to begin implementing a radically unsound approach to world affairs, an approach whose most famous manifestation has been a tragically failed effort to invade and transform Iraq. In those early post-attack months, a very broad and influential swathe of the American establishment, including many leading voices of the center-left like Friedman, chose to essentially go along with Bush and his ideas. Friedman himself explained shortly after the invasion on *Charlie Rose* that "what they needed to see was American boys and girls going from house to house from Basra to Baghdad, saying basically 'Which part of this sentence don't you understand? You don't think we care about our open society, you think this bubble fantasy we're just going to let it go? Well suck on this.' That, Charlie, was what this war was all about." Not surprisingly, policies grounded in this sort of juvenile thinking resulted only in disaster. Most spectacularly in Iraq, but also to some extent in North Korea, in Afghanistan, in Somalia, in South America, and various other fields of American policy. But rather than admit error and simply cut bait, prominent opinion leaders preferred the sort of shuffling abdication typified by Friedman's endless delaying.

About six months after FAIR released its report on Friedman, his November 8 *Times* column finally started to show some self-awareness and pronounced that it was "time to make a final push for the tolerable, and if that fails, quit Iraq and insulate ourselves and our allies from the awful."[5] Just a few weeks later, however, when he next revisited the subject of the war he was already backpedaling from the idea of leaving. "Either we just get out of Iraq in a phased withdrawal over 10 months," he wrote on November 29, "and try to stabilize it some other way, or we accept the fact that the only way it will not be a failed state is if we start over and rebuild it from the ground up, which would take 10 years."[6] No decision to accept a thorough reconsideration of the nature of the mission in Iraq had been taken by July, so in his July 11 column Friedman simply reiterated what he had said months earlier, "we must not kid ourselves: our real choices in Iraq are either all in or all out—with the exception of Kurdistan. If those are our only real choices, then we need to look clearly at each."[7] Again, nothing happened, and again in August Friedman still wasn't ready to throw in the towel, saying instead that he might change his mind "if I saw something with my own eyes that I hadn't seen before—Iraq's Shiite, Kurdish and Sunni leaders stepping forward, declaring their willingness to work out their differences by a set *deadline* and publicly asking us to stay until they do. That's the only thing worth giving more time to develop."[8] By November, Friedman was still on the precipice of giving up, but not actually doing so: "If you were President Bush and your whole legacy was riding on the outcome of this war, wouldn't you be sending your top diplomat to Baghdad to work with Iraqis and their neighbors to broker a political settlement and not let them grow complacent that they have an open-ended commitment from the American people?"

Friedman also helpfully acknowledged that his "Iraq crystal ball stopped working a long time ago."[9] And, indeed, it had. This bout of indecision came fully four years after Friedman first proclaimed that "the next six months in Iraq" would "determine the prospects for democracy-building there."

None of which would matter if Friedman were merely an idiosyncratic columnist, even an extremely prominent one. He stands in, however, for a much broader trend of conventional wisdom that's come to acknowledge that Bush's policies have led to disaster but can't quite bring itself to reject them. Meanwhile, despite some honorable exceptions, the Democratic Party's role in this has mostly been to play Charlie Brown perennially falling down as Lucy yanks away the football, swearing not to be fooled again, and then doing the same thing over and over.

They do it because they have nothing better to do.

The simple answer for Charlie Brown is that he needs a football of his own, and the same is true for the Democrats.

Rejecting not just Bush, but Bushism—the use of military force to fight a grandiosely defined "war on terror" by asserting U.S. domination of the Middle East—would require a coherent alternative. Ask a prominent Democrat to explain that alternative and you might get a long-winded, useless answer, but you're more likely to get one of many recently created dodges. What you won't get is a clearly expressed, compelling worldview. Instead, with a few honorable exceptions, America's opposition party has let its positioning be guided almost entirely by short-term thinking and a conception of "political expediency" so shallow it doesn't even work in the short term. The good news is that better principles—principles that guided the Democratic Party, and indeed the country, until very recently—exist and are as vital as ever. If anything, more so now in the twenty-first century.

All that's needed is to understand what those principles are, how they came to be discarded during the Bush presidency, and why the world desperately needs them brought back to life.

ACKNOWLEDGMENTS

Thanks are owed in the first instance to my agent, Eric Lupfer of the William Morris Agency. Before I met him, I had resigned myself to the idea that a blogger's first book had to be about blogging rather than on a topic about which he had something worthwhile to say. Without Eric Lupfer, there would be no book. Without Eric Nelson, my editor at Wiley, the book in your hands would have been much longer and quite a bit worse.

Besides those who were actually paid to work on the manuscript, I was fortunate to have complete drafts read by Jim Henley, the lovely Sara Mead, and my father, whose life also happens to be an endless source of inspiration and motivation for a young writer. I also had the good fortune of developing most of these ideas in their initial form while working for the *American Prospect*, whose editors, Bob Kuttner, Paul Starr, Mike Tomasky, Sara Blustain, and Harold Meyerson, did me enormous good and whose track record of teaching brand-new journalists how to write is without peer. While there, I also had my privilege of sharpening my thinking in constant conversation with my colleagues Spencer Ackerman, Jeff Dubner, Garance Franke-Ruta, Ann Friedman, Mark Goldberg, Ezra Klein, Ayelish McGarvey, Alec Oveis, Sam Rosenfeld, Laura Rozen, and Kay Steiger. Beyond formal colleagues, I owe a debt to the invaluable support of my informal coworkers in the burgeoning blogging sector of the economy at the Flophouse and around the neighborhood—Catherine Andrews, Brian Beutler, Krison Capps, Sommer Mathis, Rebecca Piazza, and Julian Sanchez. My editors at the *Atlantic* proved remarkably understanding about my need to finish a manuscript during my first month on the job with them, especially since I didn't bother to inform them when they agreed to hire me.

It was John Roderick Keating, my English teacher in seventh and eighth grades, who first suggested I might do well to look into journalism as a career, and despite his counsel, it never would have happened if not for the many, many people who've read my blog over the year and offered advice, support, publicity, and encouragement. Every reader and commenter deserves my thanks, but besides those already mentioned I'll single out Matt Welch, Noam Scheiber, Nick Confessore, Josh Marshall, Eric Alterman, and Andrew Sullivan as each having been especially vital.

When I started out in journalism about five years ago, I knew almost nothing about foreign policy or defense issues except what I'd gleaned from a single college course titled "War and Politics" taught by Steven Peter Rosen, but his insights have proven remarkably robust over the years. Perhaps more surprisingly, philosophy courses in which I learned about the dilemmas of multiculturalism and identity from Anthony Appiah and Michael Blake have turned out to be surprisingly relevant to my understanding of America's doomed efforts in Iraq. Mostly, though, I've been privileged to do an enormous amount of learning about these issues through real and virtual conversations with people more knowledgeable than myself who, often unwittingly, have wound up making major contributions to my ideas, though they would no doubt disavow much of what I've written here. I'm particularly indebted to Robert Wright and John Ikenberry for organizing (and inviting me to) a fascinating weekend retreat on foreign policy issues conveniently timed to occur at virtually the precise moment when I went on leave to start working on the book full time. The conversations that weekend and following the retreat with Wright, Ikenberry, Francis Fukuyama, Anne-Marie Slaughter, Hendrick Hertzberg, Michael Hirsch, David Corn, Joseph Cirincione, and Anatol Lieven were invaluable. My friend Justin Logan of the Cato Institute also introduced me to his professional thinking and that of his colleague Chris Preble, and through them I've had the opportunity to meet and talk with Robert Pape, Edward Mansfield, Jack Snyder, and others. Similarly, Steve Clemons also of the New America Foundation is not only a deep thinker in his own right, but functions as a constant hub of people and activity through whom I got the opportunity to learn from Flynt Leverett, Larry Wilkerson, and especially Daniel Levy, among others.

All this is to say nothing of what Berkeley's Brad DeLong has termed the "virtual college" of the blogosphere. It's a world that's best known for partisan vitriol, but that also includes a remarkable collection of substantive thinkers from all around the world. I've been privileged to be a member of a virtual college whose relevant members for the purpose of this book include Kenneth Baer, Rosa Brooks, Ivo Daalder, Gregory Djerejian, Daniel Drezner, Derek Chollet, Robert Farley, Henry Farrell, Shadi Hamid, Heather Hurlburt, Lorelei Kelly, Rachel Kleinfeld, Suzanne Nossel, M. J. Rosenberg, Alex Rosmiller, David Schor, Michael Signer, and, more broadly, all the many readers, commenters, and correspondents I've debated and learned from over the years.

CHAPTER 1

The Real Liberal Tradition

I n moments of conceptual confusion, it's natural to turn to history in search of lessons to learn, and many of liberalism's leading intellectuals have followed this tendency in recent years for some measure of clarity in foreign policy. The most popular analogy drawn thus far has been to the circumstances faced by Harry Truman in the election of 1948: the Democrats chose a middle ground between the Republican proposal of "rolling back" communism and the anti-anticommunism of former vice president Henry Wallace, who mounted a third-party challenge to Truman's Cold War liberalism. Truman's strategy was successful, both politically and substantively, and consequently serves as an appealing model for the present and the future. Furthermore, the main lesson learned from this analogy—that one should avoid unwise extremes and hew to a soundly moderate course of action—has the virtue of being correct.

Unfortunately, this lesson, though backed by the teachings of Aristotle, the Buddha, and Goldilocks alike, offers little in the way of practical guidance. In a world where one conservative author's proposed response to Islamist violence is to "invade their countries, kill their leaders, and convert them to Christianity"[1] and a nontrivial number of people are committed to blanket pacifism, the middle ground turns out to be an extraordinarily broad patch of terrain.

In particular, rather than provide a framework for resolving the dispute, the "What would Harry Truman do?" mode of inquiry has merely recapitulated it. The prominent war supporter Joe Biden became the first recipient of the Democratic Leadership Council's Harry S. Truman Award for his foreign policy leadership[2] even as the war was regarded by the late historian James Chace as a "stunning reversal of the policies practiced by the 'wise men'" of the Truman national security team.[3] Most tellingly of all, in late 2004 Peter Beinart, then the editor of the staunchly pro-war New Republic, published a cover story advocating Democratic emulation of the Truman approach and shortly thereafter signed a deal to write a book based on the article. While writing the book, Beinart changed his mind about the Iraq War but was nonetheless able to keep the Truman analogy at the center of his argument.[4]

The essential problem is that the international situation of 1948 simply doesn't *resemble* the current world to any great extent. The Soviets controlled a vast swath of territory inhabited by hundreds of millions of people and an enormous military establishment boasting strategic nuclear weapons. Drawing specific lessons from Truman piles one shaky parallel on top of another until the whole structure creaks: Islam = communism, bin Ladin = Stalin, Syria = Czechoslovakia, France = France. Thus, today's liberals have nothing left to draw on but the morality play of moderation. Indeed, by the time of the Vietnam War, figures who cut their teeth in the Truman years found themselves sharply disagreeing about how to apply the spirit of '48 to the era of decolonization. By the early twenty-first century the application of

Trumanism had grown sufficiently fuzzy that hardened neo-conservatives, along with Bush himself, were claiming George W. Bush as Truman's true heir.[5]

Discerning a more usable history requires recognition that Truman was but one figure in a liberal internationalist tradition that stretches both directions in time and has developed over the years in response to changing events. The policies of any given moment in the past would be inappropriate for to-day's circumstances, but the legacy as a whole has been ap-plied in various situations, and both can and should be applied today.

Indeed, the internationalist legacy was alive and well and serving the country admirably as recently as the Clinton ad-ministration. The sense that September 11, 2001, marked a great discontinuity in world affairs is, in many ways, deeply mis-leading. Unlike the dawn of the Cold War in the 1940s, the events of the fall of 2001 did not represent the emergence of a novel threat or a genuinely new situation. The new situation arose about a decade earlier, as the Cold War ended and the world entered a period of unchallenged U.S. primacy where the most pressing security problems would be transnational in nature and would not emanate from organized states. The Clinton administration had a reasonably strong grasp on the situation, including the threat of al-Qaeda, and was implement-ing policies largely appropriate to the new international context that focused on strengthening, expanding, and deepening inter-national institutions in order to foster cooperation against com-mon problems and to bring the globe closer to the long-held liberal ideal of a world governed by a reasonably just, well-enforced set of rules, rather than by the clash of rival armies.[6]

This policy was not an innovation, but merely a coming to fruition of the entire twentieth-century legacy of the Demo-cratic Party, updated for a new situation that opened up new possibilities. But the Clinton era, like any particular moment in history, is open to various interpretations, especially when viewed out of context. Some Democrats took little away from the 1990s other than that liberals, too, could be enthusiastic about the use of force. Their leadership and their misinterpretations of liberal internationalism helped to drive the party behind Bush down the disastrous road to Baghdad.

While the Goldilocks lesson of the Truman administration is clearly inadequate to resolving the question of when liberals should use force, the internationalist tradition in the United States has, since its founding as part of the Woodrow Wilson administration, genuinely sought a middle ground. When Wilson entered office, the prevailing doctrine in U.S. national security policy had been that the role of the military was to defend and expand the borders of the United States vis-à-vis its immediate neighbors—Native Americans, Mexicans, and so on—while avoiding involvement in the disputes of far-off powers, especially the European ones. On some level, this strategy was principled and deeply considered, as reflected in George Washington's farewell address and its famous injunction against "entangling alliances." On another level, however, it was born of simple incapacity—the early United States was not capable of acting as a major player on the world stage and therefore chose not to try.

In the decades following the Civil War, the United States became increasingly influential. Its newly strengthened national government, vast size, enormous natural resource base, and ceaselessly growing population and economy made it a significant actor in world commerce and a potentially major one in world politics. In turn, an important faction arose arguing that the United States should ape the nations of Europe by seeking to relate to the world through imperial domination of the weak and military competition with the strong. These imperialists (a label they did not shun at the time) were opposed by traditionalists who took the view that simply because the United States *could* intervene in European affairs was no reason to think it *should* do so.

Faced with the increasing risk that Germany might secure dominion over all of Europe, Wilson reached the conclusion that intervention was the best bet. He also accepted, however, the traditional liberal view that imperial competition and militarism were immoral and ultimately self-destructive. Thus, he sought to frame his war aims around securing victory not merely over Germany, but over the whole system of international relations as well. He rejected the shared "realist" premises of isolationism and imperialism and their conclusion that global politics is intrinsically a "brutal arena where states look for opportunities to take advantage of each other, and therefore have little reason to trust each other."[7] Liberal internationalists accepted that these problems existed (and still do), but they insisted that a better world is possible and that we neither must nor should reconcile ourselves to foreign policy being perpetually dominated by amoral power struggles between heavily armed adversaries.

Wilson envisioned the postwar world as one in which force and threats of force would no longer be the dominant element of politics among nations. Just as the rule of law in the domestic sphere makes it possible for individuals to interact with one another through commerce and friendship rather than theft and extortion, so, too, could the *international* rule of law make trade and tourism, rather than war and conquest, the main components of international relations. War, when civilized nations engaged in it at all, would be authorized by a League of Nations whose purpose was to uphold the liberal international order. If any nation attempted to violate the terms of this order, the others—under the banner of the League—would band together to crush the aggressor. This approach might not abolish war, just as domestic law has failed to abolish crime, but it would certainly mark a decisive change in the structure of world politics and, in Wilson's famous phrase, make the world safe for democracy.

• • •

Famously, it didn't work.

Wilson's specific effort to meet this aspiration—the League of Nations—was a spectacular failure. The precise problems with Wilson's approach to the end of World War I are almost too numerous to name. Put briefly, however, most of the world's major powers were simply not interested in the sort of just peace that a liberal world order could have defended. While many of Wilson's ideas about national self-determination were immensely popular with the people of Europe, they were far too vague and out of touch with realities on the ground to be rigorously implemented at the Paris Peace Conference where the League was established. What's more, Wilson's views on self-determination were flatly contradicted by his personal racism, which undercut the clear anti-imperialist implications of his views. Further worsening the situation, the newly born Soviet Union was not a member of the League. Soviet absence, in part, reflected a further problem in Wilson's thinking.

In his *Perpetual Peace*, Immanuel Kant, the first major liberal internationalist thinker, envisioned a world not only peacefully managed by a loose international confederation, but one wherein the components of that confederation would all be democratic republics, instead of the autocratic monarchies that were common in his day. Wilson took over this assumption that securing the peace depended crucially on both the League of Nations and the establishment of domestic justice (in particular, fair treatment for ethnic and national minority groups), but he had no real idea of how the latter might be achieved. Finally—the nail in the coffin—Wilson badly mishandled the domestic politics surrounding the League and the peace treaty of which it was a part, ultimately failing to secure congressional approval for U.S. membership.

Most of all, while many leaders were prepared to embrace the League, none of the major countries were interested in the sort of policies that could have established a liberal peace.

Americans were by and large not interested in accepting a permanent global role for the nation, preferring to see the war as a singular crisis whose resolution would allow for a return to the traditional policy of dominating the Western Hemisphere and ignoring the rest. England (and, to a lesser extent, France) was primarily concerned with expanding and entrenching its global empire in a manner inconsistent with the equality of nations. France, meanwhile, did not especially have faith in the League's ability to protect it from future German aggression. In place of the League's liberal peace and cooperative world order, the French government sought a punitive peace that would keep Germany weak, a strong military to deter its larger neighbor, and an alliance of viable anti-German states in Central Europe. This last goal seemed to require that the new countries formed to Germany's east be reasonably large, which in practice required Poland, Czechoslovakia, and Yugoslavia, among others, to be highly multinational rather than the smaller self-determining entities Wilson had advocated. Partially in response and partially for its own reasons, Germany continued—even before Hitler's rise—to put a primary emphasis on rebuilding military strength and seeking to revise the postwar order, rather than cooperating in stabilizing it.

Underlying all these missteps, however, was a simple hubris about the nature of the task. Wilson's aspirations for global politics were noble and even correct, but skeptics who doubted their feasibility were basically right: fundamental aspects of the human condition simply can't be radically revised overnight. Insofar as the nations of the world were unwilling to abandon imperialism and militarism as policies, formal changes in institutional structure were not going to accomplish anything. But if it was a mistake to try to move forward as boldly as Wilson intended, the arrival of World War II simply confirmed that he was correct in thinking that continuing the old ways was untenable as well. The combination of nationalism, imperialism, and militarism that fueled interwar European policies led to a collision that left everyone far worse off than they'd been before: England's empire gone, France conquered, Germany destroyed, millions dead, and civilization itself seemingly in tatters. A just peace, acceptable to all, and the creation of peaceful mechanisms to resolve disputes were more necessary than ever.

Since that time, the great goal of liberal foreign policy has been to adhere to Wilson's vision while avoiding the failures of his policy: to see the creation of a liberal world order not as a simple matter that can be accomplished with a snap of the fingers, but as an ongoing process that the United States, as the largest, richest, and strongest of the liberal powers, must consistently push forward. The question, then, that must be asked of any proposed policy is whether it advances or retards that goal; whether it brings us closer to or further from the dream of a peaceful, rule-governed liberal world order.

The attempts to implement this agenda have varied over the years according to circumstances and shifting thinking, but U.S. foreign policy has, when successful, adhered to this basic strategy. Wilson's first successor in this regard was Franklin Roosevelt, who sought to temper the liberal aspiration with a greater dose of pragmatism. His United Nations made important concessions to the realities of great power politics through the structure of the Security Council. He was also able to take advantage of shifts in world opinion. Nationalism remained a strong force, but formal imperialism was clearly on the way out, and militarism's appeal was waning—especially in Europe. The upshot was to shift the international system incrementally toward one governed by liberal ideals, rather than to transform it dramatically. As witnessed by the UN's continued existence decades after its founding, this approach was considerably more successful. But although the UN managed to endure in a way that the League never did, the onset of the Cold War led Harry Truman to recognize that the sort of cooperation FDR had envisioned between the democratic West and the Soviet Union would not be possible.

Consequently, Truman further tempered Roosevelt's vision, largely accepting that a Security Council permanently hamstrung by Soviet vetoes could not function as the major tool of U.S. foreign policy. Instead of abandoning liberal aspirations in the face of this diplomatic failure, Truman sought to enact them in miniature. He constructed a series of institutions of less-than-global scope—most prominently NATO, the General Agreement on Tariffs and Trade, the World Bank (originally, the International Bank for Reconstruction and Development), and the International Monetary Fund, which was eventually followed by the European Economic Community—so that the "free world" might be governed according to liberal principles while competing as a bloc with Soviet totalitarianism in a traditional manner.

Truman and his advisers, most famously George Kennan, believed that this struggle could be won through containment—the Soviets would not need to be defeated but merely denied victory until the communist empire collapsed by virtue of its own inherent instability. The key to making this work was preserving peaceful relations among the leading Western countries, and this task fell to the Cold War–era institutions. In this respect, their responsibilities were similar to what Wilson had envisioned for the League of Nations, which was supposed to maintain peace all around the world. In essence, Truman had devised a more reasonably scaled version of Wilson's goal—even if peace and collective security couldn't manage the whole globe, they could be made to work throughout the smaller North Atlantic community.

Critics of the liberal approach to world affairs tend to portray the role of international institutions in the Cold War years as purely incidental. According to this theory, the alliance existed because peace existed, and peace in turn existed merely because the Soviet threat provided the impetus to unite. This thinking is superficially plausible in light of the long history of nations forming coalitions to fight common threats, from the Habsburgs to Napoleon to Hitler. The salient fact about these coalitions, however, is that they were all short-lived and subject to intense instability. Even when the incentives to cooperate are strong, temptations to defect from coalitions still exist. Western unity would have needed to crack only once or twice over a period of decades for much of Europe to have gone the route of non-NATO Finland, which found itself coerced into adopting a pro-Soviet foreign policy. Grounding the anticommunist coalition in formal, rule-based institutions created the levels of trust and confidence necessary to allow the governments of Europe to choose peace rather than competition.

The pivotal test of these competing interpretations of Cold War institutions came only after the conflict ended. If the institutions played no causal role in generating unity, then the collapse of the Soviet Union should have led to the collapse of the institutions and a return to a Europe characterized by conflict between the major powers. Indeed, many observers, such as the noted "realist" international relations scholar John Mearsheimer, predicted this course of events in the early 1990s. They were, of course, proved incorrect. The institutions had a life of their own, and such conflicts between, say, France and Germany that now exist are handled through the formal mechanisms of the European Union in Brussels rather than through arms races. Truman's Wilsonian instinct that enduring peace could best be found through constructing political institutions was thus retrospectively vindicated in just the manner that liberal theory would predict. His framework established a Cold War status quo that roughly held for the next forty-five years and eight presidencies until, just as Kennan had argued, the USSR did itself in.

The United Nations could not act as the main force in world affairs in light of the realities of superpower conflict. Instead, it developed a number of useful programs as an organizer and a facilitator of what amounts to global charity work—pooling resources to pursue uncontroversial humanitarian goals like famine relief and fighting disease, scoring such notable successes as the total eradication of smallpox. Turtle Bay also developed one noteworthy contribution to international security, consensual peacekeeping, in which parties wishing to end a conflict call on third-party troops to enforce the terms of an agreement that simple distrust might otherwise render unworkable. Iraq's invasion of Kuwait just as the Cold War was winding down, however, finally gave the UN an opportunity to perform its main intended function: preventing aggressive warfare.

The first Bush administration, acting within the internationalist tradition, chose to seize the opportunity. By waging war on Iraq through the mechanism of the UN, and by fighting for the limited objectives of expelling Iraq from Kuwait and forcing it to abandon the research and development of illegal weapons, the Bush administration did more than preserve Kuwait's independence. It established a new, long-dreamed-of norm—the principle that aggressive war, long notionally banned by various treaties, would actually be repulsed by concerted international action. This achievement was—and is—fairly remarkable and, though it's seldom commented on, has held up shockingly well in the intervening years. The UN's success in the first Gulf War generated high hopes that it could become an effective enforcement mechanism for other international norms that had long existed on paper, notably in areas of human rights, unconventional weapons proliferation, and genocide. The results of these efforts were decidedly mixed, as we will see, but for now the important point is that the new world order made these hopes plausible in a way they hadn't been during the organization's first several decades of existence.

Thus, when Bill Clinton entered office as the first post–Cold War president, he and his administration inherited a world in which it was possible to raise liberal aspirations once again. Rather than attempting a renewed push for a big-bang transformation of world affairs, Clinton worked toward the basic goal along a number of tracks, including a fresh emphasis on the UN built on the precedent set by his predecessor.

Beyond the UN, efforts were made to intensify and deepen several other international organizations, often symbolized by changes in name. The General Agreement on Tariffs and Trade was redubbed the World Trade Organization, the European Economic Community was renamed the European Union, and NATO expanded to the Russian border.

Conceptual fuzziness around the precise purpose and intended scope of these groups bothered the overly fastidious. *National Review*'s Ramesh Ponnuru complained in a 1998 retrospective on the Clinton administration that "the genuine accomplishment of NATO expansion was marred by the organization's partial transformation from an alliance to a rickety collective-security arrangement."[8] Such critiques ignore the large intrinsic value of stable institutions. Even if it were true—which it isn't—that NATO accomplished absolutely nothing outside its borders, the set of institutions in which it is embedded would still be valuable.

The success of internationalism on these varying levels led to a novel situation in which the defining feature of international politics was no longer rivalry between great powers. Rather, the major countries of the world achieved a sufficient degree of consensus and peaceful cooperation that U.S. policymakers developed two new concepts—"rogue states" and "failed states." The former referred to a handful of small-to-middling countries like Serbia, North Korea, Iran, and Iraq that refused to play by the rules. The latter were states, mostly in Africa, that lacked the capacity to meaningfully control events inside their own borders. These problems proved real, but the very fact that such concerns could achieve a high level of salience indicated that the basic liberal agenda was enjoying a large degree of success.

• • •

In its early years, the Clinton administration hewed very strictly to its understanding of the first Bush administration's practices during the Gulf War, actively engaging with the world but seeking to act almost exclusively through the UN. And, on one level, the UN's surprising post–Cold War efficacy at defending the sovereignty of Kuwait stood as a great liberal victory. On another level, however, defense of the sovereignty principle proved problematic. Most liberals had been initially skeptical of the Gulf War, and it was backed by only a minority of congressional Democrats. The impetus for their opposition, by and large, was a post-Vietnam skepticism about the efficacy of U.S. arms. The swift and low-cost victory in the desert, however, proved that such fears were misguided. At least under the right circumstances, the United States could effectively project power around the world. What's more, the country had done so through the auspices of the United Nations, just as liberal pioneers had envisioned.

Superficially, this revelation made the question of national security policy after the Cold War look remarkably easy. When problems arose, the United States would go to the United Nations, secure authorization to make things right, and then use its overwhelming military power to do so. What's more, the same approach the Bush administration used to prevent Iraq from dominating the Persian Gulf's oil reserves could be applied to a wide range of circumstances, including humanitarian and human rights emergencies that were more in line with liberal instincts.

Reality proved more complicated. Soon after the Gulf War, a humanitarian crisis in Somalia eventually led to the deployment of a U.S. military force to subdue local warlords who were interfering with the distribution of aid supplies. An attempted raid on a leading warlord went badly, and several U.S. soldiers (along with huge numbers of Somalis) were killed. Gruesome images of U.S. troops being dragged through the streets of Mogadishu shocked the country. The Clinton administration decided that the public's appetite for an extended deployment in East Africa would be sharply limited, and he withdrew U.S. troops. The use of force, it turned out, was still risky and complicated.

Even worse, there turned out to be a bit of a contradiction at the heart of liberalism between a desire for a rule-governed world and a desire for the rules governing the world to be good ones.

Wilson, Kant, and other pioneering liberal internationalists had envisioned a just international order as securing and defending a block of liberal states that would themselves be domestically just. In the United Nations, the world had a rudimentary form of an organization that was prepared to prevent international wars, much as the first internationalists had envisioned. But many of the UN's member states were internally illiberal and undemocratic. Such states, including veto-wielding China, though often willing—or even eager—to embrace some aspects of the idea of a liberal international order, were loathe to countenance efforts to use the UN in ways that would undermine their sovereignty and might someday be turned against their own internal repression of their citizens. Further complicating the situation, such nations tend to be less than forthright about their stance on human rights abuses. Thus, it proves relatively easy to secure widespread international agreement on abstract treaties concerning human rights, the prevention of genocide, or the spread of weapons of mass destruction, but consistently difficult in practice to secure UN approval to take meaningful action on these fronts. The result was a dilemma pitting one set of rules—the nominal prohibitions on various abuses—against the idea of a rule-governed UN enforcement process.

These various tensions eventually came to a head, somewhat ironically, in Yugoslavia, the portion of the world whose problems were proximately responsible for the outbreak of World War I; a nation whose very existence was inextricably bound up with Woodrow Wilson's initial efforts to create a liberal peace.

The end of the Cold War set the stage for the nation's total collapse, with Croatia and Slovenia declaring independence in June 1991. Bosnia and Herzegovina—the most diverse republic, 44 percent Muslim but with large Serbian and Croatian minorities—seceded in 1992 and almost immediately became the scene of bloody three-way warfare.

The United Nations, primarily at the behest of several European nations, attempted to step into the breach. It imposed a ban on arms sales throughout the region and dispatched troops under a UN mandate—the United Nations Protection Force (UNPROFOR)—to safeguard selected sites and to ensure the flow of humanitarian aid. These steps slowed the pace of the fighting somewhat but didn't stop it. Meanwhile, images of Serb atrocities against Bosnia's Muslim population poured west on CNN and other news outlets. Clinton found himself inclined to favor more robust measures, but he was tied in knots by his internationalist commitments. NATO and the UN took different positions, and the United States siding with one would weaken the other.[9]

Eventually, a UN-approved NATO bombing campaign against Serbian targets in late August 1995 (along with diplomatic initiatives aimed at forging a Croatian-Muslim coalition) brought the Serbs to the bargaining table. There they agreed to the United States–brokered Dayton Accords, which ended the war and provided for the creation of a classic peacekeeping force for Bosnia, operated by NATO, authorized by the UN, and with a substantial U.S. military presence on the ground.

The years-long delay was not, of course, merely a temporal issue—many people died as the somewhat clumsy diplomatic gears turned. To many people, the UN and similar structures began to look like obstacles to effective action at best, and cynical pretexts for avoiding action at worst. The purpose of international law's restraints on the use of force were to guard against imperialism and aggressive wars of conquest, not to prevent benevolent powers from coming to the aid of the beleaguered and the oppressed. Surely, this line of thought went, liberals both could and should in good conscience leave the rules of the international order behind when doing so provided an expedient means of advancing substantive liberal goals.

Such sentiments came closer to the fore when the United States found itself further embroiled in the Balkans, after a crisis broke out in the Serbian province of Kosovo, populated primarily by Albanian Muslims.

The Clinton administration took three lessons away from its earlier dealings with Milosevic over the Bosnia crisis: (1) Milosevic was not to be trusted; (2) measures short of military force were less effective in changing his behavior than many had hoped; (3) air strikes were more effective than had been widely believed before their actual use. The implication seemed clear— once again, only bombing could force Milosevic's hand and bring an end to a genocidal military campaign.

The difficulty from a liberal point of view was that this time around, UN authorization was not forthcoming. A majority of Security Council members seemed willing to support intervention, but, at a minimum, China and Russia were prepared to veto any authorizing resolution.

Instead of going to the UN, NATO—using primarily U.S. forces—simply commenced the bombing campaign in late March 1999, citing previous resolutions on Kosovo and the existence of an "international humanitarian emergency" as a sufficient basis for action. Russia countered with a resolution demanding "an immediate cessation of the use of force against the Federal Republic of Yugoslavia." When put to a vote, the resolution failed 12–3, with Russia joined by Namibia and China.

Despite the lack of UN authorization, the Kosovo War fit reasonably well into the liberal framework. As we have seen, in addition to their aspirations for the UN, U.S. policymakers in the 1990s had a more robust agenda for preserving the tighter institutional web of Western Europe and expanding this web eastward. The persistent instability in the Balkans, mostly provoked by Milosevic, was a substantial challenge to this agenda. Western leaders of the period were, and are, often accused of a selective approach to humanitarianism, acting forcefully in Kosovo, while being less concerned with more serious humanitarian problems in Africa and elsewhere. The charge is essentially accurate but largely misses the point: that Kosovo presented a mixture of humanitarian and interest-based reasons for intervention was precisely what strengthened the case for playing fast and loose with the UN rules, making intervention a reasonable option.

It is necessary to examine the debates over the Balkans to understand liberal internationalist views about the appropriate use of force, since that was the most recent venue in which they have been developed. Contemporary national security debates, however, quite properly focus not on Europe's southeastern corner, which has returned to its customary obscurity, but on Islamist terrorism and related issues. The terrorist attacks of September 11, 2001, are the central event of the contemporary politics of national security, and the sense that traditional internationalism is somehow inadequate to the challenges in this area has been the crux of its eclipse.

Nevertheless, this perception, no matter how widely held, is essentially false. Indeed, the national security policies of the Clinton administration's final years were dominated by concern about the rise of al-Qaeda, something similar to, but rather different from, traditional terrorist groups—a genuinely transnational movement appealing to a universalistic Islamist identity that transcended state borders. The organization itself is part of a broader trend toward what French scholar Olivier

Roy calls "globalized Islam," a set of identities and attitudes that, crucially, extends far beyond the traditional national conflicts of the Middle East and that in many ways has its population base among Muslim communities located in—or at least highly exposed to—the West: "The new generations of radicalized Western Muslims do not go to Palestine to fight the infidels; they went to Afghanistan, Chechnya, Bosnia, and Kashmir; they go to New York, Paris, and London."[10]

What's more, despite the popular belief that "9/11 changed everything," the emergence of this phenomenon was well-understood by the relatively small number of people who concerned themselves with foreign policy during the 1990s. Two of that decade's most popular books on world affairs— Thomas Friedman's *The Lexus and the Olive Tree* and Benjamin Barber's *Jihad vs. McWorld*—portrayed the emergence of Islamist movements as the foremost symbol of resistance to the burgeoning globalized culture. A third book, Samuel Huntington's *The Clash of Civilizations*, worried that an overly aggressive pursuit of liberal globalism would provoke a major conflict between the West and a resurgent Islamic traditionalism.

As an ideology uniquely committed to the process of global integration, liberal internationalism was well-suited to an early appreciation of the nature and significance of Muslim radicalism. What's more, internationalists, committed to the view that relationships between states can and should be fundamentally cooperative, were naturally predisposed to focus on a problem that does much more to unite the interests of governments than it does to divide them.

Obviously, in light of the events of September 11, 2001, one cannot avoid wishing that more had been done against al-Qaeda sooner. But that critique, though oft-leveled at the Clinton administration, flies in the face of the reality that the Bush administration, too, had the opportunity to do more. Simply put, the sort of campaign that was eventually mounted against the Taliban in October 2001 was not realistic earlier, as a matter of either domestic or international politics. The Clinton administration did manage to foil several plots organized inside the United States, to mount a successful effort to get all but three world governments to deny diplomatic recognition to the Taliban regime in Kabul, and to launch some (admittedly, not especially effective) air strikes against al-Qaeda targets.[11]

As the bipartisan *9/11 Commission Report* notes, by late 1999 combating al-Qaeda had become a top administration priority:[12]

> The CIA worked hard with foreign security services to detain or at least keep an eye on suspected Bin Ladin associates. Tenet spoke to 20 of his foreign counterparts. Disruption and arrest operations were mounted against terrorists in eight countries. In mid-December, President Clinton signed a Memorandum of Notification (MON) giving the CIA broader authority to use foreign proxies to detain Bin Ladin lieutenants, without having to transfer them to U.S. custody. The authority was to capture, not kill, though lethal force might be used if necessary. Tenet would later send a message to all CIA personnel overseas, saying, "The threat could not be more real. . . . Do whatever is necessary to disrupt UBL's plans. . . . The American people are counting on you and me to take every appropriate step to protect them during this period." The State Department issued a worldwide threat advisory to its posts overseas.

By the Clinton administration's waning days, Richard Clarke, the National Security Council's point person for terrorism, was developing a comprehensive strategy for rolling back al-Qaeda.[13] Among other things, the plan called for "massive support to anti-Taliban groups such as the Northern

Alliance" and "to continue and expand the predator UAV [unarmed aerial vehicle] program . . . and introduce armed UAVs into Afghanistan in the Spring."[14]

These proposals were developed too late for the Clinton administration to implement, and the incoming Bush administration chose to downplay counterterrorism in favor of a focus on national missile defense and Iraq, not taking the time to review the proposal until shortly before 9/11. All indications are that even if the program had been implemented, this would not have prevented the attacks. The point, however, is simply that Bush's internationalist predecessors were already developing the substance of his response to 9/11—overthrowing the Taliban in cooperation with the Northern Alliance—*before* the events themselves occurred. Internationalists were able, moreover, to make counterterrorism a high-level security policy without making a "war on terror" the organizing principle of U.S. foreign policy. Rather, the main goal remained what it long had been: to continue to extend the effort launched by Roosevelt and Truman to bring Wilson's vision of a liberal world order closer and closer to reality.

In such a world, citizens of different countries would meet each other through commerce, tourism, and the global communications network, not as soldiers on the fields of battle. Governments would interact through diplomacy, arbitration, and international institutions, rather than through threats of force. Fighting terrorism, the visible and immediately deadly threat to this vision, was a necessary and vital task but not, itself, the animating idea of national policy.

At the same time, however, something of a new threat to internationalism began to arise, essentially from within the internationalist camp itself and including several of the architects of Clinton-era internationalism. To many liberals, and to many members of the administration, Kosovo became not an

awkward case of internationalism in action—an outlier defining the limits of when liberals would endorse the use of aggressive force absent UN authorization—but a baseline for an
ill-defined new era of humanitarian militarism. Michael
O'Hanlon, a Brookings Institution scholar who was thought
to have been in line for a top post in a hypothetical Kerry administration, penned a 1999 article advocating military intervention "whenever the rate of killing in a country or region
greatly exceeds the U.S. murder rate, whether the killing is
genocidal in nature or not," utterly without reference to the
UN or any other sort of multilateral authority. He listed
ten countries—Sudan, Somalia, Rwanda, Burundi, Liberia,
Angola, Bosnia, Chechnya, North Korea, and Kosovo—where
interventions would have been warranted by this standard
during the Clinton administration alone. Mercifully, he conceded that fighting the Russian army in Chechnya was not a
very pragmatic option (as he said, it "would have risked a
major-power war between nuclear-weapons states with the potential to kill far more people than the intervention could
have saved"[15]), but he gave no consideration to the possibility
that launching unprovoked unilateral military strikes at the
rate of one every nine months or so would destabilize the entire international system. Indeed, despite O'Hanlon's demur-
ral on the Russia front, later that year the New Republic was
lamenting that "Milosevic-like deeds by Milosevic's allies will
provoke only scolding followed by winking," rather than some
unspecified more robust action.[16]

The actual architects of the two Balkan interventions did
not implement anything resembling this grandiose agenda,
doubtless in part because they were blessed with the sensible
caution that is bestowed by the need to actually run policy.
But, significantly, a refusal to admit to any mixed feelings
whatsoever about Kosovo or to delineate meaningful limits to
the legitimate scope of humanitarian warfare eventually proved
crippling in the twenty-first century, as many policymakers

and intellectuals came to wish that something along these lines had been done. This vision of an internationalist liberalism defined by its willingness to use military force to prevent human rights violations was a significant distortion of what internationalist policymaking had looked like in practice, and it had an overwhelmingly pernicious effect on the country, the world, and progressive politics. To act in the manner suggested by the most committed interventionists would require the United States to essentially proclaim itself above the rules of the international system—free to attack any country that we deemed unworthy. The advocates of such policies fancied their commitment to humanitarian ends a crucial distinguishing factor from the unilateral nationalists of the right, but from a structural perspective their claims were essentially identical. In both cases, the key element of the international order was to be a two-tiered system of sovereignty. No country could attack or threaten to attack the United States, while we would reserve the right to use military coercion to cause other nations to alter domestic policies with which U.S. political leaders disagreed. The goal was to usher in a noble new world order, enforced not by the easily hamstrung UN Security Council, but by U.S. might. The effect was to render many liberals sympathetic to the right's view of international institutions as a kind of shackle, from which the United States needed to be freed in order to achieve its destiny. The timing of this undermining of liberal internationalism in Democratic circles at the close of the twentieth century, just as the country was about to be put under new management and suffer a dramatic new kind of threat, could not have been worse.

CHAPTER 2

The Nationalist Alternative

F oreign policy issues did not play a big role—or necessarily any role at all—in the 2000 elections that brought George W. Bush to power and provided him with the opportunity to repudiate the internationalist legacy. There is, moreover, relatively little reason to think that Bush himself was especially interested in national security policy until the events of September 11 shifted his conception of himself and his administration. Within the community of conservatives who specialize in such matters, however, a reasonably coherent critique of Clintonian internationalism had been developed during the right's long years out of power, the chief point of which was simply that Clinton had been too hesitant to assert U.S. priorities on the world stage—especially, but not exclusively, in terms of the use of military force. Clinton, in this view, was unduly interested in foreign public opinion, too haunted by the ghosts of Vietnam, too concerned with his domestic priorities, and unduly prone to worry and hand-wringing when the job called for a certain manly decisiveness.

Conservatives of this stripe had ended up disappointed with the George H. W. Bush administration.[1] In the former president's son, however, they found a man whose temperament and ideas about the world were congenial to their own and who was eager to seize such opportunities as presented themselves to cast off the internationalist tradition and replace it with the aggressive nationalism that has governed the country since his inauguration.

Unfortunately, from George W. Bush's first arrival on the national stage as a serious contender for the presidency all the way through the aftermath of the invasion of Afghanistan, liberals would persistently misunderstand and misdiagnose the agenda of their leading political adversary. Out of the gate, Bush's rejection of internationalism was consistently seen and criticized as a new form of isolationism.[2]

Ever since World War II, this has been a politically potent charge in the American context, making it tempting to apply the term wherever vaguely plausible, irrespective of its accuracy. Indeed, by the 2006 State of the Union address we had come full circle, and Bush was accusing *his opponents* of isolationism.

Political utility notwithstanding, there was in fact little sign that Bush intended to disengage the United States from the wider world as he hit the campaign trail in 2000. The Bush campaign did criticize Bill Clinton for engaging in foreign policy as "social work" and the dread "nation-building," but, as Paul Starr pointed out in one of the more perceptive pieces of foreign policy commentary during the election, when "asked specifically which foreign involvements of the past decade he would have avoided, Bush could name only one: Haiti."[3] Nor did Bush ever follow up his alleged isolationism with a proposal to reduce the size of the United States' massive military establishment. The Pentagon's budget is clearly larger than necessary for strict self-defense. Rather, it is a legacy of "the Cold War–era extended security perimeter, which necessitates forward-deployed military forces around the world."[4] A legacy, in other words, of the United States' historic postwar rejection of isolationism. Isolationism is not the only reason one might have for favoring cuts in defense spending, but no isolationist could fail to favor a significant rollback of the Defense Department.

Yet rather than see Bush's support for increasing, not shrinking, U.S. military spending as contradicting their view of him as an isolationist, most liberals chose to portray Bush as contradicting *himself*. Jonathan Chait felt that Bush's national security platform was "incoherent: a military that drains billions of dollars from other priorities but does less to promote democratic and humanitarian values overseas" and accused him of speaking in "isolationist codes."[5] In retrospect, there's no incoherence here at all. As has become clear in the intervening years, Bush simply wants a powerful military but wants it to do less humanitarian work.

Indeed, from the beginning there was little actual evidence that Bush was an isolationist, rather than what he claimed to be: a skeptic about UN-sponsored peacekeeping and humanitarian endeavors disconnected from U.S. interests. Such skepticism distinguished him from the Clinton administration but did not make him an isolationist. Rather, drawing on both the nationalist instincts of his political constituency and a long-standing body of conservative thought, his main goal in world affairs has always been to unshackle U.S. power from what he saw—and still sees—as needless restraint.

Under Bush's view, the internationalist agenda of building potent rule-enforcing institutions was doubly foolish. Such institutions allow weaker countries to neutralize the military strength of stronger ones. (Indeed, the March 2005 National Defense Strategy of the United States worries that "our strength as a nation state will continue to be challenged by those who employ a strategy of the weak using international fora, judicial processes, and terrorism."[6]) As the strongest nation on the planet by far, the United States ought, in this view, to try to dismantle and weaken potentially constraining institutions, not strengthen and expand them.

In addition to weakening the hand of the strong while strengthening the hand of the weak, internationalism, according to the right, has a second disadvantage. Liberal democracies featuring a reasonable degree of transparency, political freedom, and the rule of law are much more likely to live up to their obligations than are dictatorships that can much more effectively employ subterfuge. Under the circumstances, submitting to international rules, such as those aimed at halting war crimes or the use of certain classes of weapons, is likely to be counterproductive—the rules will be least enforced against precisely those states that are most problematic.

This worldview is very different from the liberal internationalist approach and is deeply misguided in a variety of ways. It is not, however, isolationism or anything like it. A United States governed by Bush-style assertive nationalism is less likely to use force in certain circumstances than a liberal United States is, but is more likely in other cases.

Nevertheless, faced with candidate Bush, a generation of Democrats who were proud to have overcome their party's post-Vietnam legacy on national security issues found it both politically advantageous and personally flattering to arrive at a position that fundamentally misread what was at issue. Republican skepticism regarding the Kosovo War had generated the appealing-to-Democrats notion that in the twenty-first-century world, conservatives were the new doves. In a telling 1999 *Slate* article, William Saletan simply mocked several congressional Republicans for employing similar rhetoric to the left-wing antiwar activists of yore without bothering to attempt a critique of their views on the merits.[7]

Thus, with Bush's victory, just as national security issues were about to reclaim priority on the political agenda after years of languishing in obscurity, Democrats were ill-prepared to defend the basic tenets of the internationalist worldview and its applicability to a new era in which major security threats would come from nonstate actors. In the earliest days of the Bush administration, the essential dispute over attitudes toward international institutions became obscured and conflated with the separate issue of Bush's personal unpopularity in Europe, which was held in stark contrast to the esteem won by his less overtly religious and more cosmopolitan predecessor.

The extent to which Democratic willingness to use force in the 1990s flowed from a distinctive set of principles, as opposed to being a reflection of generic "hawkishness," went unarticulated. Liberals, by not understanding where their opponents stood, wound up confusing themselves at the worst time—on the eve of a disastrous war underpinned by principles whose existence they barely understood, much less were prepared to criticize.

The picture of the pre-9/11 GOP, Bush included, as a font of isolationism derived largely from the doubts that most Republican congressional leaders expressed about the Clinton Balkans policy and the Kosovo War in particular. And, certainly, opposition to any war tends to take on a "We should mind our own business" guise at times. Nevertheless, the isolationist impulse in the 1990s remained a distinctly minority brand of conservatism, best exemplified by the failed presidential campaigns of Pat Buchanan. Buchanan was, however, something of a fringe figure in Republican circles and became increasingly so over the course of the decade. Most notably, he bolted the Republican Party *before* 9/11 to mount a third-party presidential campaign in 2000. Buchanan, the real leading isolationist in the United States, could tell the difference between his views and those of the Republican mainstream. As the journalist John Judis put it:

> [M]ost congressional Republicans were not full-fledged isolationists. They were the descendants of the Republicans of the 1920s—nationalists who applied a strict test of national interest to foreign policy. If the United States was not directly and immediately threatened or if it didn't benefit, they saw no need for it to act. They opposed the interventions in Haiti, Bosnia, and Kosovo. "We should . . . bring our troops home and let the people in Europe deal with a European problem," Indiana congressman Dan Burton declared. Said Florida representative Porter Goss of the intervention in Kosovo, "The people in my district . . . want to know how this fits into our national interest, and they want to know the costs." They disliked the U.N., opposed "nation-building," rejected money for peacekeeping forces but favored a strong defense, including national missile defense, and opposed trade protectionism.

This was a disagreement about the *aims and terms* of U.S. engagement with the world, not about the desirability of engagement as such. Republicans aggressively pushed for higher defense spending and were happy to adopt a militaristic posture when they felt circumstances were warranted.

House Majority Whip Tom DeLay, the Clinton administration's most prominent critic on Kosovo, had gone on *Meet the Press* during the war and expressed his displeasure with it and with the Clinton foreign policy in general: "His foreign policy is [a] disaster, not just Kosovo but China, North Korea, the Middle East. He has put—he has hollowed out our forces while he's running around having these adventures all over the world."[8] The military was, in other words, both underfunded and not so much overused as *mis*used. In particular, Republicans wanted force and threats of force to be used not to help defenseless Balkan Muslims but to destroy—or at least intimidate—the United States' enemies and, in particular, China. The House Republicans organized a special select committee headed by Christopher Cox that had a mandate to whip up fear and paranoia about Chinese espionage against the United States.[9] Similarly, congressional Republicans persistently criticized the administration's failure to tear up the Anti-Ballistic Missile Treaty in order to clear the path for the construction of an enormously expensive and unlikely-to-work national missile defense system to safeguard us against Russia, China, or perhaps North Korea in the future.

This dominant strain of conservatism represents what Walter Russell Meade has labeled the Jacksonian tradition in American life, a populist nationalism that, while not especially concerned with the well-being of foreigners, was not inclined to withdraw from the world either.[10] Alongside Jacksonian nationalism, a minority of Republicans, the neoconservatives, tended to take a broader view of things and were more disposed to approve of Clinton's actions against Serbia and his efforts to stabilize Haiti. This neoconservative strain is often portrayed as a fully separate school of thought, as different from Jacksonian nationalism as either one is from liberal internationalism. In fact, although the two traditions are certainly different, neither is monolithic and both share important common elements that explain why they coexist more or less happily within a single political coalition.

In particular, both traditions share a rabid detestation of the United Nations and universalistic treaties that tends, in practice, to go along with a casual disregard for international institutions generally. This goes well beyond the average citizen's oft-warranted skepticism about the practical efficacy of the UN to become the oft-paranoid loathing of the institution that is reflected in recent books such as *The U.N. Exposed: How the United Nations Sabotages America's Security and Fails the World*[11] and *Tower of Babel: How the United Nations Has Fueled Global Chaos*.[12] The FOX News host Bill O'Reilly has expressed to his radio audience his "wish that [Hurricane Katrina] had only hit the United Nations building, nothing else, just had flooded them out. And I wouldn't have rescued them either."[13] Similar sentiments are expressed by the more hot-headed conservative policy practitioners, as in John Bolton's infamous remark that "the Secretariat building in New York has thirty-eight stories. If you lost ten stories today it wouldn't make a bit of difference."

The key point is that while doubts about the feasibility of accomplishing this or that within an internationalist framework are widespread and at least somewhat warranted, the shared conservative premise—from the populist base to the intellectual elite—is that such institutions are positively malign. In his February 2004 Irving Kristol Lecture at the American Enterprise Institute's annual dinner, the neoconservative theorist and columnist Charles Krauthammer explained that "the whole point of the multilateral enterprise" is "to reduce American freedom of action by making it subservient to, dependent on, constricted by the will—and interests—of other nations." Liberal internationalists do not, in his view, disagree with the right about the best way to advance American interests. Rather, they are driven by an "aversion to national interest" that the right does not share.[14]

As Ivo Daalder and James Lindsay point out in their study of the Bush foreign policy, this idea, that "Gulliver must shed the constraints that he helped the Lilliputians weave," was Bush's agenda, not from September 11 forward, but from the very beginning. He "outlined its main ideas while he was on the campaign trail, and he implemented parts of it as soon as he took the oath of office."[15] During his first eight months in

office, Bush "rejected or gutted no fewer than six international agreements or institutions."[16] Much ink has been spilled
over the years arguing about what, if anything, is distinctively
"neoconservative" about the Bush administration's approach.
On this core principle, however, its conduct is simply nationalistic—the United States must not be constrained, and other
countries will cooperate with us because they will be either
frightened or impressed with our military might. That this
drive for domination was coupled with a rhetorical insistence
on the centrality of humanitarian aims increases, rather than
diminishes, the nationalistic elements. Nothing, after all,
could be more nationalistic than the proposition that perpetual U.S. hegemony was something we were undertaking for
the good of other people.

Democratic opposition to the phantom menace of isolation
got off to an early start in Clinton's farewell address, which
was broadcast from the Oval Office on the evening of January
19—the day before Bush's inauguration. After an eloquent account of his own administration's approach to the world, Clinton warned that "in our times, America cannot, and must not,
disentangle itself from the world," implicitly indicating that
this was the most likely alternative to continued internationalism. On February 15, the columnists Jack Anderson and
Douglas Cohn looked at Bush's efforts to reduce the U.S. presence in Kosovo and warned that "what we may be seeing here
is a resurgence of Republican isolationism," with Bush himself
(who "does not have a reputation for being cosmopolitan") as
the very "personification" of the trend.[17] About a month later,
Joe Conason surveyed clashes between Colin Powell and other Republicans, citing as a prominent example Powell's support for the Comprehensive Test Ban Treaty, whose rejection
was "one of the grossest acts of irresponsible isolationism committed in Washington since before World War II."[18]

Stepping away from the Test Ban Treaty and other dip-lomatic nonproliferation efforts could, of course, be an iso-lationist move. In particular, it might have signaled the administration's commitment to simply becoming less con-cerned about the spread of nuclear weapons and adopting a "to each his own" attitude to the weapons that various coun-tries chose to develop. The Bush team, however, believed in no such thing. Rather, their goal was to abandon traditional antiproliferation by means of international agreement with a so-called counterproliferation approach that used force or regime change to keep nukes out of the hands of rogue states. The hostility to antiproliferation agreements was driven not by indifference to foreign countries' nuclear developments, but by a desire to enhance the United States' own nuclear armaments:

> A review of U.S. defense policy published in 2000 by the neoconservative hothouse The Project for a New American Century (PNAC) argues that reducing our nuclear force is likely to be dangerous; it favors not only updating it but expanding its role beyond strate-gic deterrence. That the Bush administration has tak-en this advice to heart is no surprise. Several PNAC contributors are now running U.S. foreign policy, in-cluding Paul Wolfowitz and Stephen Cambone at the Pentagon and I. Lewis Libby in the White House. Douglas Feith (the undersecretary of defense), John Bolton (the undersecretary of state) and Robert Joseph (the National Security Council's senior counterpro-liferation official) have espoused similar views.[19]

In particular, the administration and its congressional allies were early and consistent advocates of the view that the United States ought to develop a new generation of nuclear weapons designed for battlefield use rather than deterrence. What's more, one of the main goals of these new weapons would be preventing other countries from building nukes of their own. In the wake of Israel's destruction of Iraq's main nuclear weapons facility in the early 1980s, countries had become much better at locating such facilities in underground locations that were difficult to destroy from the air. So-called bunker-buster nukes were the conservatives' answer to this problem.

The liberal approach, by contrast, would put its faith in trying to tighten inspections and enhance enforcement of the Non-Proliferation Treaty (NPT) and related agreements. The NPT, however, is based on a bargain between nuclear and non-nuclear countries. The latter agree not to construct nuclear weapons, while the former agree to, among other things, work toward the ultimate goal of total disarmament. Thus, rather than working in tandem with traditional nonproliferation, counterproliferation actually weakens it by undermining the core treaty at the heart of the nonproliferation regime. Bush's hostility to that regime and his espousal of counterproliferation aren't about isolationism but, again, about U.S. global hegemony. The counterproliferationist ideal is a world in which the United States has whatever nuclear weapons it wants and uses them to decide which other countries get to have them.

This was—and is—the general pattern of Bush's approach to the world. Liberals seek reciprocal reductions in national sovereignty wherein every nation commits to abide by certain standards in the fields of human rights, proliferation, environmental protection, and so on. An isolationist would let each country go its own way. The Bush model, in contrast to these, but in echo of the imperialist tradition, seeks an asymmetrical sovereignty wherein the United States is unencumbered by rules, while seeking to impose them on others.

Other countries, naturally, are disinclined to enthusiastically embrace the concept of a world community in which they are all destined for second-class (at best) status. The main role of U.S. force, under the circumstances, is to make other countries accept it anyway. Defiant regimes will be disciplined or, in the extreme, removed. International cooperation will be secured not through institutional arrangements designed to take everyone's interests into account, but through bold demonstrations of U.S. power that will lead farsighted foreign leaders to recognize that their nations' interests are best served through alignment with the United States.

Disagreements will exist, inside this framework, over exactly which things should be of interest to American policymakers and what kinds of priorities are worth fighting for. The framework itself, however, is the fundamental thing, and it marks a clear contrast with the liberal tradition—a dark, pessimistic vision of endless conflict, combined with a blinkered optimism about the United States' ability to perpetually prevail. The liberal alternative, by contrast, paints an optimistic picture of a better world and tempers it with experience about how far we can move toward that path in the short term. But despite the gap between these two approaches, there is room for slippage between them. Room, in particular, for liberals to grow too frustrated with the slow pace of progress toward their preferred substantive outcomes and too complacent about both the efficacy and the beneficence of U.S. arms. To its exponents, extreme forms of the humanitarian intervention doctrine remained sharply distinct from conservatism, owing to the different sort of ends they sought to promote, to the greater idealism of the left-wing strain, and so on. In fact, however, the fundamental vision of how the world should work—with policymakers in Washington, D.C., deciding what should happen around the world and then using military might to make it happen—was essentially the same as the dark visions of Bush or James Burnham. Differences remained, of course, but this basic similarity of vision would soon enough lead a substantial number of progressive leaders to back the unilateral invasion and occupation of Iraq, thereby casting their political movement into a wilderness of confusion and incoherence from which it is only slowly emerging today.

CHAPTER 3

A Tale of Two Wings

I n light of 9/11's enormous significance, captured in the cliché that "9/11 changed everything," it's worth observing that there's a sense in which very little actually changed that morning. Unlike the dawn or twilight of the Cold War or Adolf Hitler's rise to power, the destruction of the World Trade Center did not signal an important change in the objective security environment faced by the United States. The loss of life, though horrifying, was not in and of itself nearly large enough to constitute a serious challenge to the United States' stability or prosperity. Nor did anything that happened that day actually alter the risk of terrorist attacks directed at the United States.

Al-Qaeda existed before 9/11 and was known to exist. "Bin Laden [was] determined to strike in U.S." was the headline of a Presidential Daily Brief prepared for the president by the CIA about a month before the event. Islamic radicals had targeted U.S. interests throughout the 1990s and even detonated a bomb designed to destroy the World Trade Center in 1993.

A number of al-Qaeda plots had been foiled in the years before 9/11. The actual events of the day in no way altered the fact that future plots would be forthcoming or changed the ability of the relevant agencies to foil them in the future.

Rather than a change in the objective situation, 9/11 marked the beginning of an enormous *psychological* change on the part of the American people. Psychology, however, is an important matter indeed, especially in a democracy. Perceptions and states of mind have consequences in the real world. Perhaps chief among these consequences, 9/11 created a situation in which the U.S. public was receptive to listening to big ideas about the United States' role in the world and the nature of the global security situation. Previously, people had largely tuned out such debates, but in late 2001 and early 2002 they were prepared to listen. What's more, certain ideas expressed at the time swiftly became widely entrenched and difficult to dislodge down the road. The right seized advantage of the opportunity to frame issues in a way that was highly favorable to its existing policy preferences but spectacularly ill-suited to the actual situation. The left, by contrast, tended either not to seriously challenge the right's view of events or else to wrap up its critique in an unrealistic quasi-pacifism that served to obscure and discredit its more valuable ideas.

As the country prepared to devise a strategy for combating Islamist terrorism, the sensible thing would have been for the nation to immerse itself in actual empirical information about the nature of the problem. The genius of something like George Kennan's famous "long telegram," adapted into a hugely influential *Foreign Affairs* article outlining the theory of "containment" as an appropriate guideline for the Cold War, was that it emerged from intensive and accurate study of the Soviet Union.[1] Given the timing, in the late 1940s people who were determined to take the problem of communism seriously may have been tempted to simply compare it to the Nazi threat the United States had only recently overcome. Kennan's insight was to see that this was a mistake. He realized that unlike the Nazis, the fact that the communists were inspired by an evil ideology "does not mean that they should be considered as embarked upon a do-or-die program to overthrow our society by a given date."

Rather, he pointed out, the USSR's leadership was inspired by a "theory of the inevitability of the eventual fall of capitalism" that had "the fortunate connotation that there is no hurry about it." Thus, insofar as Americans believed that the Soviets were wrong and that the fall of capitalism was *not* inevitable, we could afford to simply contain and outlast them, waiting for communism's own inevitable collapse under the weight of the system's inherent problems.

Rather than embark upon a similar effort to understand what was actually happening, early twenty-first-century America tended to take refuge in a series of shopworn and flattering clichés. In part, this followed simply from the psychologically devastating impact of 9/11 itself. As Daniel Chirot and Clark McCauley point out:

> When one's own group is threatened by another group, certain reliable consequences ensue. Hostility toward the threatening group is an obvious result. . . . Less often recognized, however, are the consequences for in-group dynamics, the relations among members of the group facing a common threat. Any such group experiences an increased feeling of togetherness, which may be called cohesion, patriotism, or nationalism. Increased cohesion is associated with three other changes: increased respect for leaders, increased idealization of in-group values, and increased readiness to punish deviates from in-group norms.[2]

All three factors were prominently on display in the wake of the attacks. Increased respect for leaders is evident from the famously massive leap in approval ratings for George W. Bush on the day of the attacks.[3] The other elements of the psychology of cohesion were, however, also clearly present and quite important in shaping public comprehension—or, rather, lack of comprehension—of the issue. Notably, there was massive resistance to any serious effort to understand what motivated people to wage jihad against the United States. Rather, in keeping with the idea of increased idealization of in-group values, elite and mass opinion swiftly reached the conclusion—without any serious evidentiary backing—that anti-Americanism in the world was caused primarily by hatred of "freedom" or some other totally abstract and utterly praiseworthy concept that the United States was said to uniquely exemplify.

In her contribution to the *New Yorker*'s postattack issue, Susan Sontag contended that we had not witnessed an "attack on civilization or liberty or humanity or the Free World," but rather "an attack on the world's self-proclaimed superpower, undertaken as a consequence of specific American alliances and actions."[4]

For her trouble, Sontag was targeted for swift and furious denunciation. "Miss Sontag," wrote David Limbaugh in the *Washington Times*, "can remain in her ivory tower along with her elitist comrades, pathetically oblivious to the fact that if our commander in chief shared her views it wouldn't be long before her freedom to express such inanity evaporated."[5] Typical of the genre, Limbaugh left unsaid what was supposedly inane about Sontag's views. Thus, one saw frequent resort to the simple tactic of misrepresentation, as in a *Seattle Post-Intelligencer* op-ed accusing her of "unimaginable moral equivalencies" and "choosing . . . to blame America" for the attacks.[6]

The irony here is that nothing she wrote should have been remotely controversial. The simple observation that al-Qaeda attacked in response to U.S. policy said nothing whatsoever about the merits of the policy in question.

This is not to deny that some members of the far left responded to 9/11, in whole or part, with wrongheaded—at times, egregiously so—sentiments and analyses. Still, the sheer amount of attention paid to such statements was strangely high. The United States has, from the beginning, been distinguished from the world's other liberal democracies by the absence of a substantial left-wing political movement. The United States lacks, and has always lacked, a viable Socialist Party, and hard-left political views are essentially restricted to a small number of intellectuals, influential nowhere outside of college campuses.

Under the circumstances, it's a bit hard to understand what justified the sheer quantity of attention paid to marginal views. Typical of the era was the regular "Idiocy Watch" feature that ran from October 2001 to November 2002 in the *New Republic*. It consisted entirely of quotations—occasionally from the far right, but overwhelmingly from the far left—that the magazine's editors deemed beyond the pale. No counterarguments were offered, and the clear majority of figures quoted—including the German composer Karlheinz Stockhausen,[7] the Indian novelist Arundhati Roy,[8] the memoirist Elizabeth Wurtzel,[9] and the chess grandmaster turned lunatic recluse Bobby Fischer[10]—were completely irrelevant to actual U.S. policy debates. What was the point, at the end of the day, in bothering to highlight views deemed so absurd as to be unworthy of even rebutting? A hint is provided in the moderate conservative Andrew Sullivan's worry in the wake of the attacks that "the decadent Left in its enclaves on the coasts is not dead—and may well mount what amounts to a fifth column."[11]

The very existence of far-left viewpoints was defined as a danger to the nation, quite apart from whether those views had influence over policymakers. The idea that, say, Noam Chomsky would team up with Stockhausen, Wurtzel, and perhaps Howard Zinn in order to take up arms against the United States in the name of Osama bin Laden's holy war was, of course, a bit implausible. Hence the inclusion of the crucial weasel words "what amounts to." But what could this mean? How could the mere expression of disagreement with policy choices—whether or not the disagreements were correct—"amount to" acts of treason against the United States? The answer, most likely, can be found in the American right's valorization of willpower as the primary variable in successful war-fighting.

In this view, there are essentially no objective limits to U.S. military might. The comic book character Green Lantern, along with his colleagues in the Green Lantern Corps, is equipped with a "power ring" that is said to be the ultimate weapon in the universe. The ring can, when fully powered, create objects or energy fields of essentially any sort, subject only to the user's will and imagination. Consequently, the main factor in Corps recruiting is to find people capable of "overcoming fear" so as to be able to exercise maximum willpower in crisis situations.[12] As a premise for a comic book, this works well enough.

As a premise for a foreign policy, however, it leaves much to be desired. Unfortunately, since at least the wake of the Vietnam War, U.S. conservatives have tended to espouse a Green Lantern Theory of Geopolitics, believing that U.S. force can achieve essentially anything as long as the will to use it exists. The emotional roots of this view, in turn, lie in the rise of a school of conservative revisionist thought about the Vietnam War, holding that the conflict was in fact lost by the antiwar movement, rather than by its architects or because of the inherent flaws in the concept. The sophisticated version of this thesis, expounded by Lewis Sorley in his book A Better War, holds that following William Westmoreland's replacement as commander of U.S. forces in Vietnam by Creighton Abrams, the United States began to adopt a more effective set of counterinsurgency tactics that, in effect, won the war in the early 1970s.

A cruder version of this theory, no doubt more influential among the public at large, was expressed by John Rambo in the first film of the famous series: "I did what I had to do to win, but somebody wouldn't let us win." U.S. troops, in other words, *could* have won the war had they not been subject to undue restraint by politicians in Washington. As the Iraq War began to clearly go south, this line of thinking would be revived by the right specifically in the form that the United States was losing the war because of a stab in the back from traitorous left-wing elements.[13] In its initial post-9/11 formulation, however, the main argument made was simply that the United States had invited the attack by adopting an insufficiently aggressive posture toward the world.

The evidence for this proposition was remarkably flimsy. The two main Islamist terrorist organizations—Shiite Hezbollah and Sunni al-Qaeda—were both formed in direct response to foreign invasions of Muslim territory, Israel's incursion into Lebanon in the first instance and the Soviet invasion of Afghanistan in the latter. What's more, Islamist terrorist attacks had overwhelmingly been concentrated against countries like Israel, the United States, Russia, and India that were unusually aggressive by world standards. Were the principle "Weakness invites aggression" genuinely the appropriate dictum for understanding international terrorism, one would expect countries like Iceland and Portugal to become the main targets of freedom-hating terror-mongers. In fact, something close to the reverse is true. As the Defense Science Board's 1997 Summer Task Force study of responses to transnational threats concluded, "historical data show a strong correlation between U.S. involvement in international situations and an increase in terrorist attacks against the United States."[14]

This is not to say that the United States should never involve itself in matters abroad. Rather, it is simply necessary to be clear-eyed about what this entails. Aggressive policies may have benefits, but those benefits should be weighed against the costs, including an increased risk of terrorism. Conversely, when one is considering how to reduce the risk of terrorism, an understanding of the way that aggressive policies can create terrorism is crucial.

The postattack right, however, would have none of it. On September 21, 2001, the *Washington Post* columnist Charles Krauthammer slammed those who had the temerity to suggest that specific U.S. policies had led to terrorist attacks as "voices of moral obtuseness" when "in the wake of a massacre that killed more than 5,000 innocent Americans in a day, one might expect moral clarity."[15] A week later, he proposed his countertheory—terrorism was provoked not by U.S. intervention but by U.S. weakness. "Radical Islam," in this theory, was "riding a wave of victories," namely, "the bombing of the Marine barracks in 1983 that drove the United States out of Lebanon; the killing of 18 American soldiers in Mogadishu in 1993 that drove the United States out of Somalia; and, in between, the war that drove the other superpower, the Soviet Union, out of Afghanistan."[16]

It was true, of course, that Hezbollah's success in driving the marines out of Lebanon and the mujahideen victory against the Soviet Union offered encouragement to those who believed they could wage unconventional warfare against strong states. Nevertheless, it is also clearly the case that Hezbollah never would have targeted Americans in the first place had the marines not landed in Lebanon; that the mujahideen never would have fought the Soviets had they not invaded Afghanistan. Similarly, the implication that countries should adopt a uniform attitude of stubbornness in the face of unconventional tactics is daft. The Soviets, after all, actually did stay in Afghanistan for a very long time. And while the United States swiftly left Lebanon, Israel spent eighteen years attempting to implement a policy of stubbornness in that country. In both instances, they merely learned the same lesson the United States was taught in Vietnam and that the nations of Western Europe learned as they lost their colonial empires—it is essentially impossible under contemporary circumstances for a foreign military force to remain indefinitely in a country in the face of hostile public sentiment. By withdrawing from Beirut, Ronald Reagan did not demonstrate a weakness that encouraged further Hezbollah strikes against the United States. Instead, he demonstrated wisdom that saved a great deal of lives and largely led Hezbollah to leave the United States alone.

Despite the weak logic, however, this line of argument swiftly reached the status of conservative cliché. In the *National Review* contributor and American Enterprise Institute scholar Michael Ledeen's formulation:

When the Israelis tucked their tail between their legs and beat an ignominious retreat from southern Lebanon, the terror masters could suddenly taste victory over us. They added "our" retreat from Lebanon to our earlier retreats from Vietnam, Beirut, and Somalia, and they got a very big jackpot number, so big that they convinced themselves that our moment had passed, and theirs had come, and the evidence was all there: we wouldn't fight like real men because we were afraid to die in combat so all we could do was drop bombs from time to time, and we had stopped challenging Saddam Hussein, another sign of cowardice and fear. All they had to do was kill a lot of us, and we would yield to their more powerful will.[17]

One can easily enough understand the appeal of such statements in the wake of a monstrous calamity inflicted by vile men. The natural—indeed, appropriate—instinct in the wake of such an event is to strike back. And the "retreat causes terrorism" theory has the comforting implication that striking back *very hard* is all one needs to do. If it doesn't work, one needs merely to strike *even harder*. Such an approach is not only well-fitted to the postattack mind-set, but ideally suited to the equally comforting notion that the United States could easily enough solve the whole terrorism problem once and for all. Our military might, conveniently enough, was utterly supreme and certainly exceeded anything radical Islamists could mobilize by several orders of magnitude. Frightened, anxious, and justly outraged people are not eager for self-examination or the message that patience is needed.

As an analysis of al-Qaeda's motives, however, the resolve-centric worldview suffered from serious deficiencies. What made it especially pernicious as an approach to national policy, though, is a point clarified by Ledeen's formulation of the argument: resolve or lack thereof can be demonstrated in any number of contexts. The decision to retreat from Vietnam, for example, plainly had nothing in particular to do with Osama bin Laden or radical Islam. Nevertheless, by the right's standards, withdrawing from Southeast Asia, by demonstrating a lack of U.S. willpower, gave encouragement to terrorists decades later. If this is true, then the converse also ought to hold: *any* demonstration of implacable will anywhere would serve as a useful counterterrorism measure simply in virtue of demonstrating resolve.

Conveniently enough, this analysis led to the conclusion that the appropriate response to 9/11 was simply to implement the very same hyperaggressive, hypernationalistic foreign policy that many on the right had long advocated. That they had not earlier framed this policy as a terrorism deterrent and indeed had disparaged the threat of international terrorism as less important than other challenges was irrelevant. Arguing that we should combat al-Qaeda by attacking a target chosen literally at random was not, of course, going to convince anyone. But the underlying focus on resolve did make it plausible to simply lump together a host of very loosely related issues—often linked only by the fact that Muslims and/or Arabs were in some way involved—and argue that they should all be tackled simultaneously and forcefully. In November, Frederik Kagan explained to readers of the *Weekly Standard* that in combating terrorism, "above all, we must abandon fear and focus on our goals." In this context, however, "focus" turned out to mean something like the reverse of actually focusing. "It is not enough," he warned, "to eliminate al-Qaeda or overthrow the Taliban." Beyond these mere "immediate objectives," he proposed the following three-point plan:

- Replace the Taliban with a stable Afghan regime committed to functioning as a respectable member of the international system and preventing the use of its territory and resources for the support of terrorism.
- Eliminate to the best of our ability known terrorist organizations such as al-Qaeda, Hamas, Hezbollah, and Islamic Jihad.
- Replace Saddam Hussein's criminal regime before he finds a way to use the chemical and biological weapons we know he is developing for a devastating attack on the United States.[18]

This was, to put it mildly, an ambitious agenda. Notably, however, the article evinces no understanding of exactly how ambitious it was. Both the title, "Fear Not the Taliban," and the rhetoric surrounding the proposals are classics of the Green Lantern Theory, seeming to imply that undue hesitancy was the only serious obstacle to accomplishing all this.

A sensible person would have been ashamed to put forward this argument in the course of mentioning anti-Israel organizations like Hamas, Hezbollah, and Islamic Jihad, which, obviously, the Jewish state had been trying to eliminate for quite some time with what one could only call limited success. To be sure, the United States is a significantly more powerful country than Israel. Nevertheless, the gap in sheer firepower terms between Israel (which has a navy, tanks, and armored personnel carriers; a large and adept air force; nuclear weapons; and so on) and, say, Hamas was already so gigantic that there was no plausible case that simply throwing additional heavy equipment into the mix would achieve anything.

More consequential, though no less misguided, was the suggestion that the United States respond by attacking Iraq. By November, Kagan was far from alone in putting this idea on the table. The curious flip side of the mass movement to marginalize the extreme left's opposition to a war against the Taliban was the extraordinary speed with which the "attack Iraq" concept was mainstreamed. Jim Woolsey, appointed in a frightening misjudgment by Bill Clinton to be his first director of central intelligence and since then a consistently hysterical foreign policy commentator, was fast out of the gate encouraging Americans to "at least consider" the possibility "that the attacks—whether perpetrated by bin Laden and his associates or by others—were sponsored, supported, and perhaps even ordered by Saddam Hussein."[19] For evidence to back this assertion, he cited the work of Laurie Mylroie, who explained her thinking in a postattack article of her own. Saddam was a likely suspect for 9/11 because "Iraq was responsible" for the *earlier* attack on the World Trade Center in 1993, which "was a 'false flag' operation, run by Iraqi intelligence, with the Muslim extremists who participated in the plot left behind to be arrested and take the blame."

To say that Mylroie and Woolsey had no evidence for their assertions would be an insult to evidence-free speculation. Their theory about 9/11 was grounded in a larger theory about Saddam and the 1993 attacks that had been the subject of rigorous investigation over a period of years and been thoroughly debunked. They were, in short, crackpots peddling an absurd conspiracy theory with dramatic policy implications. But at the very same time that marginal left-wing views were subjected to an unprecedented bout of public excoriation, Mylroie and Woolsey were treated as serious figures worthy of access to the pages of the United States' premiere political magazines. With the far left marginalized and the far right still going strong, the entire spectrum of opinion became suddenly and dangerously unbalanced.

As an immediate response, however, the Bush administration wisely chose to focus on Afghanistan. The military campaign to push the Taliban out of Afghanistan eventually went smoothly, but the task was an apparently daunting one. The United States lacked close allies in the region. Afghanistan's most important neighbor, Pakistan, had historically been one of the most Taliban-friendly nations on earth. The other nearby 'stans of Central Asia, logistically essential to mounting operations in support of the Northern Alliance, were in the traditional sphere of influence of the United States' old rival, Russia. But working through the night, the State Department team came up with the outlines of a plan that Colin Powell was able to bring to the White House the next morning and that became the cornerstone of the diplomacy surrounding Operation Enduring Freedom when it was launched.[20] Beyond the initial military effort, however, there was a larger problem on the horizon of stabilizing postwar Afghanistan and neutralizing al-Qaeda around the world.

In the coming months, the same team worked to develop a strategy for these issues. The key element, coinciding with the tenets of both liberal internationalism and traditional realpolitik, was to see the tragedy of 9/11 as, in a sense, an opportunity. Nations around the world, including ones with long-standing tense relations with the United States, felt their interests threatened by the rise of transnational terrorism. An internationalist approach could have brought a vast quantity of resources from all around the world to bear on a handful of acute problems—a global alliance capable of achieving defined goals on several fronts. Following 9/11, the outpouring of sympathy and support for the United States from our traditional allies—playing "The Star Spangled Banner" at Buckingham Palace, the "We Are All Americans" headline in *Le Monde*—are justly famous. Less well-known were the cooperative feelers put out by distinctly untraditional allies. The secular Baath regime in Syria, whose leaders were drawn from the minority Shiite sect, had long felt threatened domestically by the local branch of the Muslim Brotherhood, the large Sunni Islamist organization of which al-Qaeda was an extreme offshoot. Consequently, Syrian intelligence had been monitoring al-Qaeda for some time, and the regime "had compiled hundreds of files on al-Qaeda, including dossiers on the men who participated—and others who wanted to participate—in the September 11th attacks."[21] After 9/11, the Syrians wanted to help. We had a common enemy. They had intelligence we needed, and we had the legitimacy, the allies, and the global reach they lacked.

Similarly, Syria's ally Iran had long-standing concerns about al-Qaeda. The Iranian regime and the bulk of its population belong to the Shiite sect of Islam, and they are regarded as heretics by bin Laden and his followers. More pragmatically, Iran shares a border with Afghanistan and, like all of that country's neighbors, sought to exercise influence in the country during the chaos that followed the Soviet withdrawal in the 1980s. Iranian-backed groups had battled the Taliban for years, and several Iranian diplomats (the Taliban regarded them as spies) had been killed by bin Laden's allies there, on occasion nearly leading to war. Consequently, as it became clear that the United States was planning to orchestrate the Taliban's overthrow, Iran was eager to assist in exchange for assurance that the new regime in Kabul would not be hostile to Iranian interests.

According to Flynt Leverett, the State Department's medium-term plan was to take advantage of these cooperative feelers to build something deeper. "As other state sponsors of terrorism like Iran and Syria came to the United States to offer assistance against al-Qaeda and the Taliban, that help would be accepted." Such states would learn the value of having a friendly relationship with the United States and "this tactical cooperation would then be used as a platform for persuading these states to terminate their own involvement with anti-Israeli terrorist groups in return for a positive strategic relationship with Washington."[22] In exchange, the United States would resume efforts to revive the Israeli-Palestinian peace process, creating the context in which it would be viable for rejectionist regimes to restrain or cease supporting groups like Hezbollah.

This approach represented the mainstream consensus among most relevant professionals inside and outside the government. Unfortunately, it was not to be. Tactical cooperation continued for some time, but the administration never made a serious effort to move in the direction of strategic reconciliation. By the summer of 2006, Leverett would be a prominent administration critic perched at the New America Foundation. His boss, Richard Haas, the director of policy planning at the State Department, would become chairman of the Council on Foreign Relations. Haas's bosses, Secretary of State Colin Powell and Powell's deputy Richard Armitage, were in private life and subject to regular scorn by the conservative movement.

Instead of being guided by the professional consensus, the administration followed up the operation in Afghanistan with an embrace of the far right's preferred focus on Iraq. Liberals, meanwhile, had little success in countering the discourse's rightward drift. Driving the ineffectual liberal response was the continuing near-pathological obsession with the far left, the sentiment that in a moment of national crisis the most important task facing liberalism was not to combat the errors of in-power conservatism but those of the hopelessly marginal left, who became the primary target of their rhetoric. In some cases, it seems reasonably clear that simple loathing of left-wing antiwar activists pushed liberal intellectuals into support of the Iraq War. But even many mainstream writers and pundits who would eventually reject the war contributed to the problem in the early postattack months, in effect firing in the wrong direction for so long that they wound up outnumbered and outgunned when they finally switched targets.

Michael Walzer, the distinguished moral philosopher and specialist in the ethics of war and peace, is perhaps the ultimate exemplar of this trend. A brilliant thinker who reached a correct conclusion about Iraq at the end of the day, he nevertheless completely failed to turn his insights into effective political action, choosing instead to beat up on left-wing adversaries and noticing that the leadership of the country was about to do something horribly misguided far too late for anything to be changed. An early postattack Walzer article in the *American Prospect*, for example, took to task the utterly trivial bloc of opinion that believed in excusing terrorism. Walzer's conclusion in the piece—that when faced with an ideological fanatic and/or a suicidal holy warrior, implacable opposition is the only viable option—is clearly true. Equally true, however, is that nobody remotely in the vicinity of the levers of power was proposing to do anything else. A genuine debate—one that has continued to rage to this day—was unfolding, however, on the related issue of what to do about Muslims who were not ideological fanatics or suicidal holy warriors but simply aggrieved by aspects of U.S. foreign policy, of which, as Walzer conceded, "there is a lot to criticize."[23]

The approach suggested by the State Department after the attack was to try to combine implacable opposition to al-Qaeda with concessions to others. In particular, to work toward a constructive resolution of the Arab-Israeli conflict. The goal of such initiatives would not be to appease Osama bin Laden himself or his core followers. Rather, the idea was to recognize that the looming conflict with al-Qaeda was bound to polarize Muslim opinion and that one of the aims of U.S. policy should be to ensure that as large a segment of that opinion as possible came to be polarized in our favor. Walzer does not take the wrong side in this debate; he doesn't even acknowledge that the debate exists. But by intervening solely in the irrelevant debate about the non-option of excusing hard-core fanatics, while remaining silent in the genuine debate about moderate Muslim opinion, Walzer managed, de facto, to advance the cause of implacable opposition to compromise under all circumstances.

In light of the mass outpouring of hate being directed at the far left from all directions at the time, the impulse to focus on distancing oneself from them—the effort to construct what Walzer, in a different piece, called a "decent left"[24]— was understandable. The pressure to distance oneself from "those people" was intense, and many, including myself, succumbed to the temptation to give far more emphasis to the task than objective circumstances warranted. Soon, the anathema spread beyond the far left, and liberals were also supposed to eschew cooperation with absolutely everyone whose views could not be wholeheartedly endorsed. Libertarian isolationists were out, as were cautious realpolitikers and Old Right types who were suspicious of neoconservative grandiosity. But while checking the Bush administration's wilder ambitions would have been a difficult task under any circumstances, doing it while simultaneously attacking every possible partner in forging an anti-Bush coalition was clearly a nonstarter.

The sort of decency that prioritizes abstract consistency and moral purity over the possibility of effective action has a certain obvious appeal to intellectuals. In the real world, however, decent political action is political action with decent outcomes, which means a focus on problems that may realistically arise and on what can best be done to stop them.

Instead, during the months of the immediate crisis, liberals acted—or failed to act—from a position of crippling weakness. They were isolated from potential allies in checking the conservative drive to hegemony, did little to nothing to draw public attention to the radicalism lurking inside the corridors of power, and bought into many key elements of the right's narrative. The purpose of all this was to weather the political storm resulting from 9/11 and to position Democrats for the electoral battles to come. In practice, however, the strategy that was adopted and the premises that underlay it produced a fiasco for liberals and gains for the incumbent party that were almost without precedent in U.S. political history. En route to this electoral disaster, Democrats would find themselves abandoning long-held principles in a way that has hamstrung progressive politics ever since.

CHAPTER 4

See No Evil

As the country's eyes began to shift from Afghanistan back to the domestic scene, Democrats had reason to be optimistic about the outcome of the 2002 midterm elections. First, history was in their favor—no opposition party had failed to pick up seats in a first midterm election in the modern era. What's more, ever since losing ground in the 1994 election, congressional Democrats had been steadily winning it back in 1996, in 1998, and again in 2000. Many saw these gains as tied to underlying demographic changes that strongly favored the Democrats. The U.S. population had rising numbers of Hispanics and highly educated professionals at a time when the Democratic Party had managed to stabilize its performance with the white working class. Months before the election, John Judis and Ruy Teixeira published their widely hailed book *The Emerging Democratic Majority*, making just that demographic argument and, while not venturing a prediction about the midterms as such, bolstering the general mood of optimism.

One of the Democrats' brightest hopes for the midterms came in the state of New Hampshire. To contend for an open seat in the Senate, Democrats were united around Jeanne Shaheen. As the state's popular incumbent governor, Shaheen had statewide name recognition and recent experience in running and winning statewide campaigns. The local branch of the College Democrats organized bus convoys on October weekends to take the Boston area's many students on trips out to the chilly New Hampshire countryside to volunteer for Shaheen. As such a student at the time, I made the trip twice. What I saw there encapsulated the absurdity of the Democratic strategy.

"This election," proudly proclaimed the volunteer coordinator at the Concord office in a speech designed to fire up the troops, "is about whether there is going to be war or whether there is going to be peace." Out in the field, though, the question of war hardly seemed to be on the agenda. Trudging from house to house, knocking on doors and dodging irate dogs, we handed out campaign literature or else, when the resident was unavailable or simply unamenable, left it behind for later perusal. Nothing in our arsenal of pamphlets so much as mentioned the question of Iraq.

What's more, if the looming invasion had been mentioned, it scarcely would have been the defining issue of the campaign. The vote to authorize the use of force, after all, was made before election day, making the New Hampshire race legally irrelevant to the issue. That aside, Shaheen was on record as supporting the use of force against Saddam Hussein. As, for that matter, was Tom Daschle, who would lead the Senate in the event of a Democratic majority, and Dick Gephardt, his counterpart in the House.

Shaheen's refusal to make an issue out of national security policy hardly kept it out of the campaign. On October 5, about a month before the voting began, the president came to New Hampshire to campaign for John Sununu. "In order to make sure I can do a better job" of defending the country from terrorism, he explained, "I ask the Congress to join me in the creating of a Department of Homeland Security." Sununu, Bush said, stood with him, as had the House of Representatives as a whole. "But it's tied up in the Senate" because Democrats were preventing "a president from putting the right people at the right place at the right time in order to respond to an enemy." The nation's security, in other words, depended on a Republican Senate. Shaheen got precisely no credit from the president for supporting him on Iraq. Indeed, Bush did his best to imply that the two contenders were on opposite sides of the issue. Bush's attitude put Shaheen in a situation that was intrinsically all but impossible. Protestations of support for the president's positions would do her little good, since Shaheen's backing of Bush was so very clearly not reciprocated.

What's more, there was the question of stakes. According to Bush, the Iraq situation was an important reason to send him a GOP Senate. After all, Saddam Hussein "not only has denied and deceived about possessing weapons, he's actually used the weapons of mass destruction. He's used the weapons of mass destruction against neighbors. He has used weapons of mass destruction against his own people."

The argument was a deeply misleading one. The events to which Bush referred—uses of poison gas and other chemical weapons against the Iranian military and in retaliation for an insurgency in Kurdistan—happened long ago, in the 1980s. They had no bearing on Saddam's current capacity, which had been massively degraded in the years following the 1991 Persian Gulf War. What's more, they occurred at a time when the United States was allied with Iraq, and evidence from this period had little bearing on the crucial issue of whether Saddam could be deterred from WMD use in the future. Much more relevant was the experience of Bush's father, who prosecuted a war against Saddam at a time when he certainly did possess a chemical arsenal—an arsenal that was not used against the United States specifically in response to U.S. threats of massive retaliation.

Having taken the pro-war position on the underlying issue, however, Shaheen was in no position to point out exactly how deceptive the president's claims on these and other related issues were. She was trapped in a lose-lose situation. Bush and Republicans everywhere were going to imply that voters needed to back her opponent in order to face down a massively exaggerated portrait of the threat posed by Baathist Iraq, but in virtue of her pro-war stance, Shaheen was in no position to argue that the GOP position on Iraq was chock-full of deceptions. She could have accused the opposition of outright lying about her stance on Iraq, but the facts would have been against her. Nothing in Bush's speech actually said she was an opponent of his Iraq policy; it was all a question of implication—why have a long section in your speech about Iraq and the coming congressional debate on Iraq unless it was relevant to the campaign?

Bush left New Hampshire, the campaign's final weeks played out, and when the voting was done, Shaheen had lost—47 percent to 51 percent.

The Shaheen strategy of attempting to avoid a debate on national security policy was odd, but it was by no means unusual. Indeed, Shaheen's strategy was in essence the party's official plan for waging the midterm. The general feeling was that Democrats were well positioned for gains. Bill Clinton had captured the White House in 1992 on his "It's the economy, stupid" platform and had managed to deliver—by his second term the pace of growth was furious and for the first time in decades prosperity was so robust as to clearly reach all segments of U.S. society. Then came the election of 2000. And, with timing so perfect one nearly suspected that the

Democratic National Committee was somehow responsible, the economy fell into recession almost exactly as George W. Bush took office.

For many years following the gas lines and the inflation of Jimmy Carter's administration, the question of managing the economy had been an albatross around the Democrats' necks. But now, with the clear Bush-Clinton-Bush recession-prosperity-recession pattern established, the roles were reversed. Democratic strength on the economy, or so optimists believed, was strongly bolstered by a series of corporate scandals that broke in early 2002. These cast big business under suspicion—good news for liberalism. Even better news: the scandals were epitomized by the gross misconduct of Enron, a company with close ties to the Republican establishment and to Bush personally.

Last, but by no means least, there was the simple matter of Bush.

Presidents normally take office riding a wave of public esteem. That, after all, is how you win elections. But the 2000 election was different. More voters chose Al Gore than Bush—his win was a simple fluke of the United States' odd electoral college system of choosing presidents. And even in Florida, Gore was preferred by more voters than Bush. His win in that state was based on a combination of the flawed ballot design in Palm Beach County that led many Gore voters to mistakenly cast their votes for fringe right-winger Pat Buchanan, and a court-ordered halt to a recount process that would have added many votes to Gore's column. What's more, both in Florida and nationwide there was a clear majority for the center-left once Ralph Nader's supporters were added to the equation. Bush was president, but the underlying public opinion favored Democrats.

Most observers had expected Bush to cope with this difficult situation by significantly curtailing his agenda and governing in a bipartisan manner. It hadn't happened. On his signature proposal for gigantic tax cuts overwhelmingly tilted in favor of the wealthy, Bush had brooked no compromise and had gotten his way. This was an unpredicted strategy, but it had predictable results—months after taking office he was mired in unpopularity, and the moderate Republican senator Jim Jeffords had switched parties and thrown control of the Senate to the Democrats by a single vote.

But there was a cloud on the horizon. Unpopular as Bush may have been in the summer of 2001, his ratings were sky-high in mid-2002. The reason was obvious: 9/11. The attacks prompted a massive "rally 'round the flag" effect and sent his poll numbers to unprecedented heights. His base of support had eroded steadily after that, but only slowly, and it began from such a momentous peak that he was still very popular as the 2002 campaign season began. The rally effect was bolstered by the perception that he had in fact done a good job in responding to the attacks. In its very initial weeks, Bush's military campaign in Afghanistan was looking somewhat troubled, and a certain amount of talk of a "quagmire" could be heard in the press. With remarkable speed, however, the situation turned around. Backed by U.S. special operations forces, intelligence and logistical support, and precision air strikes, the fighters of the opposition Northern Alliance began to rout Taliban forces and captured Kabul by November. What's more, all this was done with remarkably few casualties for U.S. troops.

Democrats had been essentially unanimous in their support for regime change in Afghanistan, so the war's success was not, as such, an enormous problem. It did, however, ensure that Bush would hold on to most of his post-9/11 popularity surge. That created a problem—the risk that Bush's security-related popularity would be wielded as a bludgeon to block Democratic hopes of making electoral gains.

This left the Democratic Party with a choice. On the one hand, it could choose to face the Republican strong point head-on. This would entail simply *assuming* that national security was bound to play a major role in the campaign, that high GOP ratings on the issue were bound to be a problem for the Democrats, and that the Democratic Party had to use the months at its disposal to try to take Bush down a peg or two. The alternative was to reject this task as too difficult and unnecessary anyway. Congressional elections normally turn on domestic issues, and domestic issues were the party's strong suit. On this theory, what Democrats needed to do was strive as diligently as possible to take national security "off the table" as a point of political controversy and fight things out on more promising terrain—corporate scandals, a prescription drug benefit for Medicare recipients, the lousy state of the economy, and so on.

Democratic leaders chose this second option and they chose poorly. Very poorly.

Most simply, the strategy failed. Rather than making significant gains, Democrats suffered serious losses. In the House, no Republican incumbents were defeated and eight Democrat seats flipped to the GOP. In the Senate, the Republican senator Tim Hutchinson, rendered unpopular by his decision to divorce his wife and marry a young staffer, lost to the moderate Democrat Mark Pryor. Meanwhile, Republicans gained Senate seats in Minnesota, Missouri, and Georgia. The Democratic Party's high hopes were dashed.

Worse than the loss of a single election, however, were the long-term implications of the choice to try to take national security off the table. At the very same time that congressional Democrats were determined to avoid a debate over foreign policy, the White House was determined to invade Iraq. Consequently, the Democratic leadership wound up endorsing Bush's war and encouraging dissenting rank-and-file members to keep their complaints low-key. Cover was given for this move by a cadre of "liberal hawks" in the policy and punditry communities, who sought to defend the invasion on liberal terms. As a result, when the invasion eventually was launched and went sour, Democrats, rather than being able to exploit these problems for electoral gain and with it the political power to set the country on a better course, were hobbled by their own history of backing the war and their consequent inability to articulate a coherent alternative approach to the world.

Since the main political aim that Democrats hoped to achieve by backing the war was to avoid the need to talk about the administration's plans for war, congressional Democrats have left us a very thin record of their official thinking about the issue. In addition, the 2003 Iraq War was a curious one, in that its proponents never articulated a single clear-cut argument in favor of the march to Baghdad. To many war supporters, such as the *National Review* editor-at-large Jonah Goldberg, this was a feature, rather than a bug: "There are plenty of excellent geostrategic, legal, and political arguments in favor of regime change in Iraq" and the tendency toward shifting rationales simply indicated how compelling the policy was.[1]

Still, unlike Democratic politicians, liberal writers and intellectuals tended to try to explain themselves in some detail, and it's possible to group the genuine "liberal hawks" into three broad, albeit somewhat overlapping, families.

On the one hand was a group of Democrats who favored invading Iraq for straightforward national security reasons. The most famous and influential of this group was Kenneth Pollack, the director of Persian Gulf Affairs on the National Security Council at the end of the Clinton administration and the author of the celebrated-at-the-time book *The Threatening Storm: The Case for Invading Iraq*. The book, as Fred Kaplan put it, "convinced hundreds of otherwise liberal opinion leaders—and, in turn, thousands and possibly millions of their readers and viewers—that invading Iraq was a good thing to do."[2]

While the Bush administration was putting forward the argument that Saddam Hussein would soon be in possession of a nuclear bomb that he was likely to give to al-Qaeda or otherwise use to mount a first strike against the United States, Pollack pushed a considerably more subtle line. In Pollack's view, as in Bush's, Saddam was likely to build a nuclear weapon within a relatively short time frame. The problem with this was that once nuclear-armed, Saddam was likely to view himself as immune to U.S. military retaliation and might recommence his efforts to conquer Kuwait. Once this happened, a future U.S. leadership would be faced with the unpalatable options of either allowing Saddam to dominate the Persian Gulf and its oil supplies or else making war on a nuclear power.

Under the circumstances, argued Pollack, it made sense to strike sooner rather than later—to wage a preventative war in order to avoid the war Pollack foresaw down the road if Saddam went nuclear.

The book took what passed at the time for an even-keeled tone. Pollack leveled the typical Munich analogies: "Just as Britain and France should have taken up arms in 1938, I believe that the United States should take up arms against Iraq to end the threat from Saddam Hussein's regime once and for all." Then he countered with a dose of fair-mindedness: "This is not to insinuate that those who wish to contain or deter Saddam are somehow equivalent to those who opposed a war with Hitler—that they are appeasers."[3] The antiwar faction was, in Pollack's view, simply mistaken and not, as most of the right would have it, essentially treasonous.

The book's argument struck many liberals, myself included, as exceedingly credible. Pollack was no lunatic right-winger. Indeed, during the 1990s he had coauthored an impressive smackdown of regime-change hyperenthusiasts like Paul Wolfowitz.[4] Because Pollack had served in the

Clinton administration, his view of the state of Iraq's nuclear program and the unlikelihood of keeping it at bay through containment appeared quite plausible. It was also, as we know now, quite mistaken. This is not, however, merely a question of 20/20 hindsight. The intelligence being marshaled to create a sense of urgency about the war was badly flawed in ways that were knowable at the time.

In the first half of 2002, the Intelligence Community's assessment of Saddam's nuclear capabilities was distinctly not alarmist, as John Judis and Spencer Ackerman pointed out in the first comprehensive assessment of the prewar manipulation of intelligence:

> CIA analysts also generally endorsed the findings of the International Atomic Energy Agency (IAEA), which concluded that, while serious questions remained about Iraq's nuclear program—many having to do with discrepancies in documentation—its present capabilities were virtually nil. The IAEA possessed no evidence that Iraq was reconstituting its nuclear program and, it seems, neither did U.S. intelligence. In CIA Director George Tenet's January 2002 review of global weapons-technology proliferation, he did not even mention a nuclear threat from Iraq, though he did warn of one from North Korea.[5]

The solution, rather famously, was to bring pressure to bear on the CIA and other agencies to toe the line. This approach succeeded in creating a dynamic where the aim of the intelligence analysis process was not to discern the truth, but rather to provide evidence for the conclusion that hawks already knew to be true—that Saddam was a serious short-term threat to the United States. Consequently, bits of information that tended to support the administration's view made it into the press, into official documents, and into statements intended for public consumption. Contrary information was buried. The prominence of any given fact—or pseudo-fact— was determined by the degree to which it supported the pre-war view, rather than by its actual reliability.

Casual observers of the scene had little way of knowing pre-cisely how controversial these alarmist assessments of the Ira-qi WMD program were inside the Intelligence Community. For an administration to distort evidence in its public procla-mations was hardly unheard of, but this, or so one might think, is what an opposition political party is for. Some of the Bush administration's claims—most prominently of tight links between al-Qaeda and Iraq—were hotly contested by Democratic elected officials and national security analysts. But on the core contentions about Iraq's nuclear program, Democrats offered little dissent. Indeed, most of the party's leaders in both houses of Congress were backing the war or, at a minimum, not demonstrating much eagerness to chal-lenge the administration's push for a resolution that might authorize a war.

What's more, many people who had some doubts about the cogency of Bush's case chose to focus their energies not on pushing back but on developing a different—a more dis-tinctly liberal—line of pro-war argumentation. This second group of hawks came from the school of what one might call humanitarian militarism.

Leading the charge in this regard was the *New York Times* columnist Thomas Friedman, who explicitly disavowed the WMD argument in a September 2002 column: "I think the chances of Saddam being willing, or able, to use a weapon of mass destruction against us are being exaggerated." Rather than dwell on the point, Friedman put forth a different ration-ale for war, namely that "what the Arab world desperately needs is a model that works—a progressive Arab regime that by its sheer existence would create pressure and inspiration for gradual democratization and modernization around the region."[6] Iraq, it was hoped, could be such a model.

The desirability of transforming Iraq from a brutal dictatorship into a shining exemplar of pluralistic liberal democracy was hard to doubt. Nevertheless, the actual policy doctrine that proponents of this view were putting forward was quite radical. To its liberal proponents, however, the war was seen as a more-or-less logical extension of 1990s-vintage foreign policy. As George Packer explained in his prewar account of the liberal hawk phenomenon:

> The history goes back 10 years, when a war broke out in the middle of Europe. This war changed the way many American liberals, particularly liberal intellectuals, saw their country. Bosnia turned these liberals into hawks. People who from Vietnam on had never met an American military involvement they liked were now calling for U.S. air strikes to defend a multiethnic democracy against Serbian ethnic aggression. Suddenly the model was no longer Vietnam, it was World War II—armed American power was all that stood in the way of genocide. Without the cold war to distort the debate, and with the inspiring example of the East bloc revolutions of 1989 still fresh, a number of liberal intellectuals in this country had a new idea. These writers and academics wanted to use American military power to serve goals like human rights and democracy—especially when it was clear that nobody else would do it.[7]

Packer's tone was one of approbation, but his precise choice of words was both apt and telling. Rather than liberals deriving some specific doctrine from Bosnia, that war "turned these liberals into hawks"—militarists—driven by a vague notion of deploying "American power on behalf of American ideals."

This way of framing the issue generated the liberal hawk equivalent of the right's will-centered Green Lantern theory— a tendency to see the Bush administration's sincerity about a desire to produce a democratic Iraq as the crucial issue. Peter Beinart fretted on the war's eve that "liberals support this war because they hope it will bring certain political results but they have limited influence over whether it will be prosecuted with those results in mind."[8] Similarly, according to Packer's account, Christopher Hitchens, who departed the left-wing *Nation* over his support for the Iraq War, "agree[d] with the 'decent skepticism' of liberals who distrust the administration's motives, but he has decided that hawks like Deputy Defense Secretary Paul Wolfowitz aim to use a democratic Iraq to end the regional dominance of Saudi Arabia." Similarly, Bill Keller, then a *New York Times* columnist (now the paper's editor), described the importance of *The Threatening Storm* as having "provided intellectual cover for every liberal [including Keller] who finds himself inclining toward war but uneasy about Mr. Bush."[9]

Bush's intentions, his sincerity, and other aspects of his precise mental state were, of course, entirely unknowable. Consequently, this particular line of concern provided reasonable fodder for showy hand-wringing but no kind of platform for effective opposition to the march to war, even for those who had some doubts about the war's wisdom.

Meanwhile, the actual connection between the topic at hand—war to topple Saddam Hussein—and the emotional and historical roots of the liberal hawk movement in the Bosnian civil war was left distinctly underexplained. The two issues were, simply put, quite different. The best anyone could come up with was the *New Republic* literary editor Leon Wieseltier's observation that "Morally, there is no significant difference between Halabja and Srebrenica."[10] Srebrenica was the site of particularly egregious Bosnian Serb human rights abuses that shocked the conscience of the world and spurred the West to intervene more decisively to bring the conflict to an end, while Halabja was a town in Kurdistan subjected to chemical weapons bombardment as part of Saddam Hussein's quasi-genocidal efforts to put down a Kurdish rebellion. Denying a morally significant difference between the two events is arguably correct, but there was a very significant *chronological* difference. In particular, at the time of NATO's UN-authorized intervention on behalf of the Bosnian Muslim cause, the war that had led to Srebrenica was still ongoing. Timely military action forced the Serbs to draw their forces back to some extent and created the opportunity to separate the Muslim population from the reach of the Serbian military.

The Halabja massacre, by contrast, happened in 1988, and there was nothing in particular that could be done about it by 2003. What's more, a series of somewhat Bosnia-esque military operations designed at establishing a Kurdish safe haven in northern Iraq had already been undertaken in the early 1990s. Though still nominally part of Iraq's sovereign territory, Kurdistan was, at the time, de facto self-governing, and the northern no-fly zone enforced by U.S. and British air power protected the Kurds from Saddam's military. Halabja was, in other words, a total non sequitur and rather clearly so to anyone who had passing familiarity with the Kurdish issue.

What the liberal hawks had learned from Bosnia was not a doctrine about the use of force or the role of human rights in foreign policy, but a kind of disdain for the aesthetics of antiwar politics. Thus Packer opened his profile of the liberal hawk movement complaining that at antiwar rallies "speakers . . . voice[d] unnuanced slogans like 'no sanctions, no bombing' and 'no blood for oil.'"[11] Years later, in his celebrated history of how the Iraq War went sour, *The Assassins' Gate*, Packer was still giving prewar invasion opponents short shrift, citing the online political organizers behind

MoveOn.org as the only exemplars of antiwar thinking and finding their comprehension of geopolitics wanting.

But *of course* the slogans on offer at antiwar rallies were unnuanced and simplistic. They were slogans at rallies. Call-and-response chants are an inevitable element of political mass gatherings, but everyone understands them to be a poor medium for sophisticated argumentation. What's more, it's hardly as if the grassroots mobilization in favor of the war consisted entirely of subtle treatises on the deep questions of war and peace. Leave aside the prominence of right-wing demagogues like Bill O'Reilly, Ann Coulter, and Rush Limbaugh in building support for war. The president of the United States himself was touring the country telling palpable untruths about links between the Iraqi government and al-Qaeda. Members of the administration's war council were in thrall to crackpot conspiracy theories holding Iraq responsible for 9/11 itself and had managed to convince vast swathes of rank-and-file conservatives that Saddam was somehow behind the attack. And yet according to liberal hawks, the case *for* war was to be judged according to its very best arguments, while the contrary case was rightly judged by its very worst.

A person seeking the best available arguments about the war would not have found it difficult to locate a bevy of former military, intelligence, or diplomatic professionals or academic students of these issues, the region, or international relations generally prepared to provide serious arguments about the war. Such arguments would not call into question the desirability of eliminating Saddam's regime and replacing it with a model democracy, but the feasibility of doing so with anything resembling a reasonable price with any decent prospects of success.

What makes this inattention to serious objections to the war especially galling was that liberal hawks clearly weren't unaware of their existence. Indeed, many of the objections were raised by the hawks themselves. A proponent of war no less strident than Pollack himself concluded his book with a chapter on the prerequisites for a successful operation that were nothing short of daunting. Noting the need for a broad diplomatic coalition in order to give war political legitimacy, he made the fundamental internationalist point that "the United States is not a rogue superpower determined to do what it wants regardless of who it threatens or angers. If we behave in this fashion, we will alienate our allies and convince much of the rest of the world to band together against us to try to keep us under control." Obtaining such legitimacy and international support was not merely desirable but actually essential, because "rather than increasing our security and prosperity, such a development would drastically undermine it."[12]

Pollack further recognized that stabilizing the postwar situation, rather than toppling Saddam as such, was "likely to be the most important and difficult part of the policy, and we would be living with the results or suffering from the consequences for many decades to come." Maintaining the necessary security would require a large quantity of boots on the ground. In order to provide those troops on a sustainable basis, Pollack hoped that after an initial U.S.-dominated phase, "fairly quickly we could transition to a more multinational force by bringing in contingents from our European, Asian, and regional allies," further necessitating a broad coalition, and we could persuade the United Nations to take the lead in managing the postwar political situation.[13] On top of all that, Pollack held that taking a serious bite out of al-Qaeda and restarting the Israel-Palestine peace process were necessary preconditions to war.

Anyone could see that the Bush administration was doing no such thing. Instead of identifying Iraq as a separate issue that should be pursued after al-Qaeda was contained, the White House was both pushing the notion that an invasion of Iraq would constitute an important blow against bin Laden and acting on that rhetoric. Already in early 2002 resources that included unmanned aircraft, intelligence operatives, and special forces troops were being pulled out of the fight against al-Qaeda in and around Afghanistan in preparation for redeployment to Iraq. Similarly, Bush and his allies regarded war against Saddam Hussein as a substitute for action on the Middle East peace process. The slogan for this rather fantastical theory was that "the road to Jerusalem runs through Baghdad," meaning that "to topple Saddam would be to remove a leading supporter of Palestinian terrorism; moreover, a stable, democratic Iraq would light a blazing trail of freedom across the Middle East."[14] As best one can reconstruct the daft thinking behind this notion, the idea was that a democratic Iraq would lead to the emergence of a democratic process for the Palestinian Authority. This, in tandem with the removal of Saddam's rhetorical and financial support for Palestinian rejectionist groups, was supposed to lead to the emergence of a more pliant generation of Palestinian leaders who would agree to make peace with Israel on terms that were acceptable to the Israeli right.

A related theory had actually been pitched in the mid-1990s to the then prime minister of Israel Benjamin Netanyahu by a group of U.S. advisers in a document given the menacing title "A Clean Break: A New Strategy for Securing the Realm." In this version, Israel was instructed to pursue regime change in Iraq with an aim to the utterly implausible goal of restoring that country's former Hashemite dynasty to the throne. The purpose of this was that "were the Hashemites to control Iraq, they could use their influence over Najf to help Israel wean the south Lebanese Shia away from Hizballah, Iran, and Syria. Shia retain strong ties to the Hashemites: the Shia venerate foremost the Prophet's family, the direct descendant of which—and in whose veins the blood of the Prophet flows—is King Hussein."[15] Minor details like the fact that the Hashemite dynasty practices Sunni Islam and has no actual influence over Shiite public opinion were brushed under the rug. Netanyahu, no dove, but also not a fool, quite rightly rejected this proposal.

Indeed, the "Clean Break" strategy was so bizarre that it would be funny were the subject matter not so deadly serious, for several of the authors of the paper, including Richard Perle, and especially Douglas Feith and David Wurmser, were actually involved in shaping the Bush administration's Iraq policy. Perle held a position on the Defense Advisory Board and by most accounts had the ear of Secretary Don Rumsfeld. Feith, as undersecretary of defense for policy, was the civilian in overall charge of the Pentagon's approach to Iraq, and Wurmser was his key deputy for that issue.

Consequently, it could be seen in advance that even by the liberal hawks' own standards, the most enthusiastic backers of war with Iraq inside the administration were pursuing a policy that was likely to fail. Under the circumstances, the substantive points made in most liberal hawk commentaries could just as easily have been construed as arguments against launching a war as they were arguments in favor. Rather than pitch their views in this way, however, liberal hawks continued with the tradition commenced in late 2001 of treating disagreements with people to their left as more significant than disagreements with those to their right, even though the reins of power were exclusively in the hands of the right. The motivations for taking this stance were complicated, but prominent among them was the illusion of control. Casting one's lot with the antiwar faction meant disavowing any effort to influence the course of national policy. Casting your stance as an argument *for war*, by contrast, kept you on the team and perhaps in a position where policymakers in positions of actual power might listen to you.

This was fundamentally more an ego trip than anything else, as it was abundantly clear that the Bush administration had no particular interest in outsiders' opinions, especially outsiders who had no loyalties to Bush, the Republican Party, or the conservative movement. It was, however, an ego trip that was very much encouraged by the media climate of the era. This was a time in U.S. political life when favoring an invasion of Iraq was unquestionably a smart career move. Certainly, the reverse posture could be deadly. As of February 2003, Phil Donohue was the host of the most popular prime-time program on the struggling MSNBC cable network. Ratings notwithstanding, his show—unlike those of his peers on the channel—was canceled. According to a leaked internal memo, the concern was that the program could become "a home for the liberal anti-war agenda at the same time that our competitors are waving the flag at every opportunity." Under the circumstances, Donohue was "a difficult public face for NBC in a time of war," who "seems to delight in presenting guests who are anti-war, anti-Bush and skeptical of the administration's motives."[16]

Other media outlets were no less vigilant in their efforts to avoid becoming a home to the liberal antiwar agenda. According to an analysis by Paul Waldman, during the run-up to the war just 18 percent of the members of Congress to appear on the influential Sunday morning television political talk shows were opponents of the invasion.[17] Under the circumstances, people with mixed opinions had every reason to emphasize their hawkish credentials and downplay their caveats, a process the explicitly conservative branches of the media were happy to facilitate.

The result of this dynamic was a vicious cycle leading to war. Motivated in part by simple fear, leading congressional Democrats backed the invasion. They recalled all too well the first

Gulf War, which most Democrats had opposed, only to pay the price when the war ended surprisingly quickly and with few U.S. casualties. Democratic support for the war in turn encouraged the media to marginalize and neglect antiwar voices and views in favor of a pseudo-debate between conservative hawks and liberal hawks. This naturally helped to build public support for the war because the electorate had scant exposure to the other side of the argument. But the more the public supported the war, the more intense the pressure became on Democratic candidates to do likewise.

This led to the rise of a third school of hawks: political opportunists who wanted to project "strength" to stay politically viable in red states or for a presidential campaign. This group was primarily composed of practical politicians and the staffers and the consultants who surrounded them. Members of the group could be identified when people with no previous record of interest in national security suddenly developed strongly held views about Iraq that precisely mirrored the president's, or when longtime internationalists discovered a sudden, newfound enthusiasm for U.S. unilateralism.

Somewhat similarly, the national security analysts residing at places like the Brookings Institution and other Washington think tanks are not, in reality, the independent experts they appear to be. Rather, such institutions tend to serve as a kind of unemployment insurance for people who expect—or at least desire—political appointments when partisan control of the White House flips. Consequently, when it became clear that leading Democrats would support the war, it was useful from a careerist perspective to likewise back the war, cast doubts about its feasibility only in the form of advice about its conduct, and mute or otherwise downplay criticism. This, however, merely served to further entrench the cycle. The more Democratic politicians supported the war, and the more liberal analysts did likewise, the more rank-and-file liberals became inclined to favor it as well. This made highly public opposition more politically problematic and reinforced the sense that the smart play was to back the war with caveats, rather than couch the caveats as reasons to weigh in against the drive to war.

Eventually, the caveat crowd got a chance to make something of its hand-wringing when the president asked Congress to pass a resolution authorizing the use of force in Iraq in October 2002. The timing of the request was rather sudden, and not merely because it happened to come immediately before a midterm election. Instead, the truly shocking element of the request was that it came at a time when the administration was not actually proposing to start a war and indeed was busy denying that it had even made up its mind as to whether a war was necessary. Instead of touching off an invasion, the resolution was merely supposed to initiate a series of diplomatic initiatives aimed at building an international coalition to tackle Iraq and seek UN action on the subject. The outcome of these initiatives was not yet known and indeed was inherently unknowable. Similarly, Saddam Hussein's response to Bush's demands was unknown, as was the actual content of what Bush would be demanding. Nevertheless, the White House wanted Congress to authorize war *in advance* at a time of the president's choosing, irrespective of the circumstances that might or might not be prevailing at the time.

This naturally provoked some dissent from members of Congress, including most Democrats, along with some Republicans who had moderate views on foreign affairs, such as Senators Richard Lugar and Chuck Hagel. Carl Levin, the top Democrat on the Senate Armed Services Committee, introduced text that would have authorized war only if the president was able to secure authorization for such action from the UN Security Council. Most of the Democratic leadership, however, rallied behind an alternative resolution by Lugar and Joe Biden, the senior Democrat on the Senate's Foreign Relations Committee. The Biden-Lugar resolution put only the mildest constraints on Bush's authority to wage war. It enjoined the president to seek Security Council approval for war but also permitted the White House to "make available to the Speaker of the House of Representatives and the President pro tempore of the Senate his determination that the threat to the United States or allied nations posed by Iraq's weapons of mass destruction program and prohibited ballistic missile program is so grave that the use of force is necessary, notwithstanding the failure of the Security Council to approve a resolution."[18]

What, exactly, this would have amounted to in practice is a bit difficult to say. The political message it was intended to send was that Congress, while not willing to rule out unilateral war, was not convinced of its necessity either. Legally, however, the resolution seems unlikely to have tied the president's hands. Nevertheless, the White House appears to have found the distinction salient. As Tom Daschle, the leader of the Democratic caucus at the time, recalls in his memoir, "the President and his key officials, National Security Adviser Condoleezza Rice, Secretary of State Colin Powell, and Secretary of Defense Donald Rumsfeld, lobbied hard for his position," leaning on moderates in both parties.[19] Joe Lieberman, who'd consistently staked out the most-hawkish-possible position on foreign policy issues, was in the administration's camp.[20] More surprisingly, Dick Gephardt, the Democratic leader in the House of Representatives, defected to the administration's side as well.

Gephardt had no particular record as a foreign policy hawk in general, an Iraq hawk in particular, or even a noteworthy level of interest in national security questions. Virtually nobody understood his support for the president's position as driven by conviction. Rather, just as a cynical desire to take national security off the table for the midterms had pushed the Democratic leadership as a whole toward a more hawkish stance on Iraq, Gephardt's move was all about the

internal Democratic jostling for the 2004 presidential nomination. Conventional wisdom in Washington had it that only
a hawkish profile could put a Democrat into the White
House, just as the three Democratic candidates to appear on
national tickets since 1992 had all been chosen from the few
members of the Democratic Party who had backed the first
Gulf War. Consequently, all the congressional Democrats
with presidential aspirations were backing war. Aligning himself more closely than the rest with Bush was a way for
Gephardt to separate himself from the pack.

With Gephardt and Lieberman on board with Bush, Republican support for the Biden-Lugar compromise effort vanished, and it was dropped. Democrats were then left with a
choice—they could support the White House's blank-check
authorization, or they could vote for Levin's resolution. This
latter would still have authorized war in the event that the
Bush administration secured Security Council approval.
What's more, it would have allowed Bush to return to Congress later to ask for a new resolution if things went poorly at
the United Nations. As an antiwar measure, in other words, it
wasn't much. Nevertheless, it was still too much for Congress,
including most Democrats. The majority of the party's Senate
caucus, including Daschle, Biden, Daschle's deputy and
eventual successor Harry Reid, and presidential hopefuls John
Kerry and John Edwards, backed the Bush resolution. In the
House, most Democrats were opposed. Gephardt, however,
was obviously in favor, as were the bulk of the members in
competitive races and challengers in swing districts.

The floor speeches given by pro-resolution Democrats
were oddly incoherent. In his address, Daschle warned that
the intelligence backing the president's case for war was likely
flawed. He referenced a *Washington Post* article warning that
"an increasing number of intelligence officials, including former and current agency employees—are concerned the [CIA]
is tailoring its public stance to fit the administration's views."

He also cited the need to "make every reasonable effort to secure a UN resolution." Nevertheless, he was backing a resolution that took no such concerns into account. Jay Rockefeller, meanwhile, who served on the Senate Intelligence Committee, rehashed the administration's worst distortions. "There is unmistakable evidence that Saddam Hussein is working aggressively to develop nuclear weapons and will likely have nuclear weapons within the next five years," he warned. "We also should remember we have always underestimated the progress Saddam has made in development of weapons of mass destruction." Not only was this all wrong, but Rockefeller was in a position to know it. What followed was worse:

> But this isn't just a future threat. Saddam's existing biological and chemical weapons capabilities pose a very real threat to America, now. Saddam has used chemical weapons before, both against Iraq's enemies and against his own people. He is working to develop delivery systems like missiles and unmanned aerial vehicles that could bring these deadly weapons against U.S. forces and U.S. facilities in the Middle East.
>
> And he could make those weapons available to many terrorist groups which have contact with his government, and those groups could bring those weapons into the U.S. and unleash a devastating attack against our citizens. I fear that greatly.[21]

Members of the public could be forgiven for putting a lot of stock into Rockefeller's words. They—we—lacked access to classified intelligence and to the personnel charged with analyzing it. The president of the United States has such access and was making similar claims. As an opposition party member of the committee charged with overseeing the United States' intelligence agencies, Rockefeller was precisely the sort of person one would expect to speak up if, as was the case in this instance, the president was offering a distorted picture of the facts. Rather than doing so, he echoed the administration's claims. As Thomas Ricks pointed out, doing something as simple as reading the classified version of the National Intelligence Estimate on Iraq's WMD programs would have revealed that it "contained a host of doubts, caveats, and disagreements with Bush's assertions." The job of Congress, one might think, would be to bring these awkward facts to light. In fact, however, "only a handful of members of Congress ever read more than its five-page executive summary. Delving into the dissent in the intelligence community would only have gotten a politician on the wrong side of the issue with the president," precisely the outcome that election-minded Democrats were seeking to avoid.[22]

As an electoral strategy, the Democrats' approach failed miserably. Just about one month after the vote on the authorizing resolution, Americans went to the polls and delivered a nearly unprecedented win for the Republican Party. Karl Rove's strategy of advising Republicans to "focus on war" for the midterm elections was a success. Muting criticism of the administration utterly failed to take national security issues off the table as a voting concern. It failed to do so for two simple reasons. On the one hand, these are very important issues that, the experience of the 1990s aside, *usually* play a role in political campaigns. On the other hand, a strategy of taking the issue off the table could succeed only if both parties agree to try it, and the Republicans didn't want to. Instead of muffling the appeal of the GOP's security focus, the decision to avoid challenging the administration's approach simply denied Democrats any opportunity to undermine Republican strength.

Pessimism among Democratic political operatives about the possibility of winning a debate with the Republicans over security was not necessarily unwarranted. The GOP had enjoyed a generic political edge on foreign policy issues since the early 1970s. The president of the United States has a lot of intrinsic advantages in debates on these subjects and tends to get his way no matter what anyone else may do. What's more, at the time Bush was quite popular, his handling of terrorism was especially popular, and the press was disinclined to seriously challenge him. A stronger, more principled stance against the march to war might well have brought electoral defeat to Democrats.

The strategy they actually adopted, however, simply guaranteed defeat. Declining to engage the debate seriously didn't stop the debate from happening; it just ensured that only one side even bothered to try to make its case persuasively. Like ostriches with their heads in the sand, party leaders believed they could make the security issue go away by ignoring it, but instead they only made it easier for their adversaries to devour them. Even worse, by assenting to so much of the administration's narrative and rhetoric, Democrats wound up desperately compromising their own *long-term* posture once reality began to make trouble for Bush's strategy.

What's more, in this particular instance the long term didn't even take especially long to materialize. The war, after all, came not in October 2002, but in March 2003 after months of activity at the UN and elsewhere had radically undermined the case for an invasion. At the apparent insistence of the British prime minister Tony Blair, Bush went to the United Nations soon after the midterm elections in an effort to obtain Security Council authorization of an invasion of Iraq. What he got was Resolution 1441, demanding that Saddam readmit UN weapons inspectors and fully cooperate with their efforts lest he face "serious consequences."

Thanks to these efforts, by March 2003, the two inspectors had been in the country for months and were able to report clearly that there was no significant security threat from Iraq.

Hans Blix's UNMOVIC (United Nations Monitoring, Verifi-
cation, and Inspection) team found no evidence of the stockpiles of chemical and biological weapons that Iraq allegedly
had. Nor did they find evidence of programs to make such
weapons. They did find several missiles whose ranges were
slightly higher than what Iraq was permitted to have, and
those missiles were being duly dismantled. Mohammed
ElBaradei, the director of the International Atomic Energy
Agency (IAEA), was in charge of the crucial issue of Iraq's nuclear weapons program. His team was able to verify that the
State Department and the Department of Energy were correct
and that Iraq's aluminum tubes were not for a nuclear program. They determined that documents presenting evidence
that Iraq had sought to purchase uranium from Niger were
"in fact not authentic." Indeed, *none* of the specific allegations brought to demonstrate that Iraq had reconstituted its
nuclear program were verifiable. Thus, the IAEA concluded
that there was "no evidence or plausible indication of the revival of a nuclear weapons programme in Iraq," much less
one likely to bear fruit in the near future.[23]

Under the circumstances, UN support for an invasion was
naturally not forthcoming. Remarkably, although many liberal hawks took note of the near-total absence of international
backing for a war, virtually none paid any attention to the *reason* that Bush's position had so little support. Or, rather, in a
theme that would become more prominent in years to come,
they agreed with Joshua Micah Marshall in attributing the situation to "the Bush administration's incompetence" in managing the diplomacy, rather than to a flawed underlying
policy. The country was said to face a problematic choice between a poorly executed war and a situation where "we let
Saddam remain in power now without even having made a
nod to disarmament."[24]

Had Democrats not been so eager to avoid making a big
deal out of the fact that the administration's Iraq intelligence

claims had always been fishy, Americans would have been prepared to notice that the inspectors' work was demonstrating that the administration was simply wrong—the nuclear menace didn't exist. Foreign governments weren't supporting the U.S. position because the U.S. position made no sense. Instead, it was simply assumed that the advanced WMD programs were there and that the inspectors' failure to uncover them represented a failure of the inspections process to succeed in producing disarmament. War was, in a sense, more necessary than ever. Some liberal hawks argued in favor of a thirty- or forty-five-day delay before beginning the war, in an effort to garner more international support for the invasion.

The Bush administration, however, rejected this path. Late in the evening of March 19, the president addressed the nation and informed the public that "at this hour, American and coalition forces are in the early stages of military operations to disarm Iraq, to free its people, and to defend the world from grave danger." The speech had an air of anticlimax about it since the inevitability of war had been clear for several days before the fighting actually commenced. In my college dorm there was even serious disagreement as to whether it was worth changing the channel—everyone knew, after all, what the president was going to say. And so, the liberal hawks, including the leadership of the Democratic Party, put their caveats aside and, when the chips were down, backed invasion. "It appears that with the deadline for exile"—referring to a last-ditch opportunity Bush granted Saddam to vacate power voluntarily and go into exile somewhere—"come and gone," read Senator John Kerry's statement the morning after Bush's speech, "Saddam Hussein has chosen to make military force the ultimate weapons inspection enforcement mechanism. If so, the only exit strategy is victory, this is our common mission and the world's cause. We're in this together. We want to complete the mission while safeguarding our troops, avoiding innocent civilian casualties, disarming Saddam Hussein, and engaging the community of nations to rebuild Iraq."

Soon enough, it would become clear that the rationale for launching the war was gravely mistaken, the war itself incredibly costly, and the underlying strategy fundamentally flawed. The opposition political party, however, was largely unable to reap the benefits one might expect from such a disaster for the simple reason that when given the opportunity to point this out in advance, its leaders instead endorsed Bush's strategy.

CHAPTER 5

Opportunism
Knocks

I n January 2003 I found myself walking from the
Burlington, Vermont, bus station to the then headquar-
ters of Howard Dean's presidential campaign in what
passes for the city's downtown. It was cold that week like I'd
never experienced and with any luck will never experience
again. Friends and family who'd been informed of my plan
to spend a week with his campaign were puzzled. "Howard
who?" was the overwhelming reaction, even from politically
aware people.

"The governor of Vermont," I explained. "He's running
for president."

Nobody had heard of him because nobody thought he
had a chance. Because nobody thought he had a chance, nobody was covering his campaign. Because nobody would cover it, nobody had heard of him, making his chances even
dimmer. And, of course, the conventional wisdom eventually
proved correct—Dean did not become the Democratic Party's
nominee for president of the United States. In another sense,

however, the conventional wisdom proved badly wrong. The actual thinking as of January 2003 wasn't merely that Dean would lose, but that he'd be an utter nonfactor, someone who stood no chance whatsoever. His campaign was viewed as so quixotic that even his wife thought running was a silly idea.

A year later, nobody was laughing. Dean's chances looked very good indeed, and his campaign was something like a national obsession. Once he got big enough, accounts of Dean's unexpected rise tended to emphasize the unorthodox nature of his campaign—the enthusiasm he generated among progressive bloggers, the use of MeetUps and other Web-based tools to organize volunteers, his unprecedented success in raising funds from small-dollar donors.

Those explanations were exciting and trendy and even contain a large measure of truth, but they also miss a banal and crucial point. Dean worked his way into the hearts of Democratic voters by being loudly and consistently right about Iraq, and he worked his way back out when he muddied his message and his opponents succeeded in convincing the base to put their actual views aside in favor of the theory that the party needed a combat veteran as nominee more than it needed a sound foreign policy.

January 2003 was before all that; the term *netroots* didn't exist. Joe Trippi, who would eventually pioneer the use of new media in campaigning, hadn't joined the team yet. Dean had a campaign staff of maybe a half-dozen people. The press coverage he did receive was generally positive but also rather dismissive of his chances. Jonathan Cohn, a health policy specialist and an admirer of Dean's track record on this issue in Vermont, was the first national political journalist to profile Dean's campaign back in June 2002. Making the case for why we should care, he more or less assumed that Dean—called the "Invisible Man" in the article's headline—would lose but that "Dean might succeed in 2004 even if he doesn't win the nomination."[1] Cohn drew an analogy to John McCain, who lost his 2000 bid for the Republican presidential nomination but succeeded in pushing campaign finance reform onto the national agenda and forcing the presidential winner to sign the bill. This was, in a sense, prescient, but Cohn's theory was that Dean would have an impact on health policy, not on national security issues.

Democratic thinking during the 2002 congressional Iraq debate about the politics of national security was heavily influenced by a rather simple-minded reading of the lessons of the first Gulf War. Roughly speaking, most Democrats had opposed it, and many paid a price for it at the polls. That group included then senator Sam Nunn, one of the country's most respected thinkers on defense and foreign policy issues. The senator, in light of his long and solid track record on national security, had been chosen to take the lead in explaining Democratic opposition to the war. Yet he couldn't save his job in the face of security-related attacks from an undistinguished Republican opponent. Many opponents of the first Gulf War, of course, didn't wind up losing their jobs. They did, however, wind up being shut out of national politics. Bill Clinton, Al Gore, and Joe Lieberman all got spots on national tickets, and all were among the few Democrats who had supported the war. The lesson, or so it was thought, was clear—opposing wars is a bad idea.

A more nuanced take was always available. The Democrats' political problem with the Gulf War wasn't that they'd opposed it, but that they *wrongly* opposed it. They should have fully endorsed it as a necessary and practical step in strengthening global institutions and restoring international stability. Instead, the Democratic mainstream seriously underrated the ability of the U.S. military to cripple Saddam Hussein's armed forces and to coerce him into withdrawing from Kuwait. Had war opponents' warnings of a quagmire in the desert proved prescient, they would have been in a strong political position for years to come. In fact, however, such warnings were anything but prescient, and the politicians who offered them quite reasonably suffered for it.

The second Gulf War was, however, a rather different beast from the first. In January 2003, the United States was preparing to invade unilaterally, with the support of just a few allied governments, with virtually no support in international public opinion, and without the legitimacy provided by the backing of an international institution. The mission, meanwhile, was substantially more ambitious—to conquer and reconstruct the entire nation of Iraq. The relevant consideration, even in cynical political terms, was not how the war and its critics looked at the time of its launching, but how they *would* look in the months and years to come as events unfolded. By that standard, absolutely nobody would turn out to be perfectly prescient, but skeptics of the invasion eventually came off looking much better than their opponents did. This, ultimately, would prove to be the strength of Howard Dean's campaign.

While most of the U.S. press was gushing over Colin Powell's presentation of evidence of the need for war to the UN Security Council, for example, Dean was skeptical. "Secretary Powell's recent presentation at the UN showed the extent to which we have Iraq under an audio and visual microscope," he told an audience gathered on February 17, 2003, at Iowa's Drake University. "Given that, I was impressed not by the vastness of evidence presented by the Secretary, but rather by its sketchiness." This was, at the time, an unpopular opinion to voice. Within months, however, it would be a clear political asset. Powell's evidence was in fact remarkably sketchy, and after the invasion it was exposed as almost entirely bogus.

The Dean speech was part of the long-standing campaign tradition of candidates stepping back from the hurly-burly of the campaign trail to offer a more high-minded address on foreign policy so as to demonstrate presidential gravitas. Given the timing, the focus of the speech was naturally on Iraq. "We have been told little about what the risks will be if we do go to war," Dean warned. "Iraq," he noted, "is a divided country, with Sunni, Shia, and Kurdish factions that share both bitter rivalries and access to large quantities of arms" while "Iran and Turkey each have interests in Iraq they will be tempted to protect with or without our approval." Most of all, "there is a very real danger that war in Iraq will fuel the fires of international terror." He concluded his Iraq section with a statement of the classic internationalist view: the problem of Saddam Hussein should be addressed, but in a way that strengthens, rather than weakens, the global framework that his alleged quest for WMD threatens to disturb.

> Some people simply brush aside these concerns, saying there were also a lot of dire predictions before the first Gulf War, and that those didn't come true. We have learned through experience to have confidence in our armed forces—and that confidence is very well deserved.
>
> But if you talk to military leaders, they will tell you there is a big difference between pushing back the Iraqi armed forces in Kuwait and trying to defeat them on their home ground.
>
> There are limits to what even our military can do. Technology is not the solution to every problem. And we can't assume the Iraqis have learned nothing over the past twelve years.
>
> In short, America may have to go to war with Iraq, but we should not rush into war—especially without broad international support. Now, I am not among those who say that America should never use its armed forces unilaterally. In some circumstances, we have

no choice. In Iraq, I would be prepared to go ahead without further Security Council backing if it were clear the threat posed to us by Saddam Hussein was imminent, and could neither be contained nor deterred.

However, that case has not been made, and I believe we should continue the hard work of diplomacy and inspection.[2]

The speech was not exactly clairvoyant. But compared with statements made by other contenders, it holds up remarkably well to this day. And, indeed, it started to look rather smart as early as the summer of 2003, putting Dean's political fortunes on an upward trajectory. By November 2004, it would look even more prescient and the speech could, in principle, have been a valuable asset in a general election.

Needless to say, it did not turn out that way. Equally clearly, there's no guarantee that had Dean received the nomination, he would have won the general election. He was, in various respects, a less-than-ideal candidate for reasons that had nothing to do with his stance on Iraq. And a Dean-esque Iraq message might have failed, even as events on the ground were demonstrating its correctness. But a straightforward competition between Bush's hegemonic worldview and the liberal alternative could well have proved compelling. At a minimum, equipped with such an alternative, Democrats would have stood a fighting chance, and the election would have hinged on the two parties' ability to convince the American public of the soundness of their approaches.

On some level, we can never know for sure because Dean did not in fact prevail, and none of the other candidates who shared his opposition to the war got a real shot at winning the nomination. Even stranger, Democrats did end up embracing a pro-war candidate but not because they decided to embrace *the war*. Instead, John Kerry, a pro-war senator who managed to stand out from the pack by virtue of the tepidness of his support for the invasion, took the nomination. He took it, moreover, not by convincing primary voters that his view of national security policy was superior to Dean's. Rather, in an odd recapitulation of the failed strategy of 2002, he sold himself as the candidate of "electability" and his stance on Iraq as part of a necessary package of tactical positioning. The 2004 primary offered the best possible opportunity for a Democratic course correction: a chance to reject the errors of the congressional leadership in favor of the greater wisdom demonstrated by the bulk of the party's rank and file, in and out of Congress. But that opportunity was squandered, and the Democrats wound up deeper in a political quagmire of their own making.

There's more to life, and even to contemporary foreign policy, than the invasion of Iraq, and it's not the case that nominating any old war opponent on whatever platform would have been a smart move. In particular, the other candidates who joined Dean in early opposition to the war were offering ideas that like Bush's, though in a different way, repudiated the internationalist tradition. Most prominently, the marginal candidates Carol Moseley Braun, Al Sharpton, and Dennis Kucinich *really were* the dubious left-wingers Dean is sometimes made out to be. Kucinich, who, to his credit, unlike the other two, made much of his view explicit about world affairs, was a fan of some eccentric notions like the creation of a Department of Peace that would "support disarmament, treaties, peaceful coexistence, and peaceful consensus-building," along with steps toward unilateral nuclear disarmament.[3]

Indeed, Kucinich adhered to a kind of crypto-pacifism in foreign policy. True pacifists, of course, utterly reject the legitimacy of violence and war as tools of politics under any circumstances. Kucinich, in principle, did not adhere to that view. He voted, for example, to authorize the use of force in Afghanistan. Several months after doing so, however, in a speech to the Southern California branch of the liberal organization Americans for Democratic Action, Kucinich complained that although Congress had "licensed a response to those who helped bring the terror of September 11," they "did not authorize the bombing of civilians in Afghanistan" or "ask that the blood of innocent people, who perished on September 11, be avenged with the blood of innocent villagers in Afghanistan."[4]

Of course, Congress did not authorize the deliberate targeting of Afghan civilians as some form of revenge for the terror of 9/11. But the resolution most certainly did authorize the president "to use all necessary and appropriate force against those nations, organizations, or persons he determines planned, authorized, committed, or aided the terrorist attacks that occurred on September 11, 2001, or harbored such organizations or persons." Everyone understood this to mean a war whose aims would include dislodging the Taliban government from Kabul and ending its control over Afghanistan. Simply put, there was no way to accomplish this without spilling at least some of the blood of innocent Afghan villagers. This is the tragedy of war—mistakes happen and innocent people die. The inherent tragedy of military conflict is a good reason to hesitate before resorting to military force, but to insist that civilians never be killed is simply to insist that wars never be fought.

Similarly, although Kucinich frequently expressed admiration for the United Nations, his brand of internationalism was unrealistic, somewhat mystical, and fundamentally phony. On the campaign trail, with the invasion of Iraq already done, Kucinich was an early voice for the withdrawal of U.S. forces from Iraq under the slogan "it is time to get the US out and the UN in."[5] At the time, many Democrats and outside analysts were proposing superficially similar ideas about the need to "internationalize" the administration of postwar Iraq. In April 2003, the Brookings Institution analyst Ivo Daalder observed that in Afghanistan, "a U.N. conference provided the forum for setting up a representative interim administration," and he argued that a "similar U.N. process should be used to help establish a representative Iraqi authority charged with administering the country and drawing up new constitutional arrangements."[6] Two weeks later, Daalder's colleague Kenneth Pollack said that "there is no reason on earth that the United States and the UN cannot handle the operation [in Iraq] jointly," just as hybrid systems had been developed for postconflict reconstruction missions in Haiti, Bosnia, Kosovo, and East Timor.[7]

The purpose of such proposals was twofold. On the one hand, they were intended to entice a broader range of nations to contribute manpower, money, and expertise to the daunting task of running Iraq. On the other hand, they were meant to enhance Iraqis' trust in the international forces that were in charge of their country, to provide reassurance that they were living through a genuine attempt to help them, rather than an effort to exploit them or recolonize their country. A major role for the world's premiere international institution was available, in other words, to provide *legitimacy* and to permit the United States to engage in a distant corner of the world while avoiding the taint of imperialism. These ideas came in a variety of forms at different points in time, but all still envisioned a leading role for the United States government as the main foreign presence in Iraq.

The reasoning behind this was fairly simple. Contra Kucinich's notion that we could "get . . . the UN in," there simply is no "the UN" that can go in and administer a country the size of Iraq or even a much smaller place like Kosovo. A wide variety of missions are undertaken under UN auspices, but the actual cash, equipment, and people doing the mission need to come from somewhere—from the UN's member states. As the wealthiest nation on earth by some margin, and the planet's greatest military power by an even wider one, the United States would naturally be expected to be the largest contributor to any Iraq-scale undertaking. What's more, since the United States had mounted the invasion, foreign leaders would naturally expect Americans to shoulder as much of the load as feasible. Simply put, if the United States had simply gotten out in 2003, gesturing vaguely at "the UN" would not have inspired any actual countries to undertake the responsibility.

Kucinich's view of the situation was in many ways a mirror image of the right's account of international institutions. Conservatives see flaws in existing institutions and wish to use these flaws as an excuse for destroying them. To Kucinich, the flaws are in fact *virtues* that allow the institutions to be used as cover for what amounts to retreating from the United States' leadership role in the world and hoping things will work out for the best if we mind our own business. In the traditional liberal view, by contrast, shortcomings of existing institutions are just that—shortcomings to be coped with and hopefully remedied over time. In terms of the immediate problem, greater UN involvement was vital but could in no sense substitute for U.S. effort. It was hoped that the UN could enhance the United States' odds for achieving success. In the longer term, for years now various proposals have existed to create a standing international force of some sort to allow the UN, as such, to do more in these situations, independent of member state willingness to make contributions.[8] At no time, however, did Kucinich express any notable interest in these ideas or other ways by which the UN could be rendered capable of actually accomplishing the sort of things he wanted it to do in the world.

The point of this is not to pointlessly pile on criticism of a marginal figure in U.S. politics. Rather, Kucinich's very marginality is the essence of the point. During the 2004 primary and general election, and continuing to this day, a concerted effort has been made to associate Dean, the enthusiasm his candidacy generated, and opposition to the Iraq War with an abandonment of the liberal internationalist tradition. Peter Beinart has written of a Democratic Party that, controlled by a "Wallacite grassroots that views America's new struggle as a distraction, if not a mirage," has turned away from the internationalist legacy of Truman and Clinton.[9]

This view has oft been criticized as a straw man, but in fact it isn't quite that. People holding this view do exist, and indeed there are politicians who represent their views, of which Kucinich is one. Were there a large constituency for this approach to the world, it could have easily rallied to his banner, but almost no one did. By and large, and quite in contrast, people supported Dean on the nonmysterious grounds that a unilateral preventative war against Iraq stuck them as a bad idea at the time, and the idea looked worse and worse as it became clear that no advanced nuclear program existed in Iraq and that the occupation of the country was going poorly. This was neither nutty thinking nor a departure from the internationalist tradition.

Perhaps the fate of Wesley Clark makes the point. He was right about the war but was rejected by primary voters—did the activist base reject him for being too interested in national security issues? As a Southerner, a decorated combat veteran, and a retired general, he was, after all, a better-suited messenger for making the case against the Iraq War and for the liberal internationalist alternative than was Dean in almost all respects. Clark had no particular expertise in counterterrorism or Middle Eastern issues, but his experience as a military commander put him closer to the mark than anyone else on the scene. He had led NATO's successful military campaigns against Serbia in the 1990s and was ideally suited to make arguments about the interrelatedness of force, diplomacy, legitimacy, and international institutions.

Indeed, it was for exactly these reasons that Clark's candidacy attracted a great deal of enthusiasm when it was first announced. Soon enough, however, it fizzled. Not, however, because liberals were fundamentally unmoved by a campaign with national security issues at its heart. Rather, Clark failed for the banal reason that he was a bad campaigner who ran a poor campaign. His original sin was simply starting too late— in September 2003, when the other major candidates had already been in the field for months. This made it extremely difficult to catch up in terms of raising money, recruiting and organizing volunteers, and getting field operations up and running.

Beyond that, Clark was a political novice with no time to learn the requisite skills. As a consequence, his campaign was plagued by gaffes of the sort that a veteran politician would have avoided. A typical incident arose when Clark sat down for an interview with Joseph McQuaid, the publisher of the conservative *Manchester Union-Leader*. McQuaid wanted to know Clark's views on abortion, and the following debacle ensued:

> "Let's take an issue—abortion. Are there any limits on it in your mind?" McQuaid asked Clark.
>
> "I don't think you should get the law involved in abortion," Clark said at the time.
>
> "Late-term abortions? No limits?" McQuaid asked.
>
> "Nope," Clark said.
>
> "Anything up to the head coming out of the womb?" McQuaid asked.
>
> "I say that it's up to the woman and her doctor, her conscience, and the law—not the law," Clark said.[10]

As one might expect from a career military man, Clark was unfamiliar with the ins and outs of the law and politics of abortion. He was clearly trying to express an orthodox liberal pro-choice view on the subject. In fact, however, he wound up articulating a position far more extreme than anything any major reproductive rights group advocates. Trivia-obsessed campaign reporters delighted in such Clark gaffes and successfully sought opportunities to create further awkward situations and play them up. This caused the sheen to rapidly come off Clark's theoretically promising candidacy.

On the Dean front, it's noticeable that at the time, few of Dean's antagonists seemed to doubt that national security questions were important to him and to his supporters. Instead, they simply argued that he was wrong; liberal internationalism was being pushed to the margins of the political debate. At the Democratic candidates' first debate, on the evening of May 4, 2003, moderator George Stephanopoulos opened with a focus on security, and the pro-war candidates defended their views on the merits. "I would have preferred if we had given diplomacy a greater opportunity," said John Kerry of the six-or-so-week-old Iraq War, "but I think it was the right decision to disarm Saddam Hussein, and when the president made the decision, I supported him, and I support the fact that we did disarm him."

Joe Lieberman agreed. "We have evidence over the last several years he was cooperating with terrorists and supporting them. We did the right thing," he explained, "and tried everything short of war to get him to keep the promises he made to disarm at the end of the Gulf War. We did the right thing in fighting this fight, and the American people will be safer as a result of it."

"I wish [Bush] would have gotten the UN finally with us," conceded Dick Gephardt in a brief cautionary note, "but getting rid of these weapons of mass destruction—and we're going to find them, they may have gotten rid of, tried to get rid of them the week before we went in—but I'm convinced, and I think everybody is convinced, that these weapons were there and they could have found their way into the hands of terrorists and found their way into the United States, and that's what we had to stop."

By contrast, even at the height of the war's apparent success, Dean was unapologetic, calling it "the wrong war at the wrong time." He criticized the administration for having "set a new policy of preventive war in this country," on the internationalist grounds that, by having done so, we'd undermined the cause of liberal world order and "sooner or later, we're going to see another country copy the United States." As for Iraq itself, "sooner or later," Dean warned, "we're going to have to deal with the fact that there may well be a Shi'a fundamentalist regime set up in Iraq," which could emerge as a greater danger to the United States than prewar Saddam ever was.

By the May debate, there were already signs that not all was well in Iraq. The Baath regime's collapse had been greeted by the Iraqi population not with the "flowers and sweets" for U.S. soldiers that neoconservatives had predicted but with a situation of total chaos and massive looting. In a reaction that would become typical of the Bush administration's handling of Iraq, Defense Secretary Don Rumsfeld used an April 11 press conference to deny that the looting was as bad as the press was reporting. And even if it *was* bad, Rumsfeld insisted, that wasn't such a big deal. "Freedom's untidy," Rumsfeld noted, "and free people are free to make mistakes and commit crimes and do bad things." A further observation: "Stuff happens."[11]

And indeed stuff did happen in April, including the assassination of Sayyid Abdul Majid al-Khoei, a major moderate Shiite leader, likely by followers of the more radical upstart Muqtada al-Sadr. What didn't happen was the discovery of the sort of WMD programs whose alleged existence had been cited as the rationale for war. Hawks were initially unimpressed with these results. On April 22, 2003, the American Enterprise Institute, ground zero for the most extreme neoconservative thinking in town, held a "black coffee briefing" on the progress of the war, featuring Newt Gingrich and Charles Krauthammer, among others. "Hans Blix had five months to find weapons," Krauthammer noted, "he found nothing. We've had five weeks. Come back to me in five months. If we haven't found any, we will have a credibility problem."[12]

War supporters were not, of course, especially eager to revisit this point as time passed. There was no single dramatic moment when it became clear that the weapons *wouldn't* be found, but as the weeks passed it became harder and harder to deny. The reason Blix had failed to locate advanced chemical weapons programs wasn't because the UN inspections process was somehow inadequate. Rather, the inspectors found nothing because there was nothing to find. In particular, the IAEA's prewar assessment that there was no evidence of an Iraqi nuclear weapons program was entirely correct, and the main premise of the war—that it was necessary to prevent Saddam Hussein from acquiring a nuclear bomb—was entirely wrong.

With Dean emerging as a major contender, the stage appeared to be set for a useful and clarifying debate about where the Democratic Party stood on the leading issue of the day. This scenario would have played out with Dean more or less representing continuity with the liberal internationalist tradition in foreign policy, repudiating the congressional leadership's decision to abandon that tradition in favor of support for the Iraq War. His opponents, by contrast, would have an opportunity to outline a coherent "liberal hawk" alternative vision, and the voters would choose where the party would stand.

In reality, however, the issues almost immediately became clouded. Dean's adversaries portrayed him as a throwback to post-Vietnam quasi-isolationism and left-wing radicalism. Dean himself wound up reinforcing elements of this view by increasingly portraying his candidacy as a repudiation not of a relatively short period of bad decision-making by the Democratic leadership, but of the party's entire trajectory throughout the 1990s.

Ironically, before the outbreak of the Iraq debate, Dean had always been regarded as very much a moderate governor. While running Vermont, he made balanced budgets a top priority and made their pursuit a key element of his political persona. His main claim to fame was spearheading a third-way style series of successful incremental health-care policy shifts. He backed Clinton's welfare reform initiative and the NAFTA agreement. As a moderate governor of a liberal state, Dean even faced significant political challenges in the form of an unusually potent left-wing statewide third party.

That, however, was all in the past. Subjected to scathing attacks from the Democratic Leadership Council (DLC) and other centrist Democrats, Dean chose to make a virtue of necessity and recalibrated his political profile in order to seize advantage of pockets of long-simmering discontent with Clinton's approach. He became a trade skeptic, arguing in November 2003, "NAFTA and the WTO help large multinational corporations but ignore the needs of the people who work for them."[13] Later that same month, Dean called for a wide-ranging "re-regulation" of U.S. business, breaking with a trend of bipartisan support for deregulation that is often associated with Clinton but that actually reaches as far back as Jimmy Carter's administration.[14] Dean broadened his critique of the war—and of his Democratic opponents' support for it—to a sweeping condemnation of "Washington insiders" who'd been in the business of selling out progressive principles for years. On a symbolic level, he adopted a favorite catchphrase of the late Senator Paul Wellstone, hero to the anti-Clinton left faction of the party, proclaiming himself a member of the "Democratic wing of the Democratic Party."

These gambits succeeded, to an extent, in broadening Dean's appeal. He earned the support of two major labor unions, the Service Employees International Union (SEIU) and the public employees' behemoth American Federation of State, County and Municipal Employees (AFSCME). Well-informed liberal stalwarts mostly found the whole thing puzzling, with the Boston Globe columnist Robert Kuttner referring to "the right movement yoked to the wrong guy . . . a progressive grass-roots army in love with a rather tightly-wound centrist candidate," but from the Dean campaign's point of view, the important point was that the army had assembled and the candidate succeeded in convincing the movement that he was in fact the right guy.[15]

These successes did, however, end up making Dean's foreign policy line appear more radical and innovative than it really was. In particular, if the Democrats' sins in embracing the Iraq War were of a piece with the alleged sins of Clinton's domestic policies, then it seemed to follow that embracing the Iraq War was perfectly consistent with the internationalist foreign policy of the 1990s. This, conveniently enough, was precisely what liberal hawks wanted to say about the war. Dean became a critic of DLC-style domestic policy, so his views on Iraq were folded into the shift and seen as a departure as well. In fact, the hawks had shifted views on foreign policy, but their espousal of the mantle of Clintonism, combined with Dean's rejection of it, maintained an appearance of continuity, and thus the banishment of Dean and the correct view of Iraq to the radical fringe was complete.

The move toward a rejection of Clintonism also fed doubts about Dean's viability as a general election candidate, doubts that included his dovishness, his Northeastern background, and his indifference to religion.[16] Ultimately, this nexus of doubts about Dean and his efforts to build a broader-spectrum critique of his opponents helped to muddy the waters around the very divide over Iraq that propelled his campaign in the first place. The tendency of Dean and his backers to emphasize his campaign's unique organizational qualities, rather than its policy message, further exacerbated the problem, energizing core Deaniacs but making the broader movement simply look odd to most outsiders. Still, the combination of fund-raising, endorsements, and the increasing unpopularity of the war led Dean to emerge by December 2003 as the most unlikely of phenomena—the outsider as front-runner.

Then, after a period of roughly a year in which everything seemed to go right for Dean, things began to fall apart. On December 13, Saddam Hussein was captured after being found hiding in a small underground facility known as a "spider hole" at a farmhouse approximately ten miles south of Tikrit. His capture would, in retrospect, have no meaningful impact on the course of events in Iraq. At the time, however, it was widely misperceived as a major turning point. As the situation had deteriorated throughout the year, the Bush administration consistently sought to attribute blame to a handful of "dead-enders" and "former regime elements" said to be fighting on Saddam's behalf. The capture of their alleged leader would, according to this theory, break the back of the resistance to U.S. occupation. The press largely bought into this account and loyally relayed it to the American public, which responded with a sharp boost in approval ratings for the president and his war alike.

Dean responded to the news defiantly, observing correctly that "the capture of Saddam Hussein has not made America safer." The public, however, was not especially open to this message at the time. Dean's Democratic opponents, moreover, didn't back him up. Instead, they piled on with savage criticism that further marginalized accurate assessments of what was taking place.

Joe Lieberman said that Dean was in a "spider hole of denial," while John Kerry opined that "no one can doubt or should doubt that we are safer—and Iraq is better—because Saddam Hussein is now behind bars."

Kerry and Lieberman were wrong, as events in Iraq over the subsequent months and years would make clear, but this was little appreciated at the time. What's more, even among those inclined to agree that Dean might have a point, the consensus was overwhelming that he'd committed a major gaffe. The *New Republic* senior editor Jonathan Chait conceded that "on a narrow, technical level" Dean was correct, but Chait slammed him nonetheless. The observation, according to Chait, "demonstrates once again Dean's incurable habit of handing Karl Rove the rope he'd use to hang Dean if nominated."[17]

Coming just about one month before the Iowa caucuses, Saddam's capture managed to seriously derail the Dean campaign. The upsurge in optimism about Iraq deflated his momentum, while opening the door for the electability concerns that were eventually his undoing. And further problems developed. Dean's main rival in Iowa was thought to be former House leader Dick Gephardt, and the two campaigns traded a series of expensive and vicious negative advertisements that ultimately served to make both candidates look less appealing. Meanwhile, two contenders who'd flown under the radar screen for much of the recent past—Kerry and John Edwards—were rapidly on the rise. By concentrating their efforts on Iowa, both had managed to acquire high profiles in the state, despite a relative lack of national attention to their campaigns over the past several months. What's more, both, in their different ways, suggested themselves as appealing general election candidates, an impression reinforced by the fact that they hadn't been subjected to much in the way of attacks from their rivals.

Edwards's appeal stemmed from his youthful good looks, his Southern background, and his undeniable charisma and skill as a public speaker. Kerry, though significantly less charismatic, had a tall, gaunt look and a craggy mien suggestive of presidential qualities. Indeed, his name had been bandied about as someone who might be president someday, dating all the way back to his days as an antiwar activist in the early 1970s. Both men had backed the Iraq War but somewhat tepidly. Unlike Gephardt and Lieberman, they'd done little before the war in terms of acting affirmatively to make it a reality, seemingly dragged along despite some reservations, and both registered large objections to the *manner* in which it had been conducted. Kerry, moreover, had a trump card—his status as a decorated combat veteran—which he argued gave him a unique credibility to campaign against Bush on the national security issue. His courage and patriotism, the argument went, were beyond question.

January polling indicated that both Kerry and Edwards were making headway in Iowa. Signs and bumper stickers with the slogan "Dated Dean, Married Kerry" began to appear. The line of argument was a somewhat unusual one for a presidential campaign to pursue, but it proved curiously effective. In essence, it conceded that Dean was the one primary voters *really* wanted in their hearts—an antiwar candidate whose views mirrored theirs. Kerry, however, was the responsible, adult choice. A candidate who lacked flash but had establishment appeal. A nominee you could settle down with for the long haul, someone who could be counted on to provide for the Democratic family by delivering the greatest prize of all—victory over George W. Bush. Best of all, with just a couple of weeks left before the caucuses, and opinion shifting rapidly, there was little time for anyone to call this narrative into question and ask whether Kerry was really such a formidable contender.

Instead, Dean counted on several aces in the hole. One was his organization on the ground in Iowa, powered by vast throngs of volunteers. The other was his organization *outside* Iowa, much more substantial than what the other candidates had been able to put together. This, in turn, reflected his third advantage—the huge sums of money his campaign had been able to raise.

All three ultimately proved to be mirages.

Dean's ground organization in Iowa was enthusiastic and innovative. It also turned out to be an absolute disaster—disorganized and often counterproductive as orange-hatted out-of-state Deaniacs alienated local voters. Caucus organizing turned out to be one of those things best done by tried-and-true methods and old-school operatives. When the votes were counted, Dean did much worse than anticipated, securing a third-place finish behind Kerry and Edwards with just 18 percent of the vote. Worse, he greeted the result with a soon-to-become-infamous scream that a hostile press adduced as further evidence of his unsuitability to serve as a candidate for national office.

The money turned out to have been largely spent. The campaign had been blowing cash at just as fantastic a rate as it had reeled it in. The broader campaign infrastructure, meanwhile, was all but useless. Kerry and Edwards emerged from Iowa with vast momentum and positive media coverage, and the New Hampshire primary was just around the corner. The "scream" hurt Dean badly, and he faired poorly in the Granite State as well. From there, the nomination was all but sealed. The Democrats had adopted a compressed primary schedule specifically designed to pick a nominee rapidly, and the system functioned as designed. There was no opportunity for anyone to recover from early missteps, and the post–New

Hampshire campaign proved to be a desultory affair. Suddenly, the race was in effect down to Kerry and Edwards—the two candidates who emerged from Iowa and New Hampshire looking good—with the latter trying to catch the former in a manner consistent with being polite enough to get tapped as a vice presidential candidate down the road.

After more than a year of build-up, the actual race was over in practically a blink of an eye. Kerry, who'd been the subject of shockingly little critical scrutiny, was going to be the nominee, even though enthusiastic Kerry supporters were virtually unheard of. He had sold himself not as the candidate you love, but as the candidate you settle for. Not the candidate you agree with, but the candidate who could win in November. And then, in an irony that should have been predictable, the candidate who'd sold himself to the primary voters as the choice of political expediency came to be haunted by charges that he was merely the candidate of political expediency, a man lacking in convictions and principles, a man who was therefore unfit for the White House.

CHAPTER 6

Evasive Action

The 2004 Democratic National Convention was held in Boston; about a month later, the Republicans would gather for their own convention in New York City. At the time, many liberals worried about the symbolism. The GOP would be just miles from Ground Zero, ready, willing, and able to exploit the imagery and memories of September 11, while Democrats would be saddled with the baggage of the nation's most infamously liberal state. Optimists believed it would be possible to rebrand Boston, appealing to an older tradition of the city as the cradle of American patriotism—the freedom trail and Paul Revere, not Ted Kennedy and judicial legalization of gay marriage. The candidate to be nominated there attracted the same hopes. Tall, fit, diligent, hardworking John Kerry, decorated combat veteran and former prosecutor, would rebrand Democrats as the real party of toughness and national security, in stark contrast to George W. Bush, draft-dodger, layabout trust-funder, failed businessman, and alcoholic.

The center of action was the Fleet Center, the city's snazzy new successor to the storied Boston Garden. Speeches droned on all day in the arena's main floor, perorations from the party's second- and third-tier figures. People one might actually want to see were scheduled for prime time, so journalists, activists and sundry hangers-on milled through the arena hallways chatting, doing spots on the dozens of talk radio shows that had set up booths in the facility, and darting to the temporary structure erected next door where journalists could file their stories and enjoy some complimentary refreshments. There in the hall, alongside the pretzel and nacho stands, where in normal times one might find an homage to Larry Bird or Paul Pierce, was a large photo essay depicting the life and times of John Kerry.

It was, however, a somewhat strange take on those times, offering essentially nothing, for example, of the events that had actually made Kerry famous—his role in Vietnam Veterans Against the War. Nor did one see much of John Kerry, United States senator, a curious choice considering he'd held that office for almost two decades and presumably the policies he'd been espousing there bore some relationship to his agenda for the White House. Instead, we saw Kerry with his guitar and Kerry in the war, sitting on his boat, posing with his gun. The sole focus of the display was not John Kerry, antiwar activist, or even John Kerry, politician, but rather John Kerry, macho man.

From the stage at the heart of the arena, the message was the same. "When our national security requires military actions," Jimmy Carter informed the audience, "John Kerry has already proven in Vietnam that he will not hesitate to act." Al Gore observed that the party's nominee "showed uncommon heroism on the battlefield of Vietnam." Hillary Clinton, making an actual policy argument about benefits and equipment for those serving in the military, dropped in a little reminder that—yes!—Kerry fought in a war: "We need to take care of our men and women in uniform who, like John Kerry, risk their lives." Keynote speakers, their texts coordinated and managed by the same cadre of political consultants, all hit upon the theme. "During the Vietnam War, many young men, including the current president, the vice president, and me," said Bill Clinton on a self-confessional note during the convention's second day, "could have gone to Vietnam and didn't. John Kerry came from a privileged background. He could have avoided going, too, but instead he said: 'Send me.'"

When, on day three, the spotlight shifted to Kerry's running mate, John Edwards, the Vietnam things only grew more extended. What we didn't hear from Kerry's allies was anything about *how* he was planning to keep America safe, anything about the shape of a Kerry foreign policy. A heavy focus on symbolism was probably a smart move. Politics is largely symbolic, and this is perhaps more true of the politics of national security than of other topics. Still, the extraordinary lengths to which the convention sought to emphasize Kerry's personal qualities rather than his ideas was quite odd. Indeed, the nearly exclusive focus on symbolism was actually bad symbolism, suggesting that Democrats didn't really have anything to say. The party was acting as if the post-9/11 world needed a president like Harrison Ford in the silly *Air Force One*, a combat veteran who wound up needing to personally fight terrorists who'd hijacked the president's airplane in an effort to wring concessions out of the government.

This approach was odd, but it was adopted for a reason—it was necessary to maintain the veneer of party unity that was an important element of Democratic strategy in 2004. Traditionally the more fractious of the two parties, Democrats had looked deeply divided throughout 2003, with the controversial Dean campaign gaining support for itself by running against a semi-mythical "Democratic establishment" in Washington. Kerry, however, managed to secure the nomination less by winning the intraparty debate than simply by *transcending* it with his argument about character and electability. He followed up his win by choosing Edwards, a darling of journalists, as his running mate. Edwards had personal ties to the DLC (Democratic Leadership Council) faction of the party, and his more recent rhetoric had thrilled progressive economic thinkers. The choice helped to usher in a nearly unprecedented era of good feelings inside the party. People on different sides of disputes—both long-running and new—inside the progressive coalition were ready, even eager, to put their differences aside and unite around the higher goal of kicking the Bush administration out of power.

The process of achieving unity did not, however, come about because of any compromise that actually bridged the divide. Instead, disagreements over the war and other issues were simply papered over, making it imperative to try to avoid talking about them. In the place of either embracing or criticizing Bush's post-9/11 *strategy*, the party united around a critique of his *tactics*, laying the groundwork for the notion that the problem with the war was incompetent implementation, rather than anything more conceptual.

Meanwhile, having sold himself to Democratic primary voters as the candidate of political opportunism, Kerry spent the entire 2004 general election campaign dogged by accusations of being the candidate of political opportunism. In particular, Kerry was said to be a "flip-flopper," a charge that primarily focused on his decision to vote "no" on an $86 billion supplemental defense department appropriation bill aimed at funding the ongoing wars in Iraq and Afghanistan. The specific charge was unfair, but the larger sense that Kerry wasn't taking a clear position on the leading issue of the day was perfectly accurate, and the image of Kerry as an unprincipled flip-flopper was a consistent drag on his campaign throughout the election.

The gravest damage, however, was that the need to combat the charge boxed Kerry in and made it difficult for him to do what all smart politicians do—engage in the occasional flip-flop. Committed to demonstrating his consistency, Kerry was unable to seize advantage of developments on the ground in Iraq since the October 2002 vote to authorize the use of force. In particular, he was unable to articulate the simple point appreciated by a growing body of the political center— the factual underpinning of Bush's argument that the war was necessary for U.S. national security was mistaken, and that absent WMD stockpiles, an advanced nuclear program, or significant ties to terrorism, the invasion made no sense. But instead of making the straightforward case that the war was a mistake, Kerry mostly stuck to criticizing the *conduct* of the war, rather than the war itself.

Though an inability to articulate a clear and consistent critique of Bush's national security policies ultimately did Kerry in, his campaign did grope toward an effective message from time to time. The substance of national security policy was downplayed at the Democratic Convention but did come up in Kerry's own speech, the closing address of the event.

"Saying there are weapons of mass destruction in Iraq doesn't make it so," he pointed out, before promising to "ask the hard questions and demand hard evidence" and "immediately reform the intelligence system, so policy is guided by facts and facts are never distorted by politics." The argument about the distortion of intelligence was used to set up an argument that actually connected Kerry's record of wartime service to a policy argument:

> I know what kids go through when they're carrying an M-16 in a dangerous place, and they can't tell friend from foe. I know what they go through when they're out on patrol at night and they don't know what's coming around the next bend. I know what it's like to write letters home telling your family that everything's all right, when you're not sure that that's true.

As president, I will wage this war with the lessons I learned in war. Before you go to battle, you have to be able to look a parent in the eye and truthfully say, "I tried everything possible to avoid sending your son or daughter into harm's way, but we had no choice. We had to protect the American people, fundamental American values against a threat that was real and imminent."

The point, in other words, was not that Kerry's experiences in Vietnam showed that he was "tough." Rather, as a veteran, Kerry knew war in a way that Bush and the neoconservative fantasists controlling the policy agenda in his administration did not. A person who had commanded soldiers in battle would not send future generations into combat lightly, on a whim, or for esoteric or panicky reasons. Under a Kerry administration, he promised, "any attack" on the United States "will be met with a swift and certain response," but lives and national treasure would not be wasted on peripheral ventures. Meanwhile, he promised to "rebuild our alliances" in order to "make America once again a beacon in the world" that would be "looked up to, not just feared," in order to put us in a position "to lead a global effort against nuclear proliferation" on a sustainable basis, rather than the failing ad hoc strategy Bush had pursued in Iraq.

The implication of this argument seemed rather clear. The threat from Saddam Hussein was, absent the manipulation of intelligence, neither real nor imminent and therefore didn't come close to meeting the standard Kerry had laid out for the use of force. An antiwar tilt played into one of Kerry's major potential strengths down the stretch of the campaign—the defection of large numbers of national security specialists from Bush's camp. Rand Beers, for example, was a longtime professional member of the National Security Council staff, serving through the administrations of Ronald Reagan,

George H. W. Bush, and Bill Clinton. Under George W. Bush, he rose to the position of special assistant to the president for counterterrorism and helped to manage the response to 9/11 and the prosecution of the war in Afghanistan. Blessed with an insider's perspective on administration thinking and access to classified intelligence information, he resigned his post five days before the invasion of Iraq. Two months later, he volunteered to work for John Kerry. In postresignation interviews with the *Washington Post*, he laid out the case against Bush in the simplest possible terms: "[T]hey're making us less secure, not more secure. As an insider, I saw the things that weren't being done. And the longer I sat and watched, the more concerned I became, until I got up and walked out."

The administration's failings were many, reported the *Post*, but the invasion of Iraq was a particular disaster, one that Beers believed had drained personnel, attention, and material resources away from a needed focus on al-Qaeda, while breeding a new generation of recruits for the cause of an anti-American holy war. The necessary war in Afghanistan, meanwhile, had been sidelined and neglected to the point of abandonment. "Terrorists," Beers said, "move around the country with ease. We don't even know what's going on. Osama bin Laden could be almost anywhere in Afghanistan."[1]

Critiques of this sort from a credible counterterrorism professional—one Bush himself had relied on as a fairly high-level adviser—should have been devastating to a president whose foremost political argument was his role in combating al-Qaeda. And Beers was far from alone. Indeed, his boss at the NSC, Richard Clarke, also a veteran of every administration since Reagan's, likewise resigned in early 2003. He did not jump onto a Democratic presidential campaign but instead directed his energies to the composition of a book, *Against All Enemies*, that served as a cutting indictment of the

Bush administration. In the book, as well as in roughly con-
temporaneous public testimony before the nonpartisan commission charged with reviewing U.S. counterterrorism policy
(the so-called 9/11 Commission), Clarke laid out the ways in
which the Bush administration had downplayed al-Qaeda in
its early months, exacerbating, rather than mitigating, shortcomings in Clinton-era policies.

More damningly, Clarke emphasized that after an early
effective response in Afghanistan, Bush had returned to mess-
ing up the struggle against al-Qaeda. Bush was, as Clarke put
it on CBS's 60 Minutes, doing a "terrible job" of managing
terrorism policy. In particular, the administration had erred
massively by invading Iraq. "Osama bin Laden had been saying for years, 'America wants to invade an Arab country and
occupy it—an oil-rich Arab country,'" Clarke observed. "He'd
been saying this. This was part of his propaganda. So what did
we do after 9/11? We invade and occupy an oil-rich Arab
country which was doing nothing to threaten us. In other
words, we stepped right into bin Laden's propaganda. And the
result of that is that al-Qaeda and organizations like it, off-
shoots of it, second-generation al-Qaeda, have been greatly
strengthened."[2]

Other distinguished officials shared Clarke's judgment.
In July, writing under the name "Anonymous," Michael
Scheuer, a former head of the CIA's al-Qaeda task force,
published *Imperial Hubris: Why the West Is Losing the
War on Terror*. This wide-ranging attack on prevailing U.S.
counterterrorism policy was especially scathing in regard to
the Bush administration and the Iraq War. Nor was opposition limited to the intelligence community. General Eric
Shinseki, the army chief of staff at the beginning of the Bush
administration, had famously warned before the war that an
occupation of Iraq would require more troops than the
United States actually had at its disposal. U.S. Marine Corps
general Anthony Zinni, a former chief of USCENTCOM

(United States Central Command) charged with the Middle East region who had enthusiastically backed Bush's 2000 campaign and been appointed as the president's special envoy to the Middle East in 2002, fell out with his former allies over the war and was sharply critical of the administration before the election.

These and other attacks on the administration's Iraq policy from inside the country's national security apparatus varied somewhat but also included strong common elements. All agreed that the administration had massively overstated the threat from Iraq, in particular by greatly exaggerating the extent of the Baath regime's ties to al-Qaeda and the evidence that it had reconstituted its nuclear weapons program. The invasion, meanwhile, had pulled resources—especially special forces and language expertise—away from al-Qaeda, allowing bin Laden and other leaders to escape the war in Afghanistan unscathed and rebuild their operations. The war in Iraq had made it more difficult for the United States to secure international cooperation against al-Qaeda, while inflaming Muslim sentiments against the United States and making it easier to add converts to the al-Qaeda cause. Far from being a "tough" response to 9/11, in other words, the war was a massive strategic miscalculation that had achieved nothing of note to advance U.S. interests, while greatly complicating the overall international situation and impeding efforts to secure the country against terrorist attacks.

This line of argument, and the authorities behind it, provided the best possible means of criticizing Bush's conduct of national security policy. It was a clear, principled, and coherent debunking of administration strategy that opened the door to a positive vision based on liberal internationalism—one in which the United States' role would be to serve as a catalyst for uniting the nations of the world in a focused, coherent effort grounded in international law and multilateral institutions to combat the common threats of transnational terrorism and nuclear proliferation. It was, moreover, a line of argument the American public was open to. By fall of 2004, consistent majorities disapproved of the Bush administration's handling of Iraq—the public could see that the war was faring poorly. On the question of whether the invasion was a good idea in the first place, more variation was on display, with the results showing sensitivity to the precise wording of the question. The typical result, however, was for a narrow plurality to retrospectively endorse the war. The challenge for the opposition candidate should have been to simply do the work necessary to bring support for the war down a handful of additional percentage points by highlighting the copious evidence that the entire enterprise was ill-conceived.

Kerry, however, declined to do so and largely left the national security component of his campaign in the hands of what the *Nation*'s Ari Berman has termed an elite "strategic class" of hawkish Democratic advisers.[3] Such advisers had good reason to fear a Democratic repudiation of the Iraq War, but it wasn't necessarily grounded in the best interests of the party or the country. Rather, repudiation risked raising the question of why top jobs in a hypothetical Kerry administration were scheduled to go to people who'd made the wrong call on the war, instead of to those who'd gotten Iraq right.

Kerry, meanwhile, had reason of his own to fear that disavowing his vote in favor of authorizing the use of force in Iraq would be a flip-flop too far. Thus, in the September 30 presidential debate that focused on national security issues, Kerry maintained that he'd had "one position, one consistent position, that Saddam Hussein was a threat." The difference between his view and the president's, however, was that "there was a right way to disarm him and a wrong way. And the president chose the wrong way." In particular, Bush had erred by failing to assemble a broader coalition against Iraq: "On the day that we went into that war and it started, it was principally the United States; America and Great Britain and one or two others. That's it. And today, we are 90 percent of the casualties and 90 percent of the costs."

This was indeed a consistent position and the one to which Kerry had consistently adhered whenever the question was put to him squarely. It also, however, tended to undercut other points Kerry liked to make. "I believe in being strong and resolute and determined and I will hunt down and kill the terrorists wherever they are," he assured the audience early in the same debate, "but we also have to be smart." "Smart," Kerry continued, "means not diverting your attention from the real war on terror in Afghanistan against Osama bin Laden and taking it off to Iraq where the 9/11 Commission confirms there was no connection to 9/11 itself." That *would* have been a smarter policy, but as Kerry himself emphasized, it wasn't *Kerry*'s policy, which, according to Kerry, also would have focused national attention and resources on Iraq, albeit in a somewhat different way. This same tension ran throughout Kerry's campaign. He had persuasive criticisms of Bush's conduct in office to make, and he even made those criticisms, but the overwhelming implication of those arguments was that the invasion of Iraq—not the management of the invasion or the handling of the diplomacy surrounding it—was a mistake. Kerry, however, refused to go there, leaving himself with a perpetually muddled message. This essential dilemma was highlighted immediately around what was Kerry's best moment in the debate and perhaps in the entire campaign, his response to Bush's contention that his policies had been undertaken because "the enemy attacked us . . . and I have a solemn duty to protect the American people, to do everything I can to protect us." Kerry retorted,

Jim, the president just said something extraordinarily revealing and frankly very important in this debate. In answer to your question about Iraq and sending people into Iraq, he just said, "The enemy attacked us."

Saddam Hussein didn't attack us. Osama bin Laden attacked us. Al Qaeda attacked us. And when we had Osama bin Laden cornered in the mountains of Tora Bora, 1,000 of his cohorts with him in those mountains. With the American military forces nearby and in the field, we didn't use the best trained troops in the world to go kill the world's number one criminal and terrorist.

They outsourced the job to Afghan warlords, who only a week earlier had been on the other side fighting against us, neither of whom trusted each other. That's the enemy that attacked us. That's the enemy that was allowed to walk out of those mountains. That's the enemy that is now in 60 countries, with stronger recruits.

He also said Saddam Hussein would have been stronger. That is just factually incorrect. Two-thirds of the country was a no-fly zone when we started this war. We would have had sanctions. We would have had the U.N. inspectors. Saddam Hussein would have been continually weakening.

Invading Iraq was, in other words, a big mistake. The Saddam Hussein situation was under control, and sanctions, no-fly zones, and inspections were weakening his regime. Meanwhile, the decision to invade Iraq is what required the administration to keep the force in Afghanistan light and allowed Osama bin Laden to slip from the United States' grasp. Kerry did not, however, draw this obvious inference. Instead, he concluded that "if the president had shown the patience to go through another round of resolutions, to sit down with those leaders and say 'what do you need, what do you need now, how much more will it take to get you to join us?' we'd be in a stronger place today."

This was a more "moderate" stance than the simpler antiwar alternative and was more consistent with Kerry's voting record as well. Moderation and consistency came, however, at the cost of rendering Kerry's actual message rather unclear. His preferred strategy might have worked better than what Bush actually did, but it would not have avoided many of the problems Kerry had just identified with the war. It put Kerry's view at odds with what everyone knew to be the beliefs of the vast majority of his supporters. It undermined some of the strongest arguments against Bush. It deflected allegations of flip-flopping but actually reinforced the broader charge that Kerry was trying to have things both ways. Last, but by no means least, it may well have cost Kerry the election.

Every electoral loss spawns dozens of "What went wrong?" accounts, and Kerry's defeat was no exception. Despite the proliferation of such theories, however, alternatives to the account previously presented can be grouped into two main families. One such constellation of theories emphasizes the idea that Kerry—and by extension the Democratic Party as a whole—had simply failed to grasp the need to "get tough" in the post-9/11 era and remained unduly in hock to a dovish base. Another, somewhat diffuse, family of notions centered on the basic idea of Thomas Frank's controversial book *What's the Matter with Kansas?* "Conservatives," as Frank noted, "generally regard class as an unacceptable topic when the subject is economics . . . but define politics as culture, and class instantly becomes for them the very blood and bone of public discourse." Thus, "from George Wallace to George W. Bush, a class-based backlash against the perceived arro- gance of liberalism has been one of their most powerful weapons," especially because "with his aristocratic manner and his much-remarked personal fortune, the Democratic candidate, John Kerry, made an almost perfect villain for the backlash pantomime."[4]

This set off a series of interesting debates about the long-term trajectory of U.S. politics, but the question of what went wrong in 2004 can only be meaningfully answered if we add "Compared to what?" After three straight elections in 1992, 1996, and 2000 in which Democrats outpolled Republicans, things reversed course in 2004 and Bush substantially improved upon the weak result that allowed him to sneak into the White House four years earlier. Examination of long-term shifts in the structure of U.S. politics is an important—vital, even—task, but it does not answer the question of why *that* happened. Abortion, gay rights, gun control and all the rest were factors throughout the 1990s and did not doom Democrats to defeat. The relevant change, simply put, was the obvious one: thousands of Americans were killed by Islamist terrorists in September 2001, and the United States launched a series of initiatives, including two wars, in response. Together, these events dramatically increased the political salience of national security issues, which, in turn, was a major advantage for the party—the Republicans—that Americans had long regarded as more trustworthy on the topic.

Indeed, the eagerness of progressives of various stripes to begin searching through the annals of domestic policy for an issue to debate when the real issues of terrorism and national security policy were staring them in the face can best be seen as a manifestation of the basic problem—the ostrich impulse to shy away from national security. The first instinct of most liberals is to debate what they're comfortable debating—the domestic policy. Similarly, Democratic candidates and political operatives alike had been trained (not incorrectly) to believe that a political focus on national security was bad for them. As a consequence, they had learned to try to duck political debates over national security, a tactic that worked well during the 1990s when it was possible to duck them. After 9/11, however, this ceased to be the case and it became vital for Democratic candidates—whether they wanted to or not—to wage campaigns that had a heavy national security component and for liberals to do the work of debating and framing an alternative to Republican national security policies.

Kerry's campaign reflected, in the main, a continuation of the "politics of evasion," of the hope that the smart play was to somehow just make national security go away as an issue. Kerry did, of course, engage national security issues and especially Iraq, but he did so reluctantly. What's more, there was consistent sentiment from the bulk of his advisers that the *point* of gaining ground on the security front was to facilitate an effort to change the conversation to something else. An October 3 *New York Times* article reported that "Kerry's aides and congressional Democrats" believed that recent strong performances criticizing Bush's foreign policy "gave Mr. Kerry credibility on this subject, allowing him to pivot to the critique of Mr. Bush on the home front that Mr. Kerry has long thought is his path to victory."[5] This was slightly bizarre advice. Kerry had been trailing in late summer, and a focus on Iraq had revived his political fortunes. Why turn away from a strategy that was working? Such advice was, however, eerily widespread, coming not only from those who had long advocated for more robustly populist economic policies but also from their antagonists.

At the height of the controversy, for example, the DLC pollster Mark Penn wrote a *Washington Post* op-ed arguing that the "good news for Democrats is that the latest signals from the Kerry campaign indicate that they may now be pivoting to target" swing voters who apparently were relatively unconcerned with whether their children were going to be slaughtered by foreign terrorists. Rather, "what will bring them back is a focus on their families, the ballooning deficits and a vision for curing the domestic ills of the country." The precedent was Clinton, who "won by making the Persian Gulf War irrelevant to the election. He focused on swing voters, with plans for welfare reform and middle-class tax cuts, and he drove the economy, not the war, as the central defining issue."[6]

A worse analogy could hardly be imagined. The Gulf War was, obviously, *over* by the time of the 1992 election, which surely facilitated efforts to downplay its electoral significance. What's more, the war was, in retrospect, a widely popular Republican success, precisely the sort of thing a Democrat would want to downplay. Bush's Iraq policy was, by contrast, an ongoing and increasingly unpopular failure. Under the circumstances, national security could have been made into a Republican vulnerability. Instead, it remained a key source of GOP strength.

The other major school of thought is formed by analysts who agree that the politics of national security were *the* cardinal Democratic failing in 2004, but they ascribe this failing primarily to John Kerry's failure to be sufficiently tough or hawkish. Peter Beinart, in his initial formulation of his version of this argument, lauded Kerry's hawkish advisers, such as Richard Holbrooke and Joseph Biden and other "Democratic foreign policy wonks [who] not only supported the war in Afghanistan, they generally felt it didn't go far enough—urging a larger NATO force capable of securing the entire country. And, while disturbed by the Bush administration's handling of Iraq, they agreed that Saddam Hussein was a threat and, more generally, supported aggressive efforts to democratize the Muslim world." The tragedy of the Kerry campaign, in Beinart's retelling, was that to wrest the nomination away from Howard Dean, he was forced to vote against the administration's $87 billion supplemental request for Iraq. "His justification for opposing the $87 billion," wrote Beinart soon after the election, "was essentially isolationist: 'we shouldn't be opening firehouses in Baghdad and closing them down in our own communities.'"

This is arguably a misreading of the complaint. In context, the line was part of a laundry list of proposed increases in homeland security spending, not a plea to cut foreign aid. Indeed, Kerry owed the firefighters' union for their early support of his primary campaign, making it rather clear what he was talking about here.

Yet Beinart's larger point that Kerry's national security message was a muddle—what he terms "the Kerry Compromise"—is undeniable. The muddle was not, however, the result of a compromise between a clear-cut liberal hawk alternative and an antiwar position. Rather, the essence of the muddle, the essence of the compromise, simply was the liberal hawk view *itself*, which tried to combine sharp criticism of the Bush administration's conduct of foreign policy with endorsement of both its signature initiative and its basic underlying theoretical premises. Kerry's advisers, and Kerry himself as Beinart notes, believed that Saddam Hussein was a threat to the United States of the sort warranting military action and that "democratiz[ing] the Muslim world" was the key to combating al-Qaeda and that the invasion of Iraq was a useful means of obtaining that latter goal. Certainly, when it looked as if Kerry stood a good chance of winning, most liberal hawks were happy to embrace him as one of their own. The Progressive Policy Institute's Will Marshall, for example, argued that "the Massachusetts politician Kerry resembles most, however, is not Michael Dukakis or Ted Kennedy, but John F. Kennedy," that "for the most part, Kerry has handled the crisis [over Iraq] deftly," and that "the tough-minded internationalism of Truman and Kennedy, and now Kerry, updated to the new realities of the post–Cold War world, can succeed where conservative unilateralism has failed."[7]

The attempt to combine praise for Kerry's pro-war position with criticism of "conservative unilateralism" merely highlights that liberal hawks were offering a fundamentally contradictory story about U.S. national security. Bush's unilateralism, after all, was most distinctly manifested in his willingness to wage preventative war against Iraq without Security Council authorization or any nontrivial level of support abroad. So it went, generally. Along with supporting the war, Kerry, like most liberal hawks, also argued that Bush had unduly neglected Afghanistan, sped up nuclear proliferation in Iran and North Korea, inflamed hatred of the United States in the Muslim world, alienated U.S. allies rather than drawing them into a coalition against terrorism, and badly overstretched the U.S. military. All this was quite true, but it also left the public unclear about where the liberal hawks stood. These matters, after all, were not incidental matters—they were direct consequences of the decision to invade Iraq. Similarly, how much sense did it make to criticize the administration's manipulation and distortion of intelligence information if one was to ultimately conclude that the decision to invade was the correct one? The hawks—just like Kerry himself—couldn't make up their minds. Or, rather, they were sharply critical of the consequences of Bush's foreign policy but couldn't bring themselves to see that Iraq was the centerpiece of Bush's strategy and that the consequences they bemoaned were largely consequences of the war itself. The demand that Democrats outline a clear alternative to the conservative approach to the world was—and is—a correct one, but the failure to do so can't be laid at the feet of doves in the party's base. Rather, Kerry failed to outline a coherent internationalist alternative to conservative unilateralism simply because there is no way that support for the Iraq War *could* cohere with such an alternative.

The inherent ambiguity of the liberal hawk position can in some ways best be seen in retrospect through the lens of the further development of liberal hawk thinking. In the course of expanding his postelection critique of Kerry and the Democrats to book length, for example, Beinart came to the conclusion that Kerry's support for the Iraq War was in fact inconsistent with his internationalist vision. Nevertheless, Beinart managed to conclude that the main problem facing the party was not the undue influence of the hawks who'd betrayed liberal internationalism but a coterie of "softs" who were insufficiently serious about jihadism. But how could the side that *lost* an intraparty dispute—the side that, by Beinart's own admission, was correct about the issue at hand—be responsible for the party's postdispute failure?

Even sharper ambiguity is on display in Michael O'Hanlon and Kurt Campbell's book *Hard Power: The New Politics of National Security*. The authors hail an allegedly embattled minority of "Hard Power Democrats" (that is liberal hawks) whom they contrast with certain Democrats who "have tended to get a little squeamish when the nation goes to battle stations." "Hard Power Democrats," according to O'Hanlon and Campbell, "prefer to work through alliance and the U.N. Security Council if possible, and would heed the views of others much more than the Bush administration has, but would not insist on U.N. approval or international popular support before carrying out certain military missions." After all, "unlike the case with many on the left, however, for Hard Power Democrats multilateralism is a means to an end, not a sacrosanct principle or an endpoint in and of itself."[8]

That is from the introduction to a book that one might assume would mount a strident defense of pro-war Democrats like Kerry, Edwards, and other war supporters such as Joe Biden, Steny Hoyer, and Hillary Clinton, whose "Hard Power" orientation comes in for praise. Kerry and Edwards, however, are thrown off the bus, their loss attributed to "the appearance of a 'leftward tilt' meant to enliven the

Democratic base," signified by the vote against the $87 billion supplemental request. Yet Biden, Hoyer, and Clinton are said to have gotten things right. O'Hanlon and Campbell, meanwhile, as did their friends among Democratic politicians, supported the invasion of Iraq, but in their book, they can't make up their minds. "While the haste and hubris that characterized the Bush administration's march to war in Iraq can and should be castigated, the basic decision to confront Saddam was not unreasonable (even if it was debatable)." They concede that "the evidence never supported any operational link" between Saddam and al-Qaeda and that the administration "overstated the significance of uncertain intelligence, later proved wrong, that Saddam was making major progress toward nuclear- weapons capability," and that "it cannot be known for sure" whether the chaos into which Iraq descended after the war could have been avoided.[9] "Nevertheless, the case for war itself was both "not unreasonable" and "debatable." Meanwhile, they agree that the administration's "focus on Iraq and its doctrine of preemption created a set of circumstances that made it much harder to prevent Pyongyang"—which, unlike Iraq, had an actual nuclear program—"from roughly quadrupling its nuclear arsenal in the last half decade."[10]

This is obviously a muddle as intense as, if not worse than, anything Kerry himself managed to offer during the campaign. The problem in both cases, however, is the same. There are no actual *principles* in play here other than a determination to adhere to the wise middle ground, rather than succumbing to extremes, along with a determination to appear tough. Hence, in part, the curious persistence of the notion that the Bush administration made a mistake by failing to send enough troops to Iraq to secure the country after the invasion. This criticism is typically leveled with reference to General Eric Shinseki's prewar prediction that it would require several hundred thousand troops to stabilize Iraq. More precisely, reference is sometimes made to a long study done by James Dobbins for the RAND Corporation, which indicated that in Iraq-type situations you need about twenty foreign troops for every thousand local civilians, implying that the Iraq venture should have involved something in the neighborhood of five hundred thousand U.S. soldiers. This line allows hawks to be anti-Bush without altering any of their own strategic commitments or theories, and as a bonus counts as tough. But it ignores the fact that the U.S. Army wasn't and isn't nearly large enough to deploy that many troops to Iraq for the required amount of time. Bush deployed the number of troops he did because that was roughly the number of troops that were available. For liberal hawk politicians and journalists to adhere to this sort of criticism demonstrates the very unseriousness about defense policy of which they accuse more dovish Democrats.

This in turn was precisely the trouble with the Kerry campaign. After all, despite liberal hawk efforts to distance themselves post hoc from Kerry's efforts, at the time he was one of their number, and his campaign simply demonstrated the limited possibilities of ambiguity and opportunism. The general idea was to seize on the manifest failures of the Bush administration, while staying on the right side of public opinion polling, which still showed narrow majorities believing that the invasion of Iraq was the right thing to do. Rather than generate a wise, centrist alternative to unpalatable choices, however, it simply generated nonsense—a view that criticized Bush for bringing about the inevitable consequences of policies the liberal hawks favored, and left it unclear what the opposition party was offering as an alternative. If the public had a preexisting inclination to trust Democrats on national security issues, a hodge-podge critique of a manifestly failing incumbent might have been good enough. But Kerry, like any Democrat, had to wrestle with a historical legacy that gives Republicans a default advantage on national security debates.

Under the circumstances, he needed to demonstrate that he had a coherent, workable, and principled alternative approach to Bush's—precisely what his commitment to Bush's war prevented him from offering. Ironically, a strategy adopted out of political expediency wound up leading only to defeat.

CHAPTER 7

The Democracy Fraud

Somewhat curiously, although the Kerry campaign certainly spent a lot of energy dealing with the Iraq issue, it largely managed to avoid what had become, by the time of the election, the main intellectual controversy over the war—the idea that the invasion of Iraq could be justified primarily as an effort to transform that country into an island of liberal democracy that would spark a broader transformation of the region. The Bush administration itself had, before the war, always put overwhelming emphasis on a straightforward national security rationale for the invasion—Iraq's WMD programs, combined with its links to al-Qaeda, made it a direct threat to the United States and its allies. Even before the war, however, a substantial school of thought, primarily adhered to by liberals, held that this was the "wrong" justification for a war that was nonetheless justified.

As Thomas Friedman, probably the leading prewar proponent of this alternative theory of the war, put it, in the invasion's immediate aftermath "the 'right reason' for this war was

the need to partner with Iraqis, post-Saddam, to build a progressive Arab regime." This in turn was necessary because
"the real weapons that threaten us are the growing number of
angry, humiliated young Arabs and Muslims, who are produced by failed or failing Arab states—young people who hate
America more than they love life." The war was, in this view,
something of a bank shot. Any number of countries could
have served as our demonstration case, so why Iraq? According to Friedman, "[W]e hit Saddam for one simple reason:
because we could, and because he deserved it and because
he was right in the heart of [the Arab] world."[1]

The alleged WMD threat from Iraq was, in other words, a
pretext. A pretext for reconstructing Iraqi society along liberal
lines to replace the rampant corruption and illiberalism
among Arab states—illiberalism that, according to Friedman, was responsible for the rising popularity of violent anti-
American Islamist movements.

Indeed, in this sense the war was a *double* bank shot. After
all, though the Iraqi regime was certainly illiberal, it wasn't
Iraqis who were signing up for al-Qaeda. Rather, the organization's Arab recruits tended to come from Egypt, Saudi Arabia,
and other Arab states whose governments were aligned with
the United States. Rebuilding Iraq as a democracy, even if it
worked, could only address the terrorism problem indirectly,
by inspiring a broader wave of political change throughout
the region.

Before the war, most liberals, quite properly, found this
idea—pulling resources off the fight against al-Qaeda to
undermine al-Qaeda by invading Iraq, turning it into a democracy, then waiting for Iraq's model democracy to inspire
democratic change elsewhere—outlandish and more than a
little implausible. Others, however, found such qualms churl-
ish and objectionable. Richard Just, for example, argued in
the *American Prospect Online* that "any self-respecting liberal ought to support an invasion of Iraq," and he recognized

that "anti-war liberals have derided the prospect of a liberated Iraq serving as a model for Arab democracy—and starting a domino effect that could liberate the Muslim world from the grips of petty despots and theocratic lunatics—as fanciful." This, he replied, was "not a policy of hope" but rather one "of little imagination and puny moral spirit."[2]

Arguments of this nature were not publicly embraced by Bush or his top aides before the war. Deputy Defense Secretary Paul Wolfowitz did, however, push them to some extent. And they were echoed prewar by some neoconservative intellectuals. Joshua Micah Marshall, writing for the *Washington Monthly* in spring 2003, reported that Richard Perle told Marshall that he was unconcerned that the war might destabilize friendly regimes like Hosni Mubarak's in Egypt. "Mubarak is no great shakes," Perle told Marshall, "surely we can do better than Mubarak." Similarly, when Marshall "asked Perle's friend and fellow Reagan-era neocon Ken Adelman to calculate the costs of having the toppling of Saddam lead to the overthrow of the House of Saud, he shot back: 'all the better if you ask me.'"[3]

Bush himself does not appear to have embraced quite the entirety of this sweeping program. It does, however, seem that from the beginning, he had some version of the "regional transformation" strategy in mind. As Gareth Porter has reported, "[I]n the spring of 2003, the Islamic Republic of Iran not only proposed to negotiate with the Bush administration on its nuclear program and its support for terrorists but also offered concrete concessions that went very far toward meeting U.S. concerns."[4] The administration's decision to rebuff this initiative, rather than explore it, is hard to understand unless the White House believed that the Iraq War was likely to lead, one way or another, to regime change in Iran. Similarly, the administration's position that Israel should feel free to avoid negotiating with the Palestinian Authority until the P.A. completed a series of internal political reforms was seemingly linked to an idea about broad regional political transformation.

Whatever the administration's precise thinking at the outset (most likely, different figures took different views of the matter), by 2004 it was clear that the straightforward national security case for the invasion was mistaken. This led increasing attention to focus on the democratization issue, one that tended to further divide an already divided progressive camp in the United States since this rationale's original home had primarily been on the left. By all rights, liberals should have been able to easily dispense with what was, at the end of the day, a foreign policy doctrine so laughable that the Bush administration had been entirely unwilling to state it publicly before the war. But liberals failed to take this opportunity to react confidently, by saying something accurate but momentarily unpopular, which would have resulted in their looking wise and far-sighted when early 2005's democracy bubble burst. Instead, they largely responded with hand-wringing and paralysis that impeded their ability to take advantage of problems when these inevitably arose. In an echo both of initial Democratic support for the war and of the gushing reactions to Saddam Hussein's capture, short-sighted opportunism and inattention to basic principles would harm the party's long-term fortunes.

Various permutations of the democracy debate had brewed for years in intellectual and media circles, but it was Bush's second inaugural address that put it squarely on the political agenda for the first time. Speaking on January 20, less than two weeks from the scheduled date for Iraq's election to select a provisional government, Bush put the Iraq War firmly in the context of regional transformation. "We are led, by events and common sense," he said, "to one conclusion: The survival of liberty in our land increasingly depends on the success of liberty in other lands." Thus, according to Bush, the age-old policymaker's task of considering tradeoffs was over: "America's vital interests and our deepest beliefs are now one" and, therefore, "it is the policy of the United States to seek and support the growth of democratic movements and institutions in every nation and culture, with the ultimate goal of ending tyranny in our world."

Bush construed people's doubts about the wisdom of basing U.S. policy on this utopian belief to the fact that "some . . . have questioned the global appeal of liberty." To this, Bush replied that "the call of freedom comes to every mind and every soul. We do not accept the existence of permanent tyranny because we do not accept the possibility of permanent slavery. Liberty will come to those who love it," and, Bush assured the public, those who love freedom are found all around the world.

In making this case, Bush echoed Francis Fukuyama's famous 1990s-vintage argument that we had achieved the "end of history," in that liberal democracy's global triumph was now inevitable because only it could answer a universal yearning for autonomy and human dignity.[5] With this, Fukuyama was arguing against those who held that democracy was an eccentric quirk of Western culture and that other cultures might be permanently better suited to authoritarian forms of government.[6] How optimism of this sort about democracy was supposed to bolster the case for the Iraq War, however, was unclear. After all, if democracy's spread is inevitable—or even semi-inevitable—then it hardly seems reasonable for the linchpin of the global democratic community to undertake great risks and massive expense to try to spread it to one particular country. If anything, faith in democracy's appeal should encourage a policy of *caution*, one that takes the view—similar to the containment of the Cold War—that if the world's democracies focus on maintaining their own security, prosperity, and a reasonable degree of unity, authoritarian alternatives will eventually collapse without dramatic invasions.

What Bush did, as Fukuyama had occasion to observe after his break with neoconservatism, was put a Leninist spin on Fukuyama's essentially Hegelian idea.

Rather than see democracy as a logical end point of a process of social and political development that would play out around the world over time, it was seen as something that could—and should—be rushed into being through dramatic U.S. actions.

Meanwhile, the age-old humanitarian interest in halting or preventing wars somehow became a call to start a few more.

Dictatorships, once toppled, would on this account naturally be replaced by democratic successors so antidictator actions by the United States could swiftly permit the spread of liberty. This theory didn't fit the facts especially well—it's by no means historically uncommon for the collapse of a dictatorship to lead either to chaos or to the consolidation of a new authoritarian regime—but it did mesh nicely with the will-centered worldview of the Green Lantern Theory by implying that American boldness was the key to the future of liberty. And not just to human freedom, but to American security besides, since it was also stipulated that dictatorships were the main source of jihadist terrorism, and that promoting democratic reform in the Muslim world would also undercut the political support for radical jihadist ideology.

The empirical backing for virtually every element of this account of U.S. strategy was exceedingly poor. Integral to the argument was a widely held but almost entirely evidence-free argument about the sources of jihadist violence. Bush, again in his second inaugural, held that "as long as whole regions of the world simmer in resentment and tyranny—prone to ideologies that feed hatred and excuse murder—violence will gather, and multiply in destructive power, cross the most defended borders, and raise a mortal threat." Nor was this theory idiosyncratic to the president and his political supporters; as we have seen, the notion was originally pushed by Friedman and other liberal hawks.

What the theory had in support from a wide range of thinkers, it lacked in simple logic. If resentment generated by life under a dictatorship left people uniquely prone to radical terrorism–supporting ideologies, then why was the United States challenged by *Muslim* terrorists but not, say, Chinese ones? Leaving that aside, if terrorists were simply motivated by nihilistic rage at liberal societies, then why was *the United States* challenged by Muslim terrorists but not, say, Portugal? Indeed, Osama bin Laden himself made this point in his pre–U.S. election video aired in late October 2004 on Al Jazeera. Noting "Bush's claim that we hate freedom," bin Laden challenged Bush to "tell us why we did not strike Sweden, for example." Bin Laden's answer was a simple one—he attacked the United States because the United States actively promoted injustice in the Muslim world, both through its direct actions and through those of its client states, most prominently Israel.

One would not, of course, want to entirely take bin Laden's word for it on such a topic. Nevertheless, the stated aims of an enemy seem like a good place to start a search for his motives. What's more, the best available research supports a similar account. Shortly after 9/11, the University of Chicago professor Robert Pape set about collecting a database of all suicide terrorism attacks conducted since 1980, in hopes of identifying the common element behind them. Initially, his research was supported financially by the Department of Defense, which had an obvious interest in the question. His answer, however, was not what the Pentagon wanted to hear, and further support was not forthcoming. He was, however, able to continue his work and concluded in a 2003 paper for the *American Political Science Review* that "the vast majority of suicide terrorist attacks are not isolated or random acts by individual fanatics but, rather, occur in clusters as part of a larger campaign by an organized group to achieve a specific political goal." What's more, the political goals in question have a common theme: "Suicide terrorist campaigns seek to achieve specific territorial goals, most often the withdrawal of the target state's military forces from what the terrorists see as national homeland."[7]

The fact that "whole regions of the world simmer in resentment" is, in other words, very relevant to the sources of terrorism. The relevant sort of resentment, however, is not resentment at the absence of democracy, but resentment at the absence of democracy's logical precursor—self-determination.

Thus, despite its authoritarian government and enormous population, China does not generate vast quantities of terrorists because the overwhelming majority of China's population is *Chinese*. Such terrorism as does exist in China is perpetrated by non-Chinese Uighurs living in Xinjiang province. Similarly, terrorists do not strike Sweden because Sweden does not deploy military forces around the world in ways that generate anti-Swedish sentiment among the local population. Islamist groups, moreover, were by no means the only perpetrators of suicide terrorism. The tactic was pioneered and is practiced on a large scale by secular nationalist Tamils in Sri Lanka fighting against the Sinhalese-dominated regime that rules the entire island. Muslims perpetrate suicide terrorist attacks against Israelis who occupy Muslim land in Palestine and Lebanon, against Indians who occupy Muslim land in Kashmir, against Russians who occupy Muslim land in Chechnya, and against the United States, which stations military forces throughout the Persian Gulf and supports Israel.

In accord with this theory, anti-American terrorist attacks were actually quite rare relative to anti-Israeli or anti-Indian ones, since the connection between U.S. policies and the fight for self-determination was considerably more tenuous. The invasion and subsequent occupation of Iraq was, by this measure, flatly counterproductive, introducing a new occupation dynamic into the mix. In accord with Pape's account, previously nontargeted nations like Spain and the United Kingdom have been attacked due to their participation in the Iraq War. Similarly, the number of people interested in pursuing anti-American terrorism has gone *up*, rather than down, as a result of the war, which put the United States in the role of foreign occupier in a way it had not previously been. Indeed, an after-the-fact assessment by the U.S. intelligence community concluded as such, noting that "the Iraq conflict has become the 'cause celebre' for jihadists, breeding a deep resentment of US involvement in the Muslim world and cultivating supporters for the global jihadist movement."[8]

The idea of making the world's Muslims love the United States by invading and occupying their countries had a nice nineteenth-century ring to it, but, as we have seen, there were good reasons to doubt its merits. Combined with the debunking of Bush's initial argument for war, these facts should have constituted a perfectly adequate political response to the White House's embrace of the democracy-promotion theory of the Iraq War.

As a means of reducing the appeal of terrorism to the broad mass of the world's Muslims, invading Iraq did more harm than good. Invading Afghanistan was necessary to root al-Qaeda out of its training camps and fixed positions, but it ran the risk of prompting new resentments and new recruits. By invading Iraq, Bush managed to undercut the purpose of the war in Afghanistan by depriving the mission there of the resources needed to succeed. He did so, moreover, in order to generate a *second* U.S. military occupation of Muslim lands.

Like the situation in Afghanistan, this war risked provoking Muslims' sentiment against the United States, but unlike the war in Afghanistan, it lacked a bona fide relationship to threats to U.S. security. Rather than reducing the number of terrorists who were targeting the United States, it had—at great cost in money, lives, and opportunity for U.S. military action elsewhere—increased them.

The critique was available, but, by and large, Democrats embraced it only timidly. Instead, they recapitulated their panicky reaction to Saddam Hussein's capture in late 2003, and most members of the party allowed themselves to be pushed off track by Iraq's election ten days after the president's speech.

The scenes from Baghdad and elsewhere of long-oppressed Iraqis heading to the polls in January 2005, despite threats of violence from the insurgency, were inspiring images that made for excellent television. The underlying reality in Iraq, however, continued to be every bit as grim as it had been during the 2004 campaign. Objectively speaking, the country was still mired in chaos—chaos that was kept in check for election day by extraordinary and unsustainable security measures that severely restricted people's ability to move about the country. What's more, the greatest threat to Iraq was clearly the burgeoning ethnic and sectarian tensions, not the risk that Iraqis might prove unable to master the mechanics of voting.

Indeed, all signs were that the elections would only make ethnic tensions worse. The U.S.-installed interim prime minister Iyad Allawi was a fairly good stab at finding a leader who might be able to unify the country. Of Shiite descent but personally secular and formerly a member of the Sunni-dominated Baath Party, Allawi was the sort of person who could in principle have been able to bridge the sectarian divide. What's more, during his years in London in exile, he'd developed good ties with U.S. and other Western intelligence services. If Bush's dream of a unified, stable, pro-American Iraq were to be realized, someone like Allawi would be running the country. The problem, as preelection polls of the country made clear, was that like the United States' other favorite Iraqi exiles, Allawi had no real support on the ground. The vast bulk of Iraqi Shiites were prepared to line up behind a coalition of Islamist parties with a pro-Iranian orientation that assembled under the auspices of Iraq's leading cleric, the Grand Ayatollah Ali Sistani. Iraq's Sunnis, meanwhile, were preparing to boycott an election they regarded as being illegitimately conducted under the auspices of an illegitimate foreign occupation. The Kurdish parties put together a unified electoral list that was guaranteed to win essentially all Kurdish votes, while depriving Kurdish voters of a meaningful choice between alternatives.

When the actual results were in, pessimistic projections were completely vindicated. Allawi's Iraqi List drew just 14 percent of the vote, securing 40 seats out of 275. The Shiite Islamist coalition, meanwhile, won 140 seats on 48.2 percent of the vote, while the Kurdish bloc took 75 seats with about a quarter of the total vote. Sunnis, having mostly failed to vote, were essentially shut out of power. These results, quite predictably, set the stage for the further deterioration to come.

Iraq's new government, though in a sense democratic, was a sectarian institution, destined to be dominated by Shiite Arabs working to some extent with Kurdish parties that were fundamentally opposed to the existence of a unified Iraqi state. Under the circumstances, the Sunni Arabs of the insurgency were naturally disinclined to lay down their arms. Bringing peace to the country would require not the further holding of elections, which would merely confirm Shiite dominance, but rather a political agreement among the main factions over the terms of the Iraqi state. If some agreement could be worked out between Sunnis, Shiites, and Kurds about how to arrange Iraqi institutions in a way that would protect the core interests of all sides, then the parties could live in peace. Absent such an agreement, however, the parties were bound to fight. Either way, U.S. forces were essentially irrelevant to the outcome—if an agreement could be reached, they would be unnecessary; if an agreement could not be reached, they would be useless, incapable of addressing the fundamentally *political* roots of the conflict in Iraq.

Those of us who pointed this out were not especially popular at the time. Americans are optimistic people by nature and are disinclined to accept the view that events somewhere might be beyond our control. In addition, appreciating the extent to which elections would solve nothing in Iraq required an understanding of the depth of the Sunni-Shiite divide, something relatively few Americans were equipped to do. Nevertheless, from a purely political point of view, the most noteworthy characteristic of late January 2005 was that it was about as far as one could get from a U.S. federal election. There was, rationally speaking, absolutely nothing to fear about making unpopular statements or predictions as long as your predictions would be borne out over the following twenty-two months. Under the circumstances, the best thing to do, politically speaking, was simply to try to produce a sound analysis of the situation on the merits. Speaking the truth would entail taking a momentary hit, but by the time anyone's votes were cast in the United States, good predictions would pay off.

What's more, the general spirit of optimism surrounding the election actually provided an important policy opportunity for the United States. The year 2005 was scheduled to be a time of political transition in Iraq. The elected legislature was tasked with writing a constitution that would in turn be subjected to a vote for ratification. Following ratification, another election would be held for a permanent government.

These steps provided the United States with a golden opportunity to begin withdrawing its troops from Iraq on a note of victory. We had toppled Saddam, put a transitional government in place, organized an election, and were now prepared to leave Iraq to the Iraqis. Some optimistic analysts, like Spencer Ackerman, noting that "Iraq's Sunni and Shia Arabs are united by one thing: their desire to be rid of the occupation," felt that announcing a schedule for withdrawal could make it more likely that Iraqis would achieve a political consensus, thus making withdrawal the "last chance we have to salvage a decent and democratic outcome for Iraq."[9] Even if this hadn't worked, implementing a phased withdrawal in the wake of the election would at a minimum have allowed the United States to wash its hands of Iraq's sectarian conflicts and end the war in a face-saving manner.

The Bush administration did not, of course, implement any such policy, choosing instead to view Iraq's elections as a huge coup in terms of U.S. domestic politics and an opportunity to rebuild domestic political support for the war. Some antiwar Democrats did seize the chance to restate the basic critique of Bush's policies. Days before Iraqis went to the polls, for example, Ted Kennedy noted in an address to the Johns Hopkins School of Advanced International Studies that "the U.S. military presence has become part of the problem" in Iraq, "not part of the solution," and he called on the administration to use the election as a chance to "work with the Iraqi government on a specific timetable for the honorable homecoming of our forces."[10]

Rather than meeting Bush head-on, however, many liberals at the time seemed obsessed with pointing out that democracy promotion had played little role in Bush's prewar rhetoric. This again was true, but it was not terribly clear what was supposed to follow from it. The question that needed to be grappled with was whether the policy Bush was now outlining made sense, not whether he had consistently adhered to it over a period of years.

More hawkish Democrats, meanwhile, who had been increasingly tilting against the war during the previous year's presidential campaign, took the opportunity to flip back in the other direction. The *New Republic* published an editorial that smacked Kennedy down, arguing, strangely, that "while the presence of American troops may inflame the insurgency, it does not follow that our departure would pacify the militants," although the logical connection between not inflaming and pacifying seems fairly tight and clear.

Instead, the editorial called for the United States to remain in Iraq for the indefinite period it would take to train Iraqi security forces to be capable of tackling the various insurgents and militias that were controlling the country. It concluded by sniffing derisively that "critics of the decision to go to war would do well to recall that we are no longer debating the merits of invading Iraq" but rather "the merits of quitting Iraq" as if pro-withdrawal forces were ignorant children.[11]

In his February 3 *New York Times* column, Thomas Friedman proclaimed himself "unreservedly happy about the outcome" of the vote in Iraq. "This election has made it crystal clear," Friedman continued, "that the Iraq war is not between fascist insurgents and America, but between the fascist insurgents and the Iraqi people. One hopes the French and Germans, whose newspapers often sound more like Al Jazeera than Al Jazeera, will wake up to this fact and throw their weight onto the right side of history." This analysis—coming not from a right-wing blogger, but from the country's most prominent foreign affairs writer, one who was supposed to be a liberal, no less—was simply bizarre. Whatever else the insurgents in Iraq might be doing, they most certainly *were* fighting a war against the United States, and to imply otherwise was simply to mislead one's readers. More to the point, "the Iraqi people" did not have a side in the burgeoning conflict in Iraq, whose cause, after all, was precisely Iraq's weak sense of national identity. Kurds had their agenda, Shiites their agenda, and Sunni Arabs their own agenda.

Rather than try to familiarize his audience with the complexity of the situation, Friedman merely continued to wax enthusiastic, endorsing Bush's domino theory of democracy promotion: "Those who think that a Shiite-led government in Iraq is going to be the puppet of Iran's Shiite ayatollahs are so wrong. It is the ayatollahs in Iran who are terrified today."[12] Back in the real world, the winning coalition in the election was composed of Islamist political parties whose leaders had spent years as exiles living in Teheran and had often led anti-Saddam military forces on the Iranian side of the Iran-Iraq war, but never mind that. What's more, the notion that merely *witnessing* a somewhat free election would inspire the Iranian population to overthrow its masters was, though widely held, extremely odd. Iranians had, after all, seen television and newspaper coverage of elections around the world for years. Why the fact that Iraq was geographically closer to Iran than was Italy, Iceland, Indonesia, India, or Israel should have made a difference was unclear. What's more, the Iranian political process already features regular elections and vigorous campaigning, albeit in the context of a system where ultimate power resides with unelected clerics and their security forces.

Liberal hawk politicians largely followed Friedman's lead. During a January 30 appearance on CBS's *Face the Nation*, Senator Joe Biden whined that European sentiment at the annual World Economic Forum in Davos, Switzerland, was "a little over the top, quite frankly, in terms of anti-administration and consequently anti-American feeling" and said he "found [himself] defending the administration." Equating criticism of the incumbent administration with anti-Americanism is, of course, a time-honored political tactic. Normally, however, it's one that is employed by the incumbent administration and its allies. For the highest-profile *opposition* party's foreign policy figure to take this line was stunning. Biden went on to explain that at an upcoming meeting with the French president Jacques Chirac, he would "tell him politely that it's time for the French to step up" since the election in Iraq had created "real legitimacy" for its government. Evan Bayh, another hawkish Democratic senator and a darling of the party's centrist wing, told ABC News that the election was "a great day for democracy, and we can be particularly proud of the American troops, without whom this would not have been possible."

Rather than focus on the large and evident problems with the Bush democracy-promotion doctrine—that, for example, its main purpose was to justify a failing military adventure in Iraq, and that Iraq's elections were not solving any of Iraq's problems—many of the liberal hawk commentators became obsessed with the idea that Bush was poaching on traditional democratic terrain. "Is George W. Bush the new champion of the liberal foreign policy tradition?" wondered Peter Beinart in a February 28, 2005, *New Republic* column. Sort of, he concluded. Bush's *rhetoric* was in keeping with the liberal tradition, but "Bush's actions don't match his words. From Russia to Uzbekistan to Equatorial Guinea, the United States has actually drawn closer to a whole series of tyrannies since September 11." Beinart challenged liberals to compete with Bush on the plane of grandiose speech-making: "[U]nless they respond in kind, they'll experience the same fate that befell John Kerry. In policy terms, Kerry probably had a more serious democratization agenda than Bush. But, rhetorically, he never matched Bush's grandeur. And in the United States, where it is great causes and missionary impulses that rouse citizens to engage with the world, Bush's language captured the public imagination, and Kerry's did not."[13]

This was a rather idiosyncratic reading of recent electoral politics. More to the point, however, it was an odd reading of the liberal foreign policy tradition. The central policy question at hand, rather clearly, was not Uzbekistan or Russia, but Iraq. The president's claim was that democracy both could and should be effectively promoted through the unilateral military invasion and the subsequent occupation of that country by U.S. forces. This, of course, was something that a certain kind of liberal hawk had been endorsing before the war. It was not, however, a policy that had any genuine precedent in the liberal foreign policy tradition.

No Democratic president—no Republican president, for that matter—had ever done any such thing.

What happened instead was that liberal hawks devised the gunpoint-democratization doctrine on their own before the Iraq War, only to find the Bush administration embracing it after the fact. To acknowledge that they and the administration had hit upon a similar innovation would, however, put liberal hawks in an awkward position in terms of intraparty fights. Thus, the hawks wanted to claim that they were the true exponents of the liberal tradition, that Bush had embraced the rhetoric of this tradition, and then the hawks would explain away the evident failures of Bush's policies by questioning his sincerity in embracing it.

Democracy had, of course, long played a role in the authentic liberal tradition. Not, however, the role that Bush envisioned for the United States as a coercive democratizer of entrenched authoritarian regimes. As Michael Lind has pointed out, "Woodrow Wilson said 'we must make the world safe for democracy.' He did not say we must make the world democratic."[14]

Wilson's fear was that American democracy could not survive in a world of unchecked aggression. Isolationist retreat from the world would either imperil the security of the United States or else compel the construction of a "fortress America" for defensive purposes that would undermine democracy at home. One obvious alternative would be for the United States to simply join the imperialist competition for world domination. This, however, would likewise undermine the democratic system, as democracy is fundamentally incompatible with the idea of empire. His proposed solution, as we have seen, was the construction of a rule-governed liberal world order that would safeguard the world's liberal states in a manner consistent with their own liberalism. After World War II, Harry Truman formed a defensive alliance of democratic states, bound together with complicated diplomatic, military, and economic arrangements to strengthen the liberal community in its long struggle with communism.

Bush-style democracy promotion does bear a superficial resemblance to the notion of "Democratic Enlargement" promoted by the Clinton administration and, in particular, by his national security adviser Anthony Lake, and "Democratic Enlargement" was oft cited as a precedent for Bush's policy. This, however, was a misunderstanding based on paying attention to the title of the doctrine to the exclusion of its content.

The main focus of the strategy continued to be on deepening the ties among *existing* liberal democracies to strengthen the democratic community.

The "enlargement" envisioned was a gradual process aimed at further consolidating the democratic bloc by incorporating into the liberal system countries where authoritarian systems had *already collapsed*. The historian Douglas Brinkley recounts a 1993 meeting between the then NSC member Jeremy Rosner and the then leader of the House Republicans Newt Gingrich:

> Rosner conveyed to Gingrich an attractive shorthand model of the post–Cold War period as a battle between the "blue blob" of democracy and the "red

blob" of totalitarianism. They agreed that with the collapse of the Soviet Union the "blue blob" had an unprecedented opportunity to enlarge. Gingrich explained to the administration on a number of occasions that no congressional Republican could oppose the enlargement of the "blue blob."[15]

And enlarge it did. Not, however, through war and conquest. Rather, postcommunist regimes in Eastern Europe were encouraged, through the NATO and EU expansion processes, to commit themselves to a democratic path and were assisted in doing so. Similarly, Mexico's transition to democracy was encouraged by the creation of the NAFTA trade pact, likewise aimed at consolidating progress in an emerging democracy by incorporating it into the network of liberal diplomatic arrangements.

The only element of Clinton-era policies that closely resembled what Bush claimed to be doing in Iraq was the 1994 intervention in Haiti, aimed at overthrowing a military junta and restoring the democratically elected president Jean-Bertrand Aristide to power. Even here, however, the differences were vast and obvious. The Haiti operation was not aimed at toppling some long-entrenched dictator and creating a democratic one from scratch. Rather, it attempted to reverse a coup that had occurred in the recent past. What's more, insofar as the hope was to build a stable democracy in Haiti, the operation was not especially successful, as was abundantly clear by the time of the 2005 democracy debate. The operation *did*, however, succeed in its more modest goal of ending the refugee crisis that had begun to send huge numbers of Haitian boat people to America's shores. And while the administration surely hoped to achieve something more far-reaching in Haiti, at the end of the day dealing with the refugee problem was the basic purpose of the intervention. Armed democracy promotion was not at the center of anyone's agenda, and rightly so.

This was not, of course, because liberals doubted the desirability of democracy spreading. Quite the reverse—the liberal approach to world affairs was designed to facilitate democracy's spread in the best possible way. Rather, liberalism had historically doubted that the sort of democratization strategy Bush was pursuing in Iraq was likely to work as a means of political change or was likely to be consistent with the sort of international order that could make the world safe for democracy. A political movement in touch with its ideological underpinnings would have reacted to the superficial successes of an alternative approach by simply restating the liberal critique of such policies, confident that skepticism would be vindicated in due time.

And indeed skepticism *was* swiftly vindicated. As soon as a year after Iraq's first election, no credible people were still waxing enthusiastic about it as a historic turning point toward democracy. But before vindication could arrive, a series of superficially promising developments came together to form the so-called Arab Spring of early 2005. These, however, soon proved empty.

The Egyptian dictator Hosni Mubarak's promises of free elections were worthless, Saudi Arabia's municipal elections meaningless (a majority of seats on local councils were still unelected, and the institutions lacked any real power anyway), and the changes in Lebanon known as the "Cedar Revolution" failed to meaningfully alter the underlying problematic situation. As in Iraq, the key element of Lebanese politics was deep-seated sectarian divisions, and not whether the prevailing coalition in Beirut was in some sense "democratic." Indeed, it wasn't clear how the new anti-Syrian coalition actually was more democratic than the pro-Syrian one that had preceded it.

Meanwhile, in Iraq itself, the entire sixteen months after the country's first elections proved to be an era of lost opportunities. For the United States, it was a lost opportunity to end the American military presence in Iraq—seizing on the election or the constitutional referendum or the second election as providing the chance to declare victory and go home. Instead, blinded by the false dawn of the Arab Spring, the United States waded deeper into the quagmire, committing itself to the success of a new Iraqi government it couldn't control. Meanwhile, the opposition party once again missed the chance to be politically smart by being substantively intelligent. Pointing out in February or March 2005 that the emperor had no clothes would have been unpopular at the time, but it looked wise long before it was politically relevant. It would, moreover, have been an opportunity for Democrats to articulate principled differences with the administration's grand strategy and to lay out the existence of an alternative approach. Instead, the liberal hawks who still controlled many of the leading positions in the Democratic Party and the press let themselves get carried along with the enthusiasm and once again become obsessed with attacking their enemies to the left.

Within a year, the Arab Spring had proved to be a mirage, and the United States' position in the region was worse than ever. Perversely, during this same period, Democrats managed in many ways to put themselves even closer to the Bush administration, with many party leaders explicitly or implicitly endorsing the theories that fighting terrorism required the large-scale political transformation of the Middle East, that invading and occupying medium-size countries was a good way to spread democracy, and, even more bizarrely, that all this was in keeping with the liberal foreign policy tradition. Soon enough, the moment would finally come when events on the ground in Iraq got so bad that national security became a winning issue for Democrats. Substantive problems, however, were not resolved, and it was painfully unclear what solutions, if any, the Democrats could offer to the problems whose very severity would eventually give them a taste of power.

CHAPTER 8

After Victory

As the Arab Spring fizzled, the formerly widespread phenomenon of liberal support for the Bush foreign policy all but vanished. The opposition remained divided over any number of questions, but gone were the days when any nontrivial number of progressive figures would deny that Iraq was a disaster and was extremely unlikely to evolve into anything other than a disaster. By and large, however, chastened hawks did not change their minds and decide that the doves had been right all along. Instead, they tended to conclude that things had gone so poorly in Iraq because the Bush administration had catastrophically mismanaged the war, demonstrating a staggering incompetence that had doomed the enterprise.

The emerging incompetence narrative had many virtues to it. First and foremost, there was plenty of evidence to support it. The administration really *did* have a history of ignoring expert advice that led to any number of poor policy choices in Iraq. What's more, the pattern extended well beyond Iraq and linked the disaster of the war to other problematic aspects of the administration's record, from Katrina to the

Medicare prescription drug benefit, to congressional corruption scandals and beyond. It appealed to liberal hawks, and then later even to conservative ones, who wanted to acknowledge how bad the situation in Iraq was without admitting to any personal errors of judgment or doctrine. But it also appealed to significant elements of the left wing of the Democratic Party, to people driven by intense loathing of Bush and his subordinates, who were eager to find fault with their every move. Perhaps most of all, it appealed to the large number of progressives for whom national security issues—as opposed to economics, the environment, or other domestic topics—simply weren't a very high priority. Incompetence was a good way of at least superficially healing an awkward breach and allowing Democrats to work together on other priorities.

Useful as the incompetence line may have been—and continues to be—it suffers from a fatal flaw: it's wrong, a classic Ostrich Syndrome political concept that appeals to a wide swathe of Democrats precisely because it avoids coping with the central issues. At a minimum, there's essentially no evidence that it's correct, no reason to believe that the invasion of Iraq was a good idea ruined by poor implementation, rather than an idea whose execution went badly because the underlying idea was fatally flawed. As such, it fails to provide any principled guidance on how to deal with other pressing questions or issues that may arise. Even worse, its utility to liberal hawks is itself a major problem.

It allows the very people whose dominant position inside progressive circles helped to drive the Democratic Party off the cliff in the first place to retain their positions of influence without substantially modifying their underlying worldview.

This, of course, is an important source of its appeal. It's also the essence of the problem. The incompetence line is a dodge, a way for liberal hawks to acknowledge the grim reality of the war without rethinking any of the premises that led them to support it in the first place. From a narrowly political point of view, this may be adequate to allow Democrats to regain control over U.S. foreign policy, but it offers no assurances that doing so will actually fix any of the main problems the Bush administration has created.

On Election Day 2006, Democrats proved remarkably successful at achieving the goals they'd set for themselves. Thirty seats flipped in the House of Representatives, along with six in the United States Senate. The GOP suffered a particular electoral debacle in the Northeast. It lost Senate seats in Pennsylvania and Rhode Island, the latter state represented by the moderate Republican Lincoln Chafee, who remained popular to the end. Voters tossed him out not because of any perceived failings of his, but simply because his party had become poisonous. Even Chafee agreed with the voters' assessment, remarking after the election that if he returned to politics, it wouldn't be as a Republican. The House GOP's New England caucus was utterly devastated, with only Representative Chris Shays of Connecticut surviving the wipeout. The antiwar activist Carol Shea-Porter even won a House seat in New Hampshire that wasn't on the Democrats' target list.

The New England massacre was joined by further GOP losses in upstate New York and suburban portions of Pennsylvania, and House Republicans lost more seats in Ohio and Indiana, joined by a smattering of defeats from the rest of the country. Meanwhile, the party's message remained broad enough to win Senate seats in the border states of Virginia and Missouri, along with Montana on the plains and Ohio in the Midwest.

Calculated ambiguity was crucial to making this strategy work, meaning that the Republicans' inability to expose and exploit this ambiguity was likewise essential. The GOP's failure to do this was somewhat curious. John Kerry, after all, had attempted a fundamentally similar political strategy in 2004, and

Bush had repeatedly been able to put him on the defensive over it. The difference was that the increasing deterioration of the situation in Iraq had turned the war into an albatross around the GOP's neck, motivating Republicans to attempt their own version of the Democrats' evasion strategy from 2002. To try to exploit Democratic ambiguity on the issue, Republicans would need to be willing to talk about it. And as Election Day grew near, the GOP was eager to talk about anything else. On November 3, the *New York Times* reported that "Republicans seized on a drop in the unemployment rate to assert on Friday that tax cuts were invigorating the economy, highlighting just four days before the election an issue that party strategists are counting on to offset bad news about the war."[1] In reality, just as Democrats had learned four years earlier, candidates for office don't get to unilaterally decide what elections are going to be about. Nothing in the ups and downs of the twenty-first-century economy—neither its relatively weak condition in 2002 nor its relatively strong condition in 2006, nor the downturn that followed the collapse of the subprime mortgage market—suffices to trump the drama surrounding questions of war and peace.

"If the Democrats' election predictions are as good as their economic predictions," Bush sneered at a November 2 rally for the Missouri senator Jim Talent, "we're going to have a good day on November the seventh."

November 7, 2006, did not, of course, turn out to be a good day for the Republicans at all. Talent lost, as did GOP incumbents across the country. The *Weekly Standard*'s Fred Barnes, writing in a gloomy vein before the election, explained that "the narrative of the campaign" had shifted "from one emphasizing national security, a Republican strength, to one emphasizing Republican malfeasance in Washington and dysfunction in Iraq."[2] As Jonathan Chait observed, the purported contrast between "national security" and the centerpiece of the GOP's national security strategy summed up the depth of the GOP's problems: "If we translate that statement, then, it actually means that national security as an abstract proposition is a Republican strength, but national security as it has actually been conducted is a Republican liability."[3]

By the morning of November 8, the Democrats' long electoral nightmare was over. They'd won control of both houses of Congress and, with them, a modicum of practical political power. The very issue that had plagued them in the previous two elections was now working to their advantage. Two related questions, however, remained. First, could Democrats seize the opportunity provided by Iraq to turn national security as an abstract proposition into an electoral strength? Second, could Democrats develop a strategy for actually conducting national security better than the Republicans had? To do so, the party will need to answer the questions it left unresolved during the campaign: do Democrats have a coherent alternative to the neoconservative approach, or are they merely going to offer a purportedly more competent execution of essentially the same failed strategy?

Election victory in hand, congressional Democrats swiftly had to turn their consideration to the question of what they would actually *do* with the political power they'd obtained. On domestic issues, the agenda was reasonably clear-cut—the party's election manifesto had promised a higher minimum wage, reforms to the congressional ethics process, changes to Medicare's prescription drug benefit, labor law reform, and so on. The task, legislatively, was to write and pass those bills, and then the president would either sign them, giving Democrats a policy accomplishment, or else veto them, setting up a good campaign issue for 2008.

The dynamics of the Iraq issue proved significantly different. Practical considerations, constitutional law, and the American tradition make the president, rather than Congress, the prime mover in foreign affairs. Congressional authority over such matters, while real, is also rather crude. Legislators cannot give orders to troops, conduct negotiations with foreign governments, or force the executive branch to bargain in good faith with leaders abroad. Democrats prepared to take power with a rough consensus on what, generally speaking, they wanted to see happen in Iraq—steps toward military disengagement, negotiations with Iraqi factions with the objective of producing political reconciliation, talks with regional actors aimed at supporting the first two goals and, at a minimum, containing the fallout if the situation collapsed, and an eventual end to U.S. combat involvement in Iraq. There was, however, no obvious way to turn those goals into a legislative agenda. Nor, indeed, was there any plan for how an agenda might be formed.

Instead, the hope was that electoral victory would prove to be the key to achieving the party's goals in Iraq. The thinking, both before and immediately after the election, was that if the Democrats were able to sweep to power in part on the unpopularity of the war, then the president would naturally be driven to begin disengaging the U.S. military from Iraq. The war's end would, after all, make everyone happy. Both Republicans who wanted to get the albatross of Iraq off their necks and Democrats who were eager to talk jobs and health care could admit (though not in public) that they wanted nothing more than to make this problem go away.

It did not, of course, work out like that. Although many Republicans did indeed want Bush to wrap the war up as soon as possible, Bush and his administration had other plans. The Iraq Study Group (ISG), headed by James Baker, attempted to act in defense of this moderate Republican position and push the president toward disengaging from Iraq, but it ultimately failed to persuade and indeed may have helped to push Bush in the other direction because, according to the *Washington Post*, "how to look distinctive from the study group became a recurring theme" in the administration's internal discussions about what to do.[4] Thus, the administration eventually decided that Iraq needed *more*, rather than fewer, U.S. troops.

The move to escalate the war, rather than the reverse, was both unpopular and substantively unsound. It did, however, have the virtue of badly wrong-footing Democrats, who weren't quite sure how to respond. The need to confront the Iraq issue in an unexpected way reexposed the hawk-dove fault lines that had been somewhat submerged during the previous year's electoral campaign. More to the point, both the president's escalation plan and the ISG's alternative correctly insisted on putting Iraq in a broader regional context.

This, however, highlighted the extent to which politicians who'd belatedly come to their senses on Iraq remained unable or unwilling to articulate broader principles that could serve to guide sensible approaches to issues beyond Iraq—notably, the growing controversy over Iran.

The Democratic Party that emerged after the midterms was in many respects a significantly transformed party from the one seen during the 2002 Iraq-authorizing debate. Most notably, Nancy Pelosi, at the time second-ranking House Democrat beneath the hawkish Richard Gephardt, had replaced him as leader. John Murtha of Pennsylvania, a close Pelosi ally but a former war supporter, had disavowed his previous vote and become a leading antiwar voice from his perch as the top defense appropriator. John Kerry and John Edwards had both emerged as high-profile public figures, thanks to having run a national campaign, and both apologized for their votes and became strident antiwar voices. What's more, the election itself had resulted in the ascension of a bumper-crop of new antiwar members of Congress, including several with very strong credentials on national security issues like Senator Jim Webb of Virginia and former admiral Joe Sestak in Pennsylvania's seventh congressional district.

The members joined existing antiwar leaders like Carl Levin and Dick Durbin, the number-two Democrat in the Senate. A distinct hawkish faction, however, driven by a mix of policy conviction and political timidity, continued to exercise considerable influence and to find itself disproportionately represented in strategic security posts. Steny Hoyer, the number-two Democrat in the House, was the most senior of the hawks. In terms of practical influence, Rahm Emanuel and Chuck Schumer, whose chairmanships of, respectively, the House and Senate campaign committees during a successful midterm battle earned them considerable respect, probably have the most sway over rank-and-file members. Joe Biden, the top Democrat on the Senate Foreign Relations Committee, is a media favorite, while his House counterpart, Tom Lantos, is influential within Congress. Perhaps most important of all, Hillary Clinton, the front-running presidential candidate as of this writing, had consistently identified herself with the more hawkish wing of the party.

On the other hand, by the aftermath of the election, the "hawkish" position on Iraq had become fairly dovish. With the exception of Joe Lieberman, no major Democrat disagreed by this point that withdrawal of one form or another from Iraq was vital or that the war had been in some sense a mistake. That hawks had concluded liberals were right about the war did not, of course, prevent hawkish journalists from expressing their smug sense of superiority to the doves. "Since winning the midterms," observed George Packer in the November 27 *New Yorker*, Democrats "have been talking about the endgame in Iraq with a strangely serene sang-froid." Packer did not disagree with Democrats that the United States should begin to extricate itself from Iraq but did disagree with efforts by leading Democrats to paint withdrawal as an appealing option. "The consequences of withdrawal need not be catastrophic to American interests in the region," said former Director of Central Intelligence John Deutsch in a statement Packer found objectionable. John Murtha claimed that "there'll be more stability, less chaos" in a post-U.S. Iraq since "they have more confidence in their people than they do in ours." To Packer, "the argument that Iraq would be better off on its own is a self-serving illusion that seems to offer Americans a win-win solution to a lose-lose problem." Withdrawal might be correct, he conceded, but "we shouldn't deepen the insult by pretending that we're doing the Iraqis a favor."[5] It was all well and good, in other words, for congressional Democrats to try to end the war. Heaven forbid, however, that they try to adopt politically effective language with which to do it!

As the New Year approached, hawks and doves, liberals and moderates, were in operational agreement over the war in Iraq. Specifically, both before the election and roughly through the end of 2006, it was popular to believe that winning the election would be enough to bring the war to an end. The theory held that a war-fueled Democratic electoral victory would bring irresistible pressure to bear on the White House to begin rolling things up. Perhaps a disengagement motivated in this manner wouldn't go as quickly as liberals would ideally choose, but it would happen. Best of all, it would happen under a Republican president's watch and, nominally at least, by his own initiative. This in turn would ensure that blame for the war was permanently placed squarely on the shoulders of Bush and his conservative allies, avoiding a replay of postwar revisionism about Vietnam, where U.S. defeat came to be blamed not on the hawks who initiated the war but on the congressional doves who ended it.

Congressional Democrats weren't, of course, planning to literally do nothing with their newfound political power.

Their plans were, however, quite modest and aimed at giving small pushes to a boulder they foresaw as rolling downhill one way or the other. Days after the election, Senator Carl Levin, due to take over as chairman of the Senate Armed Services Committee, organized a conference call with reporters to explain his agenda for the coming Congress. Unlike the Armed Services chair in the House or the Foreign Relations chairs in either the House or the Senate, Levin had voted against the authorizing resolution back in October 2002, so it seemed that insofar as substantial antiwar activity would take place in the new Congress, he'd be the one spearheading it. What he had on offer was rather thin gruel. He said he expected that troop levels would start to be reduced over the coming year, though probably not at a pace he was happy with. In terms of putting pressure on the administration, Levin believed that "Republicans would take the lead" in urging the White House to begin ending the war out of, at a minimum, a desire to avoid future electoral defeats. The main role of the Democrats in all this would be to keep up the pressure on congressional Republicans, who in turn would give the White House whatever push was necessary to convince the Bush administration that it was time to start getting out of Iraq. Democrats would use their newfound power as majority party to schedule hearings aimed at exposing past misdeeds and hampering the administration's forward-looking spin-control efforts, thus rendering the war ever more unpopular and hastening its end.

This plan had a certain plausibility to it but basically flew in the face of history. Many observers had in past years looked at the extreme cynicism with which the Bush administration pursued domestic policy and assumed that the White House would attempt to "declare victory" in Iraq, withdraw troops, get the story off the front page, and reap political benefits without steering its way clear of the substantive problems in Iraq. It was particularly popular in early 2004 to believe that the handoff of power to Iyad Allawi's Provisional Government was designed to provide cover for a declaration of victory and a substantial draw-down of troop levels in anticipation of the 2004 election. The elections in early 2005 seemed to provide a further opportunity, and it was widely speculated in the winter of 2005–2006 that surely the administration was not so foolish as to be willing to wage a midterm campaign in the midst of an unpopular war with no end in sight.

Such predictions, needless to say, proved incorrect. Why, exactly, this was is a bit hard to say. On a fundamental level, however, it appears that Bush was either more stubborn than his critics dared to believe or more principled than they gave him credit for. Spun either way, the point is that Bush's belief in the United States' mission in Iraq—and his own role in that mission as God's chosen leader of the country[6]—seems to have been perfectly genuine, no matter how cynical much of the public relations surrounding the war was. Over the years, it repeatedly proved tempting to assume that Bush's talk about commitment to building a democratic future for Iraq was simply rhetoric rather than a sincere—and all the more dangerous for the sincerity—commitment to an absurdly unrealistic policy goal.

On a more crass and pragmatic level, however, the 2004 election appeared to teach the lesson that any apparent political costs the Iraq War may have entailed for the Bush administration and the wider Republican Party were entirely superficial. The reality of an ongoing war—even a war that wasn't going very well and wasn't popular—kept national security issues at the forefront, preventing Democrats from shifting the conversation to jobs and health care, where they were more comfortable. And the opposition party was itself badly divided about the war. Thus, not only did Bush plunge confidently into the midterms, but congressional Republicans plunged after him fairly uniformly, with only late and mild efforts to distance themselves from the party leader. After the electoral defeat in 2006, there was good reason to think that GOP members of Congress might change their position, but there was little reason to expect Bush to change his tune. The president had, after all, stuck to his guns on Iraq for years, contrary to expectations that he was looking for a way out. The gamble had paid off in 2004 and had cost him in 2006, but with the election done he had nothing more to lose. He wasn't on the ballot in 2008, and in a situation unique in post–World War II America the incumbent vice president wasn't running to become his boss's successor. Indeed, the Bush team had deliberately avoided designating a successor and had looked for a VP who wouldn't expect to be so designated, precisely in order to give the president a freer hand.

For the final two years of his administration, Bush would have no need whatsoever to bow to political reality. The new opposition Congress could certainly constrain his activities at home and perhaps abroad, but insofar as it simply hoped to bring political pressure to bear on him, there was little reason to think the president would feel the heat.

Nevertheless, the hope that the president would voluntarily start heading for the exits persisted until Bush himself delivered an explicit and ultimate refutation of the theory. In the interim, optimists even identified a specific mechanism by which withdrawal would occur—the Iraq Study Group, known informally as the Baker-Hamilton Commission after its cochairs, the longtime GOP fixer James Baker and the former Democratic congressman Lee Hamilton.

The commission had been created in March 2006 largely at the behest of the Republican congressman Frank Wolf of Virginia, who, following several trips to Iraq, became concerned about the course of the war. The White House was cool to the idea, but Wolf's fellow Virginia Republican senator John Warner, the chairman of the Armed Services

Committee whose support was vital to the administration, backed the proposal, forcing the White House's hand. The commission members were, like its chairs, all pillars of the Washington establishment: none on the Democratic side were affiliated with the dovish left and none on the Republican side were affiliated with the neoconservative right. The larger circle of individuals involved in its "expert working groups" was somewhat more diverse, but the members from outside the elite consensus looked like tokens and came to perceive themselves as such.

The personnel involved and the origins of the commission created the expectation that its purpose was to deliver a substantial change in Iraq policy in a way the president could swallow. As Ryan Lizza reported in mid-November of 2006, "[O]n the left, the conventional wisdom about Baker's return is that the Bush family loyalist will craft his recommendations to provide a face-saving cover for Bush's own modest course corrections in Iraq. On the right, Baker's ascent is eyed warily as an ideological rebuke to the neocons from the realist foreign policy establishment they sought to overthrow." Lizza's own analysis did not seriously dissent from this consensus. "Almost everyone," he reported, "agreed that the midterm elections will move the debate left, not right" and that "a big Democratic victory would increase Baker's leverage with Bush regarding how to proceed in Iraq."[7]

Robert Dreyfuss, writing in the *Washington Monthly*, agreed. "Anything labeled 'bipartisan commission' seems almost guaranteed to be ignored by a highly partisan White House that is notoriously hostile to outside advice and famously devoted to 'staying the course,'" he conceded, before arguing that "what makes this particular commission hard to dismiss" was Baker himself, a figure regarded as uniquely "able to break through the tight phalanx of senior officials who advise the president and filter his information." The mandate, as Dreyfuss saw it, was "to devise a fresh set of

policies to help the president chart a new course in—or, perhaps, to get the hell out of—Iraq." Once a plan was on the
table, the president would have good reason to accept it, since
if "Baker can forge a consensus plan on what to do about Iraq
among the bigwigs on his commission, many of them leading
foreign policy figures in the Democratic Party, then the 2008
Democratic presidential nominee—whoever he (or she) is—
will have a hard time dismissing the plan. And if the GOP
nominee also embraces the plan, then the Iraq war would
largely be off the table as a defining issue of the 2008 race—
a potentially huge advantage for the Republicans."[8]

The political advantage, however, would extend not only
to Republicans but also to the substantial ranks of Democratic
hawks, a group heavily represented on the commission. With
Iraq off the table, Hillary Clinton and other presidential contenders who'd badly damaged themselves in liberal eyes
through their support of the war would be off the hook. Likewise, politicians would be relieved of pressure to distance
themselves from the gaggle of mostly pro-war national security
hands whose intellectual leadership had proved so disastrous
in the years after 9/11. Not only Republicans, but a bipartisan
elite of chastened Iraq hawks had a great deal to gain from
taking Iraq off the table as a political issue, and, fortunately for them, the commission was stacked full of people just
like them. Consequently, expectations were running high
that the commission's report, when released, would change
everything and lift the obligation to actually cope with Iraq
from the shoulders of the congressional Democrats.

That, at least, was the hope. The reality turned out to be
rather different. The ISG wound up addressing itself to a
wider regional context along with Iraq, but the Iraq section of
the report was closer to a sick joke than a solution to anyone's
problems. The report contained two parts, one an analysis of

the situation in Iraq and the second a series of recommendations for coping with it. The great strength of the analytic section of the report was the emphasis it places on the need for "national reconciliation" in Iraq, a political accommodation that leaders of major Iraqi institutions and the bulk of Iraqi public opinion regard as preferable to war. In principle, such a reconciliation should have been possible. The ongoing warfare in Iraq has obviously been devastating to the Iraqi people and looks likely to become more devastating in the future. Under the circumstances, one would hope that people could find a settlement that all sides would find preferable to the continuation of fighting. Unfortunately, however, the world is filled with situations where lack of trust and a legacy of fear and bitterness keep people trapped in negative-sum conflicts. Iraq, by all indications, is just such a case. As the ISG report notes, essentially none of the influential actors in Iraq appeared interested in an agenda of national reconciliation.

As a result, many of the ISG's substantive recommendations were simply bizarre. They proposed embedding more U.S. troops within Iraqi army units. They wanted U.S. civilian agencies to do more in Iraq and help Iraqis, for example, to bolster their ability to conduct criminal investigations and put together "witness protection facilities." Clearly, however, as the commission itself understood in its analytical section, national reconciliation was the whole game. With reconciliation achieved, a large deployment of U.S. troops would be unnecessary (and probably unwelcome) and various foreign aid schemes stood a chance of helping. Without reconciliation, however, neither U.S. soldiers nor U.S. advisers nor U.S. aid and advice could accomplish anything. The only realistic option was to start planning the withdrawal of U.S. troops, hope for the best in Iraq, and work on diplomatic and other efforts to contain the damage throughout the region. Most egregiously, several commissioners appeared to recognize that withdrawal was the logic of their analysis. *Newsweek* reported in its December 18, 2006, issue that William Perry, an ISG member and a former secretary of defense, "wanted to set dates" for the departure of U.S. forces, but "Baker was concerned that Bush would write off the report as unrealistic," and Perry was persuaded to drop his objections.

The Baker-Hamilton report's serious shortcomings on this question—and the obvious procedural biases in favor of consensus and acceptability to Bush over accuracy—were the main focus of progressive attention on the report. Another aspect of it, however, was more promising: Baker-Hamilton put the Iraq conflict in a broader regional context and suggested the creation of a multilateral diplomatic forum involving the United States, the Iraqi government, and Iraq's neighbors. *All* of Iraq's neighbors, including Syria and Iran. On one level, this was a relatively minor proposal. On another level, it constituted a striking repudiation of the Bush administration's approach to the world. The premise of holding diplomatic talks about Iraq with Syria and Iran was that all three countries—more than three, when Iraq's other neighbors are counted into the mix—should work together to secure their common interests in that country. Clearly, however, the core interest of the Syrian and Iranian governments was not to be overthrown. Thus, any vision of Iraq that involved reconciling the interests of the United States, Iran, and Syria would have to be a vision in which the Iraq War was not seen as a precursor to regime change in Damascus and Teheran. That, in turn, implied a rejection of the strategic vision behind the Iraq War. Which, in turn, implied a rejection of the strategic vision of the Bush administration writ large. Read correctly, in other words, the ISG report could be seen as, in Gary Kamiya's memorable phrase, "a bombshell with a very long fuse."[9] In a similar vein, Daniel Levy, the director of the Middle East Policy Initiative at the New America Foundation, denounced the liberal tendency toward "knee-jerk rejection" of the ISG and preferred a policy of "strategic embrace," which would appreciate "that,

politically, one could read between the lines of the Report"
and see it as the implicitly rather radical rejection of Bush-
style conservatism that it was.[10]

Although this advice was not popular among progressive
pundits, it was the advice largely chosen by the Democratic
leadership, whose public statements tended to simply emphasize the positive in the ISG report and attempt to use it as
political cover to articulate some points in favor of a change
in strategy. A few Democratic politicians, including Senators
Bill Nelson, Chris Dodd, and John Kerry, went so far as to
travel to Damascus where they met with senior Syrian politicians, including the dictator Bashar Asad himself.

Neither Baker's strategy nor the Democratic strategy that
was built around Baker-Hamilton worked. Bush is said to have
told reporters from the country's top newspapers, including
the *New York Times* and the *Washington Post*, that he viewed
the ISG's recommendations as a "flaming turd," although the
papers didn't run with the quote.[11] Though possibly apocry-
phal, the anecdote captures the substance of the administration's actual response. On December 15, Glenn Kessler and
Robin Wright reported in the *Post* that during an extended
conversation with the paper's reporters and editors, Condoleezza Rice had categorically rejected the idea of engaging
Syria and Iran over the Iraq issue. Democrats and the ISG
wanted Bush to begin restraining his war aims and scaling
back U.S. military involvement in Iraq. The president, however, had other plans. He rejected schemes for diplomatic engagement with Syria and Iran, rejected calls to withdraw
troops from Iraq, rejected calls to move U.S. forces in Iraq
away from a combat mission, and rejected calls to provide any
kind of end date for U.S. military involvement in Iraq. Instead, Bush conducted his own private policy review in
December before unveiling what the White House termed a
"New Way Forward" for Iraq in a January 10 prime-time
speech. The U.S. military commitment to Iraq would be

escalated, not reduced, to the tune of 22,000 soldiers who, contrary to the advice of the Joint Chiefs of Staff, would "surge" into Baghdad and Anbar province for an unspecified period of time in hopes that 150,000 troops could bring security to a country where 130,000 had failed. Bush followed Baker-Hamilton's lead in gesturing toward the broader regional context but nodded in the other direction. "Iran and Syria," he said, "are allowing terrorists and insurgents to use their territory to move in and out of Iraq," and Iran in particular "is providing material support for attacks on American troops." Days later, U.S. forces attacked an Iranian consulate in Irbil, the unofficial capital of Iraqi Kurdistan. On January 23, Alexandra Zavis and Greg Miller reported for the *Los Angeles Times* that "the Bush administration has provided scant evidence to support these claims. Nor have American reporters traveling with U.S. troops seen extensive signs of Iranian involvement."[12]

Evidence or not, the message was clear. Bush had no intention of backing away from the war. He intended instead to escalate both U.S. military involvement in Iraq and American tensions with the other designated enemies in the region. Neither of these decisions polled well, but neither was met with the mass Republican defections that Democrats had been certain would force Bush's hand in a more dovish direction. Nor was either met with especially effective Democratic Party resistance.

In a fundamental sense, of course, the Iraq Study Group and the Democratic political strategy built around it failed simply because George W. Bush was president of the United States and, in practice, has extremely broad authority to conduct foreign affairs as he sees fit. The failures did, however, demonstrate the continued presence of certain pathological habits of mind throughout the Democratic establishment; habits that had ill-served the party during the earlier phases of the Iraq debate would ill-serve the party in the case of a future military confrontation with Iran and are, generally speaking, inimical to the task of reorienting the United States' national security policies in a sounder direction.

At the core of this pathology is a vicious cycle of neglect and failure. Democrats are reluctant to address security issues except when forced to do so, and, as a result, they discover that when they are so forced, they aren't very good at it. Political failure breeds further reluctance, which breeds further failure—no one develops the relevant ability to spin security for partisan gain, and because no one can win on security, no one learns how to campaign on it. Political operatives cut their teeth in national politics running campaigns for the House and the Senate. Because the national security issue is of limited relevance to these races, and because it's been a weak issue for Democrats for decades, the party's operatives have learned to avoid it as much as possible. On the Republican side, conversely, it's been a source of strength, and clever campaign managers have sought opportunities to turn the discussion to foreign and military policy.

This sometimes lends itself to wishful thinking, as when Chuck Schumer, the top Democratic electoral strategist in the Senate, maintained a belief that "Iraq will not be as strong an issue in the 2008 elections," even *after* Bush rejected the ISG and announced the surge.[13] Worse, when Democrats confront issues, their tendency is to confront them in a half-hearted manner, while often seeking to dodge the core question at hand. This could be seen in the early days of the Iraq debate when Democrats were much more eager to observe that Bush had to "make his case" and—especially—formally seek an authorizing resolution from Congress than they were to debate the merits of invading Iraq. Similarly, in early 2007 prominent Democrats such as Harry Reid, Jim Webb, and Hillary Clinton were eager to make the argument that the

Bush administration lacked the legal authority to initiate military action against Iran. Considering that few of the Democrats raising this point had similar procedural objections to Bill Clinton's decision to bomb Serbia in 1998 without congressional authorization, it's unclear how persuasive anyone will find this.

Again, though, it's pointless to debate the *process* by which the president ought to launch a war with Iran completely detached from the question of *whether* a war with Iran ought to be launched.

In essence, Democrats have tended to approach security debates from a reflexive posture of fear, preemptively assuming a defensive crouch from which it is impossible to practice politics effectively. The intent is usually to slice the salami as thinly as possible in order to minimize political risks, but the actual consequence is to make it hard to build support for liberal ideas and impossible to formulate a clear statement of those ideas. The ISG's effort to, in essence, repudiate the entire Bush foreign policy doctrine without saying so explicitly was part and parcel of this slicing. Some members of the commission seem to have believed that they might have the ability to trick the president into adopting policies that were deeply at odds with the premises he'd articulated throughout his administration. Others appear to have believed that the president wanted to repudiate his policies and was merely seeking "cover"—cover that the ISG might provide. Democrats, meanwhile, were eager to either believe one of those theories or else adopt the strategy of sotto voce repudiation for themselves. Generally speaking, the main impetus of Democratic strategy since the 2006 election has been to try to minimize the extent to which they are portrayed as disagreeing with the Bush administration. Leading figures like Steny Hoyer have taken to the floor of Congress to loudly denounce the idea of "cutting off funding" for U.S. troops in Iraq, embracing the Republican framing of the issue rather than seeking to evade it. On Iran, the major Democratic presidential contenders all said they favored negotiations with Iran but were at pains to emphasize that that no options were being taken "off the table." Worse than that, in early 2007 the presidential contenders all tended to talk about Iran primarily in the context of addressing extremely hawkish Jewish audiences, rather than making the issue a regular feature of their pitch. "U.S. policy must be clear and unequivocal," Hillary Clinton intoned, addressing the American Israel Public Affairs Committee (AIPAC) on February 1. "We cannot, we should not, we must not, permit Iran to build or acquire nuclear weapons. And in dealing with this threat, as I have said for a very long time, no option can be taken off the table."

Later in the speech she observed that "there are many, including our president, who reject any kind of process of any sort of engagement with countries like Syria and Iran." Then, in a gesture of outreach to an audience she feared might agree with the president, she said, "I do believe that that is certainly a good faith position to take," before offering the tepid criticism "I am not sure it is the smartest strategy that will take us to the goals that we share." For her trouble, she got booed. About a week earlier, John Edwards made some very aggressive remarks at a security conference in Herziliya, Israel, arguing that "Iran must know that the world won't back down" and that "the recent UN resolution ordering Iran to halt the enrichment of uranium was not enough." On military options, Edwards said that "to ensure that Iran never gets nuclear weapons, we need to keep all options on the table. Let me reiterate—all options must remain on the table." Edwards was roundly criticized for these remarks by many of his would-be allies in the progressive blogosphere, and in a February 2 interview with the *American Prospect*'s Ezra Klein, he appeared to substantially backpedal, coming out strongly against war with Iran.

A month later, Barack Obama got his chance to address an AIPAC regional meeting in Chicago and did somewhat better, pitching the military option more as an afterthought than a threat, arguing that "while we should take no option, including military action, off the table, sustained and aggressive diplomacy combined with tough sanctions should be our primary means to prevent Iran from building nuclear weapons." Unlike the others, Obama actually devoted substantial time to laying out the case for negotiations, rather than tossing off an aside in their favor. It was left, however, to lower-profile figures like Wesley Clark and Bill Richardson to simply argue in a straightforward manner that the idea of launching a unilateral military campaign against Iran was insane. That, as the nonproliferation experts Joseph Cirincione and Andrew Grotto argue, we "could not assume that air strikes would buy anything more than a few years' delay in Iran's nuclear enrichment program," a delay that "is unlikely" to provide an opportunity "to end Iran's nuclear program," in part because strikes "would likely consolidate support for an otherwise unpopular government" and "trigger global economic and political repercussions highly detrimental to American global security interests."[14]

To raise these kinds of issues would, however, require Democrats to be willing to bore deeply into national security debates—to take on the fundamental theoretical premises underlying the hypermilitarism of the Bush years and to outline a principle-driven alternative. Yet this is precisely what the party has spent the years since 9/11 declining to do, and there has been little indication that the average Democrat is inclined to alter this habit. In many cases, this is because many people affiliated with the Democratic Party do in fact have only shallow disagreements with the Bush administration. More broadly, though, it simply reflects the party's approach to foreign policy issues and the tendency of the larger progressive movement to neglect them relative to other priorities.

Democrats, simply put, tend to think of national security as a political problem that should be avoided to the greatest extent possible. At times, that means simply ducking the issue. When that's impossible, however, it tends to mean slicing the salami as thinly as possible—focusing on "incompetence" in Iraq, the procedural management of diplomacy, or other relatively trivial disagreements. When a fundamental difference of opinion does arise—about, say, the merits of engaging with Syria or Iran—Democrats attempt to portray themselves as offering a simple common-sense suggestion, and then they express bafflement as to why the Bush administration disagrees. Nevertheless, they know perfectly well (or, at a minimum, could easily find someone to explain it to them) why the administration does what it does. The theories underlying Bush's policies are not a closely guarded secret, nor is the neoconservative ascendancy a conspiracy conducted in the shadows. The books, the articles, and the speeches justifying Bush's approach are out there for the reading, the doctrine is available to anyone who wants to take an interest, and, being available, it is possible to *challenge it publicly*. Democrats need to stop complaining about Republicans "politicizing" national security and recognize that the country's national security policies are among the most important that we can discuss in our political system.

When it comes to domestic economic policy, Democrats do not shy away from going beyond specific critiques—Republicans cut taxes on the wealthy, Republicans want a low minimum wage, Republicans roll back environmental and workplace safety regulations, Republicans cut deals with lobbyists—to make a broad argument about principles: Democrats believe in public action in pursuit of the common good, while Republicans are captive to the interests of wealthy individuals and large corporations. On national security, similarly, conservative Republicans have not merely made some mistakes on Iraq, and some other mistakes on Iran, and some other mistakes on North Korea, plus some mistakes on Syria, while mishandling the Israeli-Palestinian conflict and, by coincidence, damaging our relationships with formerly close allies. Rather, they are making *one big mistake* in seeking to transform the United States' role in the world from that of a liberal superpower that uses its national strength to underwrite a liberal world order effectively governed by approximately just rules, to that of an imperial superpower that seeks to use its national strength to dominate the world and needlessly heighten conflicts.

A practical political debate is not, of course, ever going to look like an international relations seminar. Nevertheless, if you're going to argue in favor of a position, it *does* make sense to create a situation where you're able to explain yourself. Clinton trying to trim her advocacy of negotiations with Iran and getting booed for it nicely encapsulates the problem with downplaying disagreements. If you're going to deliver a message contrary to your audience's preexisting prejudices, you need to *make the argument* on behalf of your position, not simply soft-pedal it and hope they won't notice. The Democrats' 2002 reluctance to engage in the Iraq debate simply made it inevitable that they would lose the argument. By 2006, of course, the broader political context had become much more favorable to opposing the administration, but Democrats remained curiously reluctant to chip away at the underlying premises behind Bush's policies, depriving themselves of effective leverage with which to oppose any new blunders and raising the prospect that, in power, Democrats would simply commit new blunders of their own, rather than returning to the sounder policies of the past.

CHAPTER 9

In with the Old

By the 2006 election and its aftermath, Democrats had finally learned to grapple with the politics of the Iraq issue. This proved sufficient to guide the party to victory in the midterm elections, and—combined with Democratic strength on domestic issues—might (or, then again, might not) be enough to recapture the White House in 2008. The long years of Democratic failure on Iraq, however, had little to do with Iraq in particular and a great deal to do with a general problem of coping with national security issues. Those problems persist even today, many years after 9/11 put the politics of national security back on the table in a major way. Indeed, even the Iraq issue itself is not a self-contained box cut off from the broader questions of foreign policy. One cannot, for example, begin to contemplate the consequences of ending the United States' military involvement in Iraq in a way that minimizes the negative fallout without thinking about the broader regional context, including Turkey, Israel, Saudi Arabia, Jordan, Syria, Iran, and Egypt. Not only is the Iraq issue connected to Iran's involvement in Iraq, but any effort to discuss Iran as a player on the

Iraq front will necessarily lead to the question of the Iranian nuclear program. This in turn connects to diplomacy being waged at the UN Security Council that involves not only the United States, but also our key European allies, as well as other major powers such as Russia and China.

Logically, in other words, the tendency is for all the main issues in national security policy to link up with one another. For the purpose of any particular political campaign, these linkages may not become salient—certainly, they didn't in 2006. Then again, they might become salient in the future. More to the point, they definitely do matter when it comes to governing. And that, ultimately, is what matters most. The odds appear very good that in January 2009 the country will get a new president—probably a Democrat, but perhaps a Republican—who rejects the Bush administration's approach to Iraq. The question, however, is whether this will amount to anything more than a narrow technocratic rejection of alleged errors in the conduct of the occupation.

If Iraq remains the dominant subject of discussion, the narrow technocratic path will probably suffice politically. If Iraq does not, and issues relating to Iran, Lebanon, Somalia, or elsewhere begin to gain more prominence, then following the technocratic path will not be enough to win the election. Either way, however, the technocratic view will not provide an adequate basis for leading the country. It is uncontroversial at this point to observe that Iraq has become a disaster. Powerful forces, however, want to learn essentially nothing from this disaster except how to create a new one with slightly better toys.

In a January 31 *Los Angeles Times* column, for example, the neoconservative Max Boot denounced the Bush administration for underfunding the State Department's Office of the Coordinator for Stability and Reconstruction and suggested that this be reversed. He also fretted that the administration's newly proposed Civilian Reserve Corps would receive inadequate funding. He deemed Bush's plan to add ninety-two thousand soldiers and marines to the military over five years inadequate and called for "a larger and faster increase." In order to sustain such a larger, faster increase, Boot called for us to "open the ranks of the armed forces to recruits who are not citizens or green card holders." Conceding that there might be "concerns about turning over the defense of our nation to foreigners," Boot did propose that foreign mercenaries be capped at "20 percent of the total" force. All this would obviously cost money. But Boot felt that even without these increases, the Pentagon budget was still inadequate because "even though the defense budget has grown from $302 billion in 2001 to $432 billion this year, the armed forces are facing major equipment shortfalls that need to be addressed." How much did Boot want to spend? He wouldn't say, but he did note that "we're still spending only 3.3 percent of GDP on defense—a very low figure by historical standards," implying that he had in mind increases of hundreds of billions of dollars. He also called for the creation or the revitalization of a whole series of institutions of neocolonial governance, including "a Department of Peace, perhaps built out of a revamped Agency for International Development, so that we can be better prepared for the aftermath of future military operations than we were in Iraq"; a revived U.S. Information Agency; and "a federal police force . . . that can be dispatched to enforce the law in other lands." Last but not least, Boot called on Bush to "beef up the 'expeditionary' capacity in other civilian branches of government, ranging from the Treasury to the Agriculture Department, so that they can augment the efforts of our soldiers."[1]

This is, at its core, a chilling vision of an imperial United States, complete with giving the proposed Colonial Office (the term Boot had given it in an earlier column[2]) the

Orwellian name "Department of Peace," reliance on late Roman–style foreign legions, and the militarization of the entire government as civilian agencies are told to spend their time better-equipping themselves to serve as support for unnamed projected military adventures. Most disturbingly of all, however, Boot's suggestion that these ideas might serve as the basis for "bipartisan cooperation" under the slogan "No More Iraqs" is actually somewhat plausible.

The idea of a large increase in the end strength of the United States' ground military had in fact for years been championed by Democrats searching for a way to look tough on national defense. Back in May 2005, Third Way, a strategy group for moderate Democrats, called for a permanent increase of a hundred thousand troops, and a bill to that effect was introduced by the Democratic senators Hillary Clinton, Joe Lieberman, Jack Reed, Bill Nelson, and Ken Salazar.[3] The idea behind the Office of the Coordinator for Stability and Reconstruction was initially a progressive notion, and Boot has mostly been joined by progressives in bemoaning the Bush administration's lack of interest in funding it. Similarly, the Civilian Reserve Corps concept draws on ideas about national service that have long been pushed by elements of the Democratic Party, especially in its more centrist wing.

In part, some of these ideas have progressive support because they have some merits. Or, at least, they have some merit in the right form. Adding additional ground troops to the U.S. Army and the U.S. Marine Corps, for example, really does seem to be a smart idea. It would, however, be extremely costly. One good way to achieve this useful but expensive goal would be to follow the Center for American Progress's suggestion to economize on other areas of defense expenditure, in particular by cutting back on new weapons systems planned for a Cold War–style confrontation with another major power. Boot's proposal to simply add money to the United States' already enormous Pentagon budget—we currently account for about half of all world defense spending—is a much worse proposal. Nevertheless, it is the Boot-style version of this idea that is endorsed by the liberal hawks Michael O'Hanlon and Kurt Campbell in their book on progressive national security policy and that many Democratic politicians seem to have in mind when they embrace the concept of a bigger army. Similarly, it's hard to deny that an office aimed at better coordinating stability and reconstruction projects could be a good idea, or that making USAID work better would be useful (renaming it the "Department of Peace" we can probably do without), but context is extremely important here.

Improving our ability to execute missions abroad is much less important than improving our strategy for when and why to intervene. Better techniques are always welcome, but what the country needs to replace Bush's current failed strategy is a different strategy, not just another way to implement the same strategy. Similarly, to gain confidence in their ability to tackle Republicans on the politics of national security, Democrats need critiques grounded in clear principles, rather than in short-term opportunism. The country, in short, badly needs a different direction, but a significant number of people are proposing that we essentially keep doing the same thing, except with a larger army, and hope for better results.

At this point, of course, the idea that the country needs some big ideas about national security policy is hardly new. On the contrary, it's something of a cliché. Francis Fukuyama has called for a "realistic Wilsonianism," while Anatol Lieven and John Hulsman have called for an "ethical realism." Peter Beinart favors "multi-multilateralism," Robert Wright has advocated "progressive realism," and the Democratic Leadership Council presses for "progressive internationalism." Breaking from the semantic mold, John Ikenberry and Anne-Marie

Slaughter of the Princeton Project on National Security aim to develop "a world of liberty under law." Rather than join these worthy thinkers in the quest for new nomenclature for a new grand strategy for the United States, my suggestion is that at the end of the day the need for novelty has been vastly overstated. Many good ideas have been pushed in recent years, often by the previously named authors, and a great many new ideas have been pushed as well. What's been good in recent thinking, however, has tended not to be genuinely novel, while the quest for novelty has pushed people to embrace unsound ideas.

Liberals have delighted for years in pointing out how little of the neoconservative response to September 11 has genuinely been a response to that day's dramatic events. This is, of course, correct as even a casual perusal of, say, the Project for a New American Century's Iraq page will confirm.[4] Charles Krauthammer's bold proclamation that the United States "is in a position to re-shape norms, alter expectations and create new realities" solely through "unapologetic and implacable demonstrations of will" sounds like something written in the heady days of September–October 2001. It was, however, published in *Time* back in March 2001 as a generic statement of how the Bush administration ought to orient itself toward the world. The proclamation was, in short, a simple statement of the hegemonist approach to the post-Soviet world, one that was little altered by the actual events later that year. Liberals do well to point this out, but at the same time there's a lesson to be learned.

After all, one large part of what made the neoconservative response to 9/11 so compelling and politically powerful was precisely that it *was* grounded in a larger theory about the United States' role in the world. The theory, like any real set of principles, provides substantial guidance about how to react to unexpected events, leaving its adherents in a position to act quickly and decisively in response.

The problem with the approach outlined by the neocons in the 1990s and adopted by Bush in the twenty-first century isn't that it's insufficiently new or an insufficiently genuine response to 9/11, but simply that it's mistaken. The imperialist, hypernationalist influence has long been with us and probably will long be with us, but it's also always been wrong—from the Spanish-American War to the overthrow of Mohammed Mossadegh, to Vietnam, to the neocon critics who slammed Ronald Reagan for negotiating with Mikhail Gorbachev—and it always will be wrong. The liberal alternative, meanwhile, does not consist of "new ideas" or a search for new glib slogans.

It is rather an age-old doctrine that has been developed over time, was working well in the 1990s, provides the core that most of the proposed sets of "new ideas" have in common, and ought to once again become the basis of our policy-making in the near future. Arguably, for electoral purposes it's better not to use words like *liberal* or *international*. And, again, perhaps there is some reason to believe that the voters crave the idea of new ideas. If the polls and the focus groups say so, then that's what they say. Certainly, neoconservatives seemed to feel, perhaps correctly, that it was best to deemphasize the deep intellectual roots of their ideas.

Nevertheless, they did not actually abandon the ideas themselves but merely changed their packaging. A perceived political imperative toward novelty should not induce intellectual confusion about whether genuinely new ideas are necessary.

The evidence strongly suggests that there is in fact very little need for new ideas.

The course of world events in the 1990s was broadly favorable to both the United States of America and the world at large. What's more, while several very severe problems clearly existed during the pre-Bush period—the looming threat of global warming, the spread of HIV in the Third World, conditions of dire poverty across vast swathes of the globe—none of neoconservatism's innovations have mitigated any of those problems or indeed even attempted to address them. And, of course, it wasn't any of these lingering problems that made the departure from liberal internationalism appear plausible. It was rather 9/11 and the nexus of fears relating to terrorism, rogue states, and weapons of mass destruction that the events of that day unleashed.

This reaction, though understandable, is fundamentally irrational. The Clinton administration erred seriously in not moving forward more quickly with draft plans for aggressive action against the Taliban. That said, so did the Bush administration during its first nine months in office. When the destruction of the World Trade Center raised the political salience of al-Qaeda, the Taliban, Afghanistan, and Pakistan, politicians from across the ideological spectrum united around the need to take action. Whatever legitimate complaints one might raise about liberals' efforts to deal with this issue before 9/11, nothing in the neoconservative record suggests a superior alternative.

What's more, once the decision to topple the Taliban was made, the Bush administration botched things. It's rarely pointed out in the United States but we have, remarkably, failed to achieve virtually all of our war aims in Afghanistan. Osama bin Laden is still at large, as is his deputy Ayman al-Zawahiri, as are the Taliban leader Mullah Omar and most of his colleagues. They still retain some ability to communicate with their followers, and Afghanistan's government remains perilously unstable with little effective ability to control the countryside. Much of the country is under the de facto control of Taliban successor organizations, and al-Qaeda continues to be able to operate in the Pakistan-Afghanistan border area.

Just as with the administration's failures in Iraq, there is good reason to believe that the problems in Afghanistan are not merely the result of "bungling" but rather the visible, tactical consequences of large-scale strategic and ideological failings. It is widely understood that difficulties in Afghanistan—in particular, the failure to capture Osama bin Laden (or at least substantially crush the organized military opposition of the Taliban) at the Battle of Tora Bora—are partially attributable to the administration's unwillingness to commit large numbers of troops to Afghanistan. There is at least some understanding of the reality that more troops were not forthcoming largely because the administration was already planning for war in Iraq. Less understood, however, is that the operational requirements of the Iraq operation aside, one of the ideological requirements of attempting to pursue counterterrorism and nonproliferation goals through hegemonist methods was that the United States demonstrate a capacity to fight and win wars very quickly and on the cheap. By late January 2007, Fukuyama was observing that one of the lessons of the last five years "is that preventive war cannot be the basis of a long-term U.S. nonproliferation strategy." As he noted, Bush "sought to use preventive war against Iraq as a means of raising the perceived cost to would-be proliferators of approaching the nuclear threshold."

The trouble, however, is that "the cost to the US itself was so high that it taught exactly the opposite lesson."[5]

A similar logic applied in Afghanistan. A large commitment to that country—even if successful—would have prevented the United States from credibly threatening to launch a whole series of regime-change operations. Thus, the war had to be conducted with a light footprint, mostly from the air, even if that meant sacrificing actual success in favor of the appearance of success.

Nor were matters helped by the diplomatic fallout from the Iraq War. The very countries that were most inclined to

assist the United States—Britain, Australia, Japan, and so on—
were encouraged by the administration to focus their efforts in
Iraq rather than Afghanistan. Meanwhile, leading traditional
partners such as Canada and Germany who were playing an
important role in Afghanistan were alienated, and support of
U.S. foreign policy became a political liability, restricting the
level of risk that foreign leaders were willing to accept on behalf of a war that even the Bush administration couldn't be
bothered to make a top priority. Finally, after accepting Iran's
assistance during the early days of the war and seeking to col-
laborate on the strong joint U.S.-Iranian interests in a stable
Afghanistan and breaking the back of the Taliban, the Bush
administration labeled Iran part of an "axis of evil" and began
to none too subtly intimate that invading Iraq was but a first
step toward the overthrow of the regime in Teheran.

This series of moves has worked out incredibly poorly, but
nothing on the list constitutes a managerial error. Rather,
these are the logical consequences of the hegemonist approach, which, simply put, requires us to be able to conquer
foreign adversaries and remake their countries at radically
lower cost than is in fact possible. One could, of course, respond to this problem Boot-style, by simply increasing the vol-
ume of resources dedicated to military and defense issues,
thus enlarging the country's capacity for war making and other forms of involvement abroad. One problem here is that nobody knows what such an approach would genuinely cost.
Advocates of gigantic increases in defense spending are fond
of noting that current levels of military outlay are, at 3 to 4
percent of GDP, relatively low by historical standards. They
neglect to mention the fact that the Bush administration, in
a break with precedent, has made a habit of not counting
current military operations as part of the defense budget.
When the supplemental appropriations are included in
the picture, defense spending looks closer to five percent of
GDP.[6] What's more, this figure does not include substantial

defense-related sums spent under the purview of the Department of Energy on nuclear programs, money spent by the Department of Veterans Affairs on health benefits for former soldiers, or the price of the nonmilitary tools of foreign policy.

Aggregate spending, in short, is actually not far from its levels at the height of the Cold War. And this at a time when the objective level of threat facing the United States is radically lower than it was when a U.S.S.R. dedicated to the United States' destruction maintained a massive military establishment and a huge nuclear arsenal. In the present day, U.S. defense spending already accounts for around half of the world's total, and most of the other big spenders are close U.S. allies. Under the circumstances, arguments leading to the conclusion that we must massively increase our level of expenditure in order to execute some strategy should be greeted with instinctive skepticism, and we must seriously consider the possibility that it is the strategy, rather than the resources available, that is inadequate.

The problem with neoconservative hegemonism, however, is not merely the high costs, but also the absence of benefits. Indeed, the benefits are so hard to discern that advocates of a Bush-style approach to the world rarely even try to discuss this. Instead, there has long been a tendency to dramatically understate the price of a hegemonist strategy—hence the heavy focus on willpower and wishful thinking about Iraq being able to finance its own postwar reconstruction. In the neoconservative view, at least traditionally, global domination has been sitting within reach on the shelf ever since 1991, just waiting for national leadership that is bold enough to grab it. Six years of Bushism have largely dispelled this delusion, but without it, the underlying theory largely collapses. An alternative strategy, also seen with regard to Iraq, is to wildly misstate the nature of the situation. Thus, the absence of verifiable proof that Saddam Hussein had not revived his nuclear weapons program became certainty that the program was close to fruition, and a tight connection between Iraq and al-Qaeda was essentially concocted out of thin air. Insofar as national attention has shifted to Iran or to Syria or to North Korea or even to China, one sees the same pattern over and over again of wildly overstating the threat level.

When the situation is looked at through a more realistic lens, however, it becomes clear that under George W. Bush, hegemonism in action has accomplished virtually nothing for the United States and has done so at great cost. The world has seen more al-Qaeda terrorism since 9/11 than before it, a boom in nuclear proliferation, a truly horrifying humanitarian catastrophe in postwar Iraq, large-scale civil unrest in Lebanon, a surge in anti-Israeli terrorism, a rising tide of anti-Americanism as far afield as Latin America and South Korea, and—despite the rhetoric—basically no progress on increasing the number of democratic nations. The world certainly had its fair share of serious problems before Bush took office, but substituting neoconservatism for liberalism has ameliorated none of them, while aggravating many and creating an impressive array of new ones.

The liberal alternative to the recent disasters, emphasizing the use of U.S. power in a cooperative manner to sustain and expand a liberal world order, by contrast, was not only working well before the current administration's inauguration but is in many ways especially suited to the unique challenges posed by transnational terrorism. The issue, as Robert Wright has observed, is that "in an age when Americans are threatened by overseas bioweapons labs and outbreaks of flu, by Chinese pollution that enters lungs in Oregon, by imploding African states that could turn into terrorist havens, by authoritarian Arab governments that push young men toward radicalism . . . indifference to the interiors of nations is untenable."[7] In the wake of Bush's disastrous conduct of national affairs, it is natural for substantial swathes of the population to simply become weary of involvement with problems abroad. This is particularly true insofar as not only the president of the United States, but a substantial proportion of the press, insists on identifying global engagement with willingness to initiate ill-conceived military adventures. A January 2007 *New Yorker* article by Jeffrey Goldberg, for example, portrayed Joe Lieberman, and to some extent his fellow hawk Evan Bayh, as representing a faction of the Democratic Party interested in "enlightened internationalism." Presidential contenders such as Hillary Clinton, Barack Obama, and John Edwards were then rated as internationalists based more or less exclusively on their willingness to prolong the war in Iraq indefinitely and go to war with Sudan and/or Iran.[8]

Nevertheless, no matter how annoying the misuses to which the concepts of international engagement versus isolation have been put, the fact remains that it would be a bad idea for the United States to retreat from a concern with events in distant countries. At times such concern appears morally imperative, and at other times imperative to our interests or to those of our close allies. The trouble is that an impulse to simply meddle—whether the meddling is well-intentioned or not, whether motivated by morals or interests—in the affairs of others is, when combined with the United States' massive military power, an intolerable threat to the interests of other nations. The result, as John Ikenberry has argued, is that "When America tries to solve the nation's security problems by exercising its power or using force, it tends to produce resistance and backlash that leaves the country bereft of authority, isolated, and ultimately more insecure than it was before it acted."[9]

Neither neoconservatives nor liberal hawks have really appreciated this point, a failure that stems from a pathological unwillingness to attempt to seriously consider other countries' perspectives on events. To some critics, such as Anatol Lieven and John Hulsman, a determination to do better on this score implies a revival of interest in the foreign policy doctrine of "realism," but it is likewise integral to the liberal worldview. Where liberals and realists have traditionally parted ways is how to try to take the perspectives of others into account. Rather than simply by doing less or by seeking ad hoc arrangements with other powers, liberals seek to defend liberal societies by embedding them within liberal institutions that can uphold a reasonably just world order and thereby preserve the peace. The concept, well captured by Slaughter and Ikenberry's slogan of aiming at a "world of liberty under law," is an old and enduring one. The underlying logic of rule-governed reciprocity is, however, made all the more compelling by recent developments. It is precisely the fact that contemporary conditions make it reasonable for the United States to be concerned with what goes on inside the borders of other countries to an unprecedented degree that makes the notion of expressing that concern through stable, rule-based institutions so compelling. The alternative approach of simply asserting an American right to intrusively insert itself into issues abroad in times and places of our choosing is naturally appealing in its way to U.S. policy elites, who prefer to have as little constraint as possible on their authority.

It is not, however, ultimately acceptable to other countries around the world. Nor is it reasonable to expect that it will become acceptable in the near future. Fortunately, an alternative is available—reciprocity, rules, institutions, and cooperation. Other countries will be willing to accept intrusive safeguards on biological laboratories to ensure that they are not used to develop deadly weapons because the United States, too, will submit to those safeguards. Other nations will rally to America's lead in turning back acts of aggressive warfare, as they did when Iraq invaded Kuwait in 1991, in part because the United States agrees not to wage aggressive wars such as the 2003 invasion of Iraq.

Bush looked at the accumulation of agreements, treaties, and institutions that had built up during the Cold War and the Clinton years and saw a United States that had unduly constrained itself. Liberals saw a country that was not yet willing to go far enough—one that had signed but not ratified the Comprehensive Test Ban Treaty and the Kyoto Protocols and that was unwilling to join the Ottawa Treaty on land mines or the International Criminal Court. A Gore administration almost certainly would have taken the United States at least somewhat further down this road. The Bush administration instead tried to create "America unbound," acting from the beginning to dissolve treaties and shed international obligations in the belief that U.S. military supremacy could, if freed from its diplomatic shackles, remake the world.

Simply put, it didn't work. The Bush administration's embrace of militaristic nationalism has not brought democracy to the Middle East and has not frightened Iran or North Korea out of conducting nuclear research, nor has it intimidated Iran or Syria out of supporting Hezbollah, spooked Pakistan into ending its support for Kashmiri radicals or into clamping down on al-Qaeda sympathizers in its border areas, overawed China out of efforts to become a great power, or frightened Russia out of reasserting itself. Maintaining the freedom to act, it turns out, has little value unless it's paired with the ability to act *effectively*. And the United States, though very powerful indeed, cannot effectively tackle large problems except in cooperation with others and cannot secure that cooperation unless it acts in ways that other nations recognize as compatible with their own interests. A foreign policy that accepts more constraints on what we may try to do is likely to broaden the range of things we actually can do. As Suzanne Nossel has put it, "[A] foreign policy with legitimacy at its core both will enable the United States to restore its own standing in the world and make the promotion of its own aims easier."[10]

What conservatives miss when considering this issue is that U.S. power is an objective fact about the world, not something that can or need be created or enhanced through bold demonstrations. It is true that in a world ungoverned by law and characterized by conflict, the United States will be more successful than any other single nation at bending others to its will. Nevertheless, we will also be the most influential participant in nearly any diplomatic conference or international institution one can imagine, and for all the same reasons. The United States is the world's richest economy by a decent margin, has the world's most powerful military by far, and has the world's third largest population. We enjoy a favorable geographical location, possess a wide array of natural resources, and have a much larger, richer, and more important circle of close allies than does any other major state. These assets create substantial national power, and a determination to exercise that power in a legitimate manner doesn't change that. Instead, it makes it easier for the United States to secure the cooperation of other countries, making the exercise of power more effective.

Obviously, a need to abide by rules and take the concerns of other countries into account will limit what can be accomplished. There is, however, something perverse about claims like Bush's 2005 State of the Union proclamation that "America will never seek a permission slip to defend the security of our country." In the case of a bona fide emergency, of course, a president will have to do what he has to do, even if that means acting utterly alone. But in lesser cases, limits exist either way. As we have seen throughout the Bush years, unshackling ourselves from international rules and global norms does not grant the United States unlimited ability to shape world events. Instead, it multiplies the number of problems we face, while simultaneously making them harder to solve. Permission is not, in practice, all that hard to come by when U.S. initiatives are actually good ideas. Meanwhile, even the Bush administration recognizes that in practice, some measure of international cooperation is necessary to do anything. Formalizing cooperative relationships makes them work more smoothly, while Bush's approach has done much more to render cooperation impossible to get than to render it unnecessary. Confrontational policies are appropriate when faced with an ideologically driven adversary that is hell-bent on our destruction, such as Nazi Germany, the U.S.S.R., or indeed al-Qaeda, but the signature fact about the contemporary world is that no such challenger controls any state of consequence. The interests of the United States are not so closely aligned with those of other countries that we can reasonably expect them to meekly submit to a U.S.-led benign hegemony, but they *are* sufficiently close that it should be possible to work in a cooperative manner with the vast majority of states most of the time, thus greatly increasing the level of power that can be brought to bear on any specific point.

What would a revived liberal internationalism entail in practice? First and foremost, it would counsel that we stop digging. The next president should quickly and plainly admit what everyone already knows: the invasion of Iraq was a mistake. Not a good idea ruined by mistakes of implementation, but a strategic and moral error. The United States can and should foreswear unilateral preventive war as a tool of nonproliferation policy and commit instead to relying on legitimate methods.

In the immediate case of Iran, that means making a good-faith effort to negotiate with the Iranians. Not pointless, Bush-style negotiations where the United States simply reiterates its demands, but a meaningful effort to resolve the outstanding disputes between Teheran and Washington in a manner that will leave both countries better off than they are now. The United States currently has much less to offer Iran in terms of shaping the futures of Iraq and Afghanistan than it once did, so the likelihood is overwhelming that we will get less from the Iranians today than we could have had in 2003, and even less in 2009 than we could get today. Nevertheless, this should hardly be used as a reason for further delay to a time when the situation will be even less favorable. A serious negotiating effort should, in the meantime, make it easier to convince close allies in Europe and Asia to credibly threaten more severe economic sanctions if the Iranians adopt an unreasonable attitude. More effective pressure can be brought on Iran to deal if Russia and China are doing some of the pressuring. Here, U.S. elites will have to face the simple reality that a nuclear Iran causes much more consternation in Washington than it does in Beijing or Moscow. Hectoring *Weekly Standard* articles and whining *Washington Post* editorials about Sino-Russian perfidy are neither here nor there in terms of changing this. Realistically, our diplomats are going to have to ask their diplomats what they would like from us and what they're prepared to offer us in exchange. We must then consider whether the prices asked are worth paying in exchange for enhanced cooperation against Iran.

Acquiring better threats is, however, not the essence of the matter. There is in fact good reason to believe that the Iranian nuclear program is not going especially well and that Iran's leaders would foreswear the acquisition of nuclear weapons in exchange for an improved relationship with the United States that would allow them to revive their troubled economy and shore up their security situation. More broadly, the Iranian situation has highlighted the need to revise the Non-Proliferation Treaty in order to give the United States better assurance that other countries aren't cheating. That, in turn, will require us to get China, Russia, and the developing world on our side by addressing some of their concerns with the United States' current nuclear policy—in particular, the drive to develop a new generation of nuclear weapons should be abandoned and we should recommit ourselves to mutual nuclear reductions in partnership with Russia.

These measures lack the sex appeal of military strikes, and the diplomatic and technical details that would lie at the heart of a liberal nonproliferation campaign are, frankly, dull—a political problem that must be admitted squarely. Nevertheless, the fact remains that such an effort would be wildly more effective than the preventive war path, which has thus far produced no successes whatsoever. What's more, a nonproliferation strategy based on rules and institutions can deal with nuclear problems—loss or theft of nuclear weapons or materials, regime collapse in unstable nuclear states such as Pakistan, and so on—that lie beyond the scope of the preventive war approach and that are likely more realistic sources of nuclear terrorism than are a rogue state. Beyond nuclear weapons, there is also good reason to be concerned about the possible future proliferation of contagious biological weapons. The technical issues here are obviously different, but the overall principle is the same. The United States has an overwhelming strategic interest in preventing the development of incredibly dangerous agents of biological warfare and should push as hard as possible for the development of the toughest possible international inspections regime to prevent that eventuality and—crucially—should be perfectly willing to submit our own laboratories to the same level of scrutiny we wish to see applied to the world's most villainous regimes. At the end of the day, we have much more to fear from too little global regulation than from too much.

Taking these steps is the single best thing we can do to ensure our safety against international terrorism. Years after 9/11, it is time to admit the obvious—while al-Qaeda's members and underlying ideology are certainly worthy successors in evil to Hitler or Stalin, their actual capabilities are rather less frightening. Conventional terrorism, while certainly a problem and a great moral wrong, is simply not that deadly in the scheme of things. As Ohio State University's John Mueller has observed, "[E]ven with the September 11 attacks included in the count, the number of Americans killed by international terrorism since the late 1960s (which is when the State Department began counting) is about the same as the number of Americans killed over the same period by lightning, accident-causing deer, or severe allergic reaction to peanuts."[11] The real risk is that terrorists will find a way to close the gap between their dreams of mass casualties and the less dangerous reality, and the best way to prevent this from coming to pass is through rigorous controls on the weapons.

Nevertheless, a terrorist plotting to kill Americans is not a peanut or an accident-causing deer, and the government clearly has a responsibility to track such people down and attempt to capture or kill them. In foreign policy terms, however, this is a rather simple task that the Bush administration has needlessly overcomplicated. None of the world's existing states shares al-Qaeda's agenda, all are threatened by it, and the desire to cooperate with the United States in this regard is widespread. Indeed, not only did traditional allies come to America's aid after 9/11, but traditional adversaries like Syria and Iran volunteered assistance, hoping that a common foe could be the basis for improved relations overall. As we have seen, the Bush administration essentially spurned those countries' advances—a major error that should be reversed as soon as possible. It is possible that some future turn of events will bring to power somewhere a government that, like the Taliban, is engaged in actively supporting al-Qaeda or some other transnational terrorist group targeting the American homeland, in which case the use or the threat of military force will certainly come into play as a counterterrorism tool. Unless that happens, however, it will remain the case that, as John Kerry said during the 2004 campaign, stopping terrorism is "primarily an intelligence and law enforcement operation that requires cooperation around the world." Kerry was roundly mocked for the observation, but, as the conservative columnist George Will pointed out in a noteworthy August 2006 column, Kerry was perfectly correct, and even though the administration denies his point, its denial involves a "farrago of caricature and non sequitur . . . intellectual contortions required to sustain the illusion that the war in Iraq is central to the war on terrorism, and that the war, unlike 'the law enforcement approach,' does 'work.' "[12]

Many liberal hawks, including those who've become disillusioned with the Iraq War and even some people who never supported it from the beginning, continue to endorse important elements of the Bush administration's denial of this basic reality. In particular, there is widespread support for the notion that the country not only needs ideas that are different from those of the Bush administration, but needs specifically *new* ideas. Needless to say, there's nothing wrong with developing new ideas as such. Good ideas are always welcome, and it's always possible to improve upon existing notions. To simply accept the demand for novelty at the outset as a political, psychological, or intellectual necessity is, however, to risk adopting bad ideas simply because they're the best ones we can think of, and several ill-conceived notions have gained substantial traction on the left in recent years and they risk crowding out sounder alternatives.

Neomania draws on several sources. One of them is the simple reality that political-message managers and journalists alike enjoy novelty, and enthusiasm for it is a particular quirk of the centrist wing of the Democratic Party. Indeed, a colleague of mine was once engaged in an e-mail exchange with a prominent neoliberal writer and operative during which the operative eventually concluded, "you're worrying about the *quality* of ideas, I'm more concerned with their size and new-ness." Another source is what Joshua Micah Marshall has labeled "the Orwell temptation," a tendency "to take momen-tous, morally serious questions and make them out to be slightly more momentous and world-historical than they really are."[13] The writer's life is more interesting and more important if the challenge of al-Qaeda is world-historical in scale, and if it is world-historical in scale, then the need for dramatic new ideas is clear. Similarly, if there is a need for new ideas, then there is also a need for generalist writers and intellectuals to dream them up or, at a minimum, argue on their behalf in an excited manner. If, by contrast, terrorism will be fought primarily through careful investigative work and patient diplomacy aimed at securing global consensus around a more technically sound proliferation regime, then there is relatively little that one can say without first doing the long, boring work of learning in detail about nuclear weapons technology. On top of all that, we have simply gone through several years where it was politically taboo to tell people that on some level, the United States ought to calm down.

The tendency, in short, has been for the search for "new ideas" to be driven by a pure desire for novelty, rather than by a quest for sound ideas.

Most prominently, it was fashionable for a long time for liberals—including some hawks, some ex-hawks, and some nonhawks—to argue that the Bush administration was right about the need to promote democracy in the Middle East but wrong in the way to go about it. What was needed, perhaps, was a new national commitment to a new method of promot-ing democracy. I myself wrote some articles along these lines, and there is some truth to that way of looking at things. The problem, however, is that the "right" way to promote democ-racy turns out to be somewhat uninteresting and not the sort of thing one would want to put at the center of national poli-cy. The financing of democracy endeavors around the world through USAID and the National Endowment for Democracy, for example, has a decent record of success, combined with low costs of failure when it doesn't work. These programs deserve some enhancement of their budgets. The total amount of money involved, however, simply isn't very large—methods of accounting differ, but it's certainly much less than $1 billion in total—so even significant enhancements would leave them as a rather minor piece of the national security pie.[14] What's more, by their nature there are real limits to how much these activities can be stepped up. Any foreign organization receiving an unduly large amount of money from the United States, after all, will simply find itself discredited as a tool of foreigners. Similarly, putting too much money into the pot would risk creating a situation where U.S. democracy-promotion funding attracts hucksters and scam artists, rather than committed idealists. Finally, while money is obviously helpful in these matters, organizations like the ones behind the Orange Revolution in Ukraine are effective only insofar as they have genuine grassroots support, and larger budgets can't simply conjure such support—or the leadership qualities necessary to obtain it—out of thin air.

At the end of the day, the best thing the United States can do for the cause of democracy, both in the Middle East and elsewhere, is simply to play its role in the world in a responsible matter and seek the generic promotion of a peaceful and prosperous international system. The connection between trade, globalization, and capitalism, on the one hand, and democracy and human rights, on the other, has sometimes been overstated by the overenthusiastic, but it is real. Countries that feature very high levels of public sector employment are also countries where governments have enormous leverage to punish critics and their friends and families. Privately held wealth can, by contrast, provide the material basis for a pluralistic public sphere. Global trade provides citizens in authoritarian or semiauthoritarian nations with connections to the larger world. There is no panacea here (just look at Singapore), but it is in many ways the best thing we can do. The subject lies largely outside the scope of this book, but one of the great challenges of liberal economic policy in coming years will be rebuilding the domestic social contract in a way that once again makes further expansions of global trade acceptable—and, indeed, beneficial—to the American working class.

This all represents the common core of the liberal alternative to conservative hegemonism. Where the fetishization of "new ideas" goes most badly awry, however, is the point where a sound appreciation of the role of institutions in foreign policy and a sober assessment of the role of democracy in U.S. foreign policy blend into unsound ideas about the creation of a worldwide democratic alliance. Proposals of this sort go under a variety of names and take several forms. Ivo Daalder and James Lindsay have written of an "Alliance of Democracies." Daalder and James Goldgeier have advocated a "Global NATO." The Princeton Project on National Security advocates a "Concert of Democracies." Other thinkers, notably Beinart and Fukuyama, have spoken more generally about the need for new institutions and a "multi-multilateralism" that will allow U.S. policy to combine flexibility with legitimacy. All these ideas have some merit, but all can be—and by their authors are—taken too far and transformed into proposals that undermine, rather than enhance, the ideals of liberal order.

What's more, they tend to reek of a quest for new ideas in the worst possible sense. As Daalder and Lindsay wrote, "American leadership in creating an Alliance of Democratic States would satisfy the deep yearning on both the left and right in the United States to promote America's values while pursuing its interests."[15] This is true, but it's also the problem. These proposals are so good at satisfying a deep yearning, less on the left or the right than in the center, for a way to secure all the benefits of multilateral legitimacy and liberal order without paying the costs that they tend to leap from germination to publication without serious thought as to the consequences.

The problem in all of these cases is that the proposals involve almost incidentally mentioning the idea that a democratic bloc could replace the United Nations Security Council as a legitimate authorizing entity for the use of nondefensive military force.

The authors of these plans don't seem to consider the issue in their writing, and those to whom I've spoken about the issue deny that this is their intention, but the upshot of any such strategy would rather clearly be to provoke a new Cold War with China joined by Russia, the bulk of the Arab League, and assorted other countries on the other side. The problem is that the authors are not seriously considering the point of view of others. To be sure, from an American perspective there is a clear moral basis in differentiating the weight we give to the views of popularly elected liberal governments and those of autocracies. That a group of moderately rights-abusing dictators may oppose action to curb the more egregious abuses of one of their colleagues in the dictatoring business does not strike anyone as an appealing reason to refrain from acting. Nevertheless, insofar as the international system does in fact contain a decent number of authoritarian states, any legitimate international order is going to need to take their interests into account or else prepare itself for endless conflict.

It is one thing to argue, as Daalder and Lindsay do, that "democratic nations should rally together to pursue their common interests." It is another thing entirely to argue that said nations should decide that they—but not other nations—have the unique right to decide when the use of military force is legitimate. Simply put, no responsible and patriotic Chinese or Russian official could or would meekly accept this vision of second-class citizenship in the international community. Worse, Muslims generally, and Arabs and Pakistanis in particular, are not going to be enthusiastic about the creation of a large formal alliance that includes Israel and India but excludes all the Arab states and indeed all Muslim ones except for Turkey and perhaps Indonesia. If an alliance—even a broad one—assembled by the United States has the legal right to intervene where it sees fit, then why shouldn't a Chinese- or Russian-backed alliance have the same right? Why not the Arab League or the Organization of the Islamic Conference? The cliché question to ponder in China policy is whether Beijing can be persuaded to become a "responsible stakeholder" in the international system. The answer to that question will, however, become a rapid "no" if we change the rules of the international system in a way that enormously loads them against China.

The result could be a disaster. The animating purpose behind the idea of an alternative force-authorizing mechanism is that it might allow for coercive enforcement of human rights and nonproliferation norms when such initiatives might otherwise be held hostage by authoritarian UN members. The problem here is real, but the cure is worse than the disease. As the authors of the most recent *Human Security Report* emphasize, "the end of the Cold War brought remarkable"—and overwhelmingly beneficial—"changes to the global security climate,"[16] in particular sharp declines in the number and the severity of wars and mass killings, genocidal or otherwise. This is no coincidence. On the one hand, the end of the Cold War dried up superpower support for various forms of conflict in the developing world. On the other hand, the end of the Cold War made international institutions like the UN and regional groups much more effective, allowing these groups and the NGO community to play a much more effective role in preventing, ending, or simply limiting armed conflicts. Deliberately redividing the world along ideological lines would risk a reversal of all this when we should be continuing the trend.

Nor would it do any good in nonproliferation terms. A somewhat enhanced legal ability to drop bombs would be badly, badly offset by a decrease in the overall level of international cooperation. In the limiting case, there is essentially nothing we could actually do to prevent Russia or China from simply selling or donating nuclear weapons to another state. Even under conditions of a new Cold War, such an extreme scenario is unlikely (there are reasons, after all, that this didn't happen frequently during the original Cold War), but the limiting case serves to illustrate the broader point—ultimately, achieving nonproliferation goals depends more on international cooperation than on U.S. military force.

The basic point about all of this is that while advocates of a strong form of the democratic alliance are paying lip service to the value of legitimacy over unilateralism, they don't seem to quite appreciate what legitimacy *is*. In the most generic sense, an action might be legitimate only if it met with universal approbation. Such an arrangement would, however, obviously prevent virtually any action from meeting the standard of legitimacy. Thus, you may see universal assent to the proposition that a certain process grants legitimacy. There may even be universal assent to a method for altering the legitimization process. What can't happen, however, is for some single country or set of countries to simply decide on its own what will and will not be a legitimate move in the international realm. An action opposed by Russia and China will not suddenly gain new legitimacy in Russian or Chinese eyes simply because a group from which they are excluded says so.

If, as is widely believed, strict adherence to the UN Security Council process would not provide the United States with sufficient flexibility, then there are better options available than creating an alternative, democracies-only organization that claims authorizing power. For one thing, in the case of a bona fide instance of self-defense or defense of an ally, the UN Charter itself stipulates a right to act. Secondarily, the United States—or, indeed, any other country—could work in partnership with a local regional organization that is viewed as legitimate in the area. The *any other country* part, however, is absolutely vital. The principle being sought here would be one that would permit regional security organizations to act in cases where the UN cannot, and it would affirm their right to draw on the assistance of outside partners. In practice, that is likely to more often mean the United States of America than the People's Republic of China, but no two-tiered system of international citizenship is being set up.

Beyond that, concerns about the UN's effectiveness should primarily motivate us to push reform measures that are designed to make it work better. It is, however, always worth recalling that problems with the UN tend to be overstated. The conservative movement's long-standing hostility to effective global governance leads it and its attendant institutions to constantly harp on oft-imagined failings of the UN, while paying no attention to the successes. At the same time, reform-minded internationalists sometimes tend to overstate shortcomings for rhetorical effect. The reality is that the UN does a great deal of good as is, it could do more good with somewhat more support from the United States, and it could also be improved through reform. The United States has every reason to try to achieve such reforms, but it should also be understood that as the world's leading power, we sometimes do a cause of this nature more harm than good by putting it at the center of our agenda.

Pressing for reform, while simultaneously insulating the cause of reform from narrow U.S. interests, could be one use for a revised and scaled-back version of the democratic alliance concept. There is, as a general matter, nothing objectionable about, say, the Princeton Project's proposal to create an international organization "to strengthen security cooperation among the world's liberal democracies and to provide a framework in which they can work together to effectively tackle common challenges."[17] It is, however, best to work together to tackle these challenges in a manner that does not involve undermining the authority of the Security Council over matters of war and peace. People who cannot think of any projects worth collaborating on that don't involve staging coercive military interventions aren't thinking very hard about the subject. Similarly, the Global NATO proposal conflates two different ideas. One, an eminently reasonable one, is that NATO membership should not be arbitrarily limited to the United States, Canada, Iceland, Turkey, and states that are located in Europe. Insofar as other liberal democracies are interested in the commitments that membership entails and the existing members are willing to extend an explicit defense guarantee, there's no particular reason to let geography alone categorically prevent further expansion.

The difficulty here, applying in an even stronger form to plans for a worldwide democratic alliance, is that there's precious little indication that other countries actually *are* clamoring to sign up for new U.S.-created alliances of any form. Realistically, the damage that's been done by Bush's policies in terms of increased skepticism of the United States won't be undone in an instant simply by electing a successor. One of the next president's primary tasks, at least at the beginning, will simply be proving that America can and will play a constructive role in the world, recreating the circumstances under which closer relations with the United States were widely perceived as desirable.

This can and should be done in a variety of ways, including enhanced foreign aid, a greater level of U.S. interest in consensual UN-sponsored peacekeeping missions, and efforts to move U.S. policy on things like global warming closer to world opinion. Perhaps the most useful thing to do, not least because it serves our interests in direct ways, would be to reengage with the United States' role as a mediator and a peacemaker. During the Cold War era, as the leader of the anti-Soviet alliance, the United States knew it was crucial for U.S. policy to seek to contain and, ideally, resolve lesser local and historical disputes. Antagonism between members of the non-Soviet world opened wedges that the communists could exploit, while internal peace within the "free world" permitted the successful containment of Soviet power. Thus, the United States took a strong interest in the highly successful efforts to promote reconciliation between Germany and France and has sought to do what it takes to maintain peace between Turkey and Greece.

The Bush administration itself has not been entirely foreign to this role, dispatching Richard Armitage—at the time, Colin Powell's deputy at the State Department—to the Indian subcontinent in 2002 for some timely mediation to halt an India-Pakistan clash that could have led to nuclear war. Primarily, however, Bush has essentially abdicated this role. He has done so most clearly and most famously in the case of the Israeli-Arab conflict. At least every president from Nixon to Clinton has made it a priority for the United States to attempt to stabilize the Middle East and better secure our allies and interests in the region by promoting reconciliation between Israel and its neighbors. This process was often frustrating for those involved, but it did in fact accomplish a great deal. Henry Kissinger's shuttle diplomacy helped to end the Yom Kippur War and prevent the renewed outbreak of formal hostilities between Israel and its neighbors. Kissinger also laid the groundwork for the Egypt-Israel peace accords that Jimmy Carter shepherded into existence. The Oslo peace process, overseen by the Clinton administration but building importantly on the George H. W. Bush administration's Madrid

Conference, ultimately failed to create peace between Israel and the Palestinians but did result in the two sides' positions drawing much closer together and a peace treaty between Israel and Jordan. The self-proclaimed "pro-Israel" community in the United States tends to look askance at these peacemaking efforts, as they necessarily involve placing some pressure on the Israeli government. Therefore this "pro-Israel" group tends to take a somewhat hostile attitude toward Clinton and an extremely bitter one toward Carter.

This attitude is, however, foolishly shortsighted. For obvious reasons, Israeli prime ministers do not enjoy being pressured by U.S. presidents. Nevertheless, the clear fact of the matter is that Israel is much better off being at peace with Egypt and Jordan than it was at war with those two states. In the 1950s, 1960s, and 1970s, the Jewish state faced a plausible threat of being defeated by the combined conventional armies of its neighbors. That threat no longer exists, and the Carter administration and its Camp David Accords played major roles in eliminating it. Nothing, meanwhile, would do more to further enhance Israeli security than would a lasting settlement with the Palestinians, which, as the Arab League has made clear in recent years, would among other things provide the basis for normalizing relations with its member states.

On some level, of course, this is easier said than done. On the other hand, the Clinton administration did in fact come very close to succeeding, and in some important ways the parties on both sides of the conflict have become more amenable to compromise in the intervening years. What's more, virtually every administration that has bothered to try to work seriously on the Arab-Israeli conflict has come away with *some* important achievements.

Most fundamentally, efforts in this regard are in the vital interests of the United States. This view is sometimes caricatured as the claim that Osama bin Laden would lay down his arms or the radical factions in Teheran would start singing "God Bless America" if a Palestinian state were created. That, of course, is false. The truth, however, is that people do not become anti-American radicals out of nowhere. Concrete, specific conflicts, especially those involving Muslims on one side and non-Muslims on the other, are the mechanism by which people come to be interested in violent struggle and may eventually join the worldwide violent struggle against the United States. Bin Laden's ideological contribution to the world of Islamist thought has been to tie together a series of apparently unrelated conflicts and assert that the key to resolving them all is to wage war against the United States. As a nation, we must be prepared to defend ourselves against those who have accepted this message.

We must also, however, have a long-term strategy for ensuring that the threat diminishes, rather than grows, over time. One essential measure in this regard is for the United States to lead in seeking to resolve the local conflicts that fuel the global jihadist movement. Instead, Bush's policy has been to, for example, assist the Filipino and Thai governments in efforts to militarily suppress insurgent campaigns based in their countries' Muslim minorities, while doing little to promote political reconciliation or the settlement of grievances. Similarly, the Bush administration actively assisted the government of Ethiopia in its effort to invade and conquer Somalia in order to displace the Islamic Courts Movement that had been serving as that unhappy country's de facto government. In all these cases, the liberal alternative suggests that our main priority should be in the other direction. These conflicts are fundamentally political in nature, and it is their resolution that will undermine support for the global jihad movement. In the meantime, U.S. efforts to use our massive leverage on the world stage in order to promote peace will enhance the credibility of efforts to strengthen the mechanisms of global governance. In combination, then, a liberal internationalist approach should reduce the number of people aiming to harm Americans, reduce the risk that those who do seek to harm Americans will be able to acquire the weapons they need to do so, and maintain the general atmosphere of peace between major states that has obtained since the end of the Cold War.

The problem, according to many, is politics. Simply put, Democrats cannot be made electorally viable unless they prove their toughness, their seriousness, or some other suitable term through an embrace of the sort of militarism and hegemonism that have ran rampant in our politics since 9/11. It is impossible, unfortunately, to prove that such claims are mistaken. The evidence for them, however, is shockingly weak. Liberal hawk politics failed in 2002 and 2004, and anti-war candidates fared well in 2006. A liberal internationalist foreign policy has not really been put to the political test in the post-9/11 era, but as the United States has mostly been governed by such policies for decades, there's clearly nothing intrinsic to the national character that makes them anathema. Meanwhile, substantially endorsing key theoretical under-pinnings of the incumbent administration's failed policies has not proved itself to be a particularly effective method of opposition.

The real political difficulty with a return to international-ism is simply that it requires someone to challenge conven-tional wisdom and the entrenched dogmas of the past several years. It rarely serves the interests of any individual politician to move first against the grain. As Howard Dean discovered after Saddam Hussein's capture, sticking your neck out tends to result in decapitation, even when everyone knows you're right, and mere retrospective vindication won't save your rep-utation. This is a genuine problem, and the reluctance of politicians and their aides to risk taking a bullet for the cause is understandable. At the same time, it must be understood that the hawks and the timidity caucus are the source of this problem, not part of the solution. The events of 9/11 led to an upsurge in nationalistic sentiment, a huge spike in Bush's approval ratings, and a leap in Americans' interest in foreign affairs. This would have been a good opportunity to try to spell out the liberal international approach to national security policy and begin advocating for its suitability to the crisis at hand. Instead, the dominant impulse was to join the public in rallying 'round the Bush administration, while expending huge efforts in denouncing marginal far-left figures. Conservative dogmas were left unchallenged or, all too often, actually embraced.

Accepting the right's framing of the question dodged the difficult problem of making the case for the liberal alternative, but did not make the problem go away. The work simply must be done, and sooner better than later. Discrediting the conservative approach to Iraq—but doing so on narrow, technocratic grounds—has not served to discredit the conservative approach to Iran or to India or to anything else. Insofar as those issues continue to have low salience relative to Iraq, Democrats can expect to enjoy the sort of political success they saw in 2006. Insofar as the salience of other topics in national security rises, however, their problems of 2002 and 2004 will return. Especially if conservative blundering plunges the country into a downward spiral of hostility vis-à-vis the Muslim world, the odds are decent that we will see a return of the dynamic prevailing from 1968 to 1992, when the politics of the Cold War gave the GOP a near-stranglehold on the executive branch.

Beyond politics, of course, is the matter of substance. Too many progressives, especially those involved in funding and managing formal progressive institutions, have tended to treat national security issues as an unfortunate distraction from the "real" (that is, domestic) issues. To some, this has meant not challenging conservative foreign policy as an explicit electoral strategy. For others, it has simply rendered opposition half-hearted and ineffectual. In both cases, the effect has been to empower a smallish faction of liberal hawks who essentially share the right's vision of unilateral U.S. military hegemony over the world. It is time, however, for liberals to get serious about national security policy. Not in the all too frequently abused sense of the word in which *seriousness* means something like "proclivity for launching ill-advised wars" but actual seriousness—a commitment to laying out the liberal world-view in a disciplined, coherent, principled manner whether or not it's advantageous to do so in the short run. The point is not that politics don't matter, but rather that on the big issues the most important thing—even politically—is to develop answers that will be vindicated over time, rather than to devise talking points that are well-suited to the instinctive prejudices of the hour. Ultimately, however, the best reason to try to get these issues right is simply that they are important—quite literally matters of life and death.

The nationalistic strain in the American public that has led politicians to shy away from explicit advocacy of liberal internationalism is, after all, grounded in the long-held view that the United States has a special role to play in the world. Insofar as that view has any truth, however, it stems the fact that throughout the twentieth century, the United States has in fact usually chosen to behave unlike the great powers of the past. We have mostly eschewed the game of empire building and coercive domination, which must end in ceaseless wars and eventual collapse, in favor of efforts to construct a liberal world order that will spread and strengthen over time. Insofar as our past behavior has not fit this model, claims of divinely favored status have not saved us from disaster. The current effort to coercively dominate the Middle East is, as the United States has seen in the specific case of Iraq, no exception to the rule. For America's global role to be worthy of the great esteem in which its citizens hold it, we must return our policies to the mold that first forged that reputation, and liberals must be the ones to do the hard work of taking the lead in making sure it happens. For if we do not, no one will.

Surge to Nowhere

By the time I finished work on this book in the summer of 2007, the mood in progressive Washington was sharply different from what it had been at the beginning. A striking optimism had taken hold, and conversations frequently focused on what grand policy achievements—particularly in the fields of health care and climate change—might be forthcoming when Democrats controlled the White House and expanded their congressional majorities. The main cause of the shift, of course, was the 2006 midterm elections. More generally, the deep unpopularity of President George W. Bush continued for months to drag down the popularity of all Republicans everywhere, giving the potential Democratic nominees an edge in head-to-head polling matchups with all the potential Republican nominees. Add to that the early fundraising woes for the Republican congressional campaign committees, the fact that most of the Senators up for reelection in 2008 are Republicans, and a rash of retirements among House Republican incumbents, and one can see that the optimism has a real basis.

On the other hand, politicians wage campaigns for a reason and leads in polls that seem impressive early in the year often vanish by November. But beyond this general note of caution, liberals would do well to direct their attention to Democratic performance in *specific standoffs* over national security issues that have occurred. Despite Bush's general unpopularity, Democrats have tended to find themselves on the losing side in these concrete controversies—over troop levels in Iraq, over torture and interrogation policy, over surveillance, over Iran, and so on—and not just because of insufficient numbers. Rather, they've often lost the public relations battle as well. In particular, despite the war's leading role in driving Bush's numbers down and thus creating the overall favorable dynamic for the Democratic Party, most members in marginal constituencies continue to believe that security-related fights favor the GOP, and the Republicans agree.

Consequently, one sees what amounts to an endless repetition of the pathologies of years past: efforts to avoid talking about these issues, and, when forced into a corner, a tendency to want to duck the main issues and quibble around the margins. This reflects a lack of self-confidence, but it also makes it all but impossible to formulate a principled basis for an alternative to conservatism. It's that lack of a principles-driven framework that makes it so difficult for the Democrats to win. Thus, the cycle reinforces itself and has continued to do so right up to the present day. Campaigns play out as a series of battles over discrete topics. So if Democrats can't win these fights, there's a good chance they'll find themselves losing more elections, particularly when Bush fades into the background to be replaced by a nominee who has the generic Republican advantages of "strength" and "toughness" but lacks personal association with the widely derided ineptitude and corruption of the Bush administration.

Examples abound, from an August 2007 bill amending the Foreign Intelligence Surveillance Act, to the decision to confirm a new attorney general who refused to answer questions about the legality of certain torture techniques previously authorized by the administration, to a vote in favor of a measure backed by the Senate's two leading Iran hawks—Jon Kyl and Joe Lieberman—branding a branch of the Iranian military as a terrorist group. Still, Iraq *continues* to be *the* central example of the Democrats' problematic political and substantive approach to foreign policy. In particular, the drama surrounding General David Petraeus's September 2007 report to Congress on the project of "the surge" perfectly illustrates the persistence of all the main pathologies. Most notably, an inability to argue particular points from a position grounded in any larger strategic principle leaves Democrats perpetually vulnerable to conservative onslaughts and efforts to shift the terms of debate.

The origins of what became known as the "Petraeus Report" lay back in January 2007, when the Bush administration rejected out of hand the Baker-Hamilton Commission's recommendations of regional diplomacy and a scaled-back military mission. Instead, Bush opted for "the surge," a reshuffling of deployment schedules that would generate a temporary increase in the number of Americans serving in Iraq by about twenty-one thousand. To oversee this operation, Bush appointed David Petraeus, a highly regarded four-star general who boasted a 1987 Ph.D. from Princeton's Woodrow Wilson School of International Affairs on top of his bachelor of science degree from West Point and distinction as the winner of the 1983 George C. Marshall Award given to the top graduate of the U.S. Army Command and General Staff College.

Earlier in the war, as a major general, Petraeus had commanded the 101st Airborne Division, which was responsible for the area around Mosul in the early days of the war.

Petraeus pursued a strategy that put more emphasis on rebuilding than on fighting. This approach, combined with his impressive educational credentials and PR savvy, helped him to garner a substantial amount of favorable press coverage, including remarks like "It's widely accepted that no force worked harder to win Iraqi hearts and minds than the 101st Air Assault Division led by Petraeus"[1] (from *Newsweek*) and "From the first day they arrived in Mosul, Bravo Company and the rest of the 101st Airborne Division were saddled with dozens of other missions, all of them distinctly nonmilitary, and most of them made necessary by the failure of civilian leaders in Washington and Baghdad to prepare for the occupation of Iraq"[2] (from the *New York Times*). As the tone of the *Times* quotation indicates, the praise of Petraeus and his approach was often an implicit—or at times explicit—criticism of the Bush administration and its larger strategy in Iraq. Jacob Heilbrunn, reviewing Thomas Ricks's influential book *Fiasco* for the *New York Times Book Review*, wrote, "[A]gain and again, apart from a few exceptions like David Petraeus and H. R. McMaster who tried to work with local leaders, the military ended up humiliating and antagonizing Iraqis."[3] The *New Yorker's* George Packer wrote an influential article along similar lines, in which he primarily focused on McMaster but also observed, "In the first year of the war, in Falluja and Ramadi, Major General Charles Swannack, of the 82nd Airborne Division, emphasized killing and capturing the enemy, and the war grew worse in those places; in northern Iraq, Major General David Petraeus, of the 101st Airborne Division, focused on winning over the civilian population by encouraging economic reconstruction and local government, and had considerable success." Packer argued that the higher-ups had failed by not ordering Petraeus-style tactics implemented on a larger scale.[4]

When Petraeus later got assigned to spearhead the writing of a new field manual for counterinsurgency, his work-product got a similar response from many war critics. Upon the leak of a draft of the document, Fred Kaplan, one of Bush's most incisive critics, observed that "two messages flutter between the lines" of the manual, one of which was that "Pentagon planning for the Iraq war's aftermath was at least as crass, inattentive to the lessons of history, and contrary to basic political and military principles as the war's harshest critics have charged."[5]

Using the words and deeds of Petraeus—one of the most successful officers of the Bush era—against the Bush administration was a useful bit of political jujitsu. It turned out, however, that Bush had some moves of his own. When Petraeus was appointed as the new commander in the Iraq theater, the opposition found itself wrong-footed to some extent. Democratic senators who voted for his confirmation to the Iraq post, for example, found themselves called hypocrites for criticizing the tactics favored by the new general whom they had helped to appoint. It was possible to simply continue the jujitsu, using Petraeus against Petraeus. As Fred Kaplan observed, "The hard arithmetic indicates that Bush needs to send in a lot more troops than 20,000. The problem is, he doesn't have them, and he won't be able to get them for many years, under the best of circumstances."[6]

The general himself evidently disagreed, and the announcement of the plan gave the White House exactly what it needed: political cover for nervous congressional Republicans to continue supporting the president. In late April, the new Congress passed an Iraq War funding supplemental that would have mandated the withdrawal of American combat forces from Iraq. Bush vetoed the bill, denouncing its "rigid and artificial deadline" for American troops to start withdrawing by October 1, arguing that "it makes no sense to tell the enemy when you plan to start withdrawing." Democratic leaders like Harry Reid countered by trying to play on a sense of impatience with the seemingly endless nature of the war. "The president may be content with keeping our troops mired in the middle of an open-ended civil war," Reid said, "but we are not and neither are most Americans."[7] Politically speaking, however, the potency of the charge was blunted by the superficially temporary nature of the surge. Why not, asked Republicans, just wait a few months? Petraeus had said that it would take until the end of summer to see the surge's results, so why not let him report back on his progress in September? The efficacy of this argument was sharply limited—it didn't push public opinion back in favor of the GOP—but also quite real in that it made Republicans feel that backing the president was a safe option.

Faced with the veto, Democrats declined to force the issue by refusing to pony up funds on the president's terms. Indeed, no such option was ever seriously considered, as leading Democratic Party politicians appeared to concede in advance that acting in this manner would be tantamount to denying necessary funds to troops in the field. In reality, of course, one could just as easily have argued that it was *Bush* who was denying troops their supplies by vetoing the funding-plus-withdrawal bill. Who would ultimately have prevailed in such a contest had it been joined in earnest must remain in the realm of speculation. By going on television before the veto had ever been cast and committing to fund the war one way or another, however, Democrats merely ensured that the veto would come and not be seriously resisted by the party.

Perhaps more consequentially, while Democrats objected to the GOP's desire to wait until September before making any decisions, they didn't object to the logic of treating Petraeus's self-assessment as dispositive. Indeed, to some extent they did the reverse, attempting to continue the pre-2007 option of using Petraeus to bash Bush by insisting that Petraeus personally report back to Congress in the fall.

During the summer of 2007, it became clear that something had gone awry. On July 30, Michael O'Hanlon and Kenneth

Pollack, two leading liberal hawk think tankers, returned from a Petraeus-organized tour of Iraq to pen a *New York Times* op-ed arguing that "the administration's critics . . . seem unaware of the significant changes taking place" in Iraq and that "there is enough good happening on the battlefields of Iraq today that Congress should plan on sustaining the effort at least into 2008."[8] Just as in the liberal hawk heyday, the pair were promptly paraded on FOX News and across conservative media outlets, with their status as leading proponents of the invasion kept mostly under wraps.

And they weren't alone. More and more people seemed to be coming back from tightly controlled visits to Iraq with very favorable views of the situation there. Liberals began to worry that they had misjudged the situation. On August 28, the *Washington Monthly*'s Kevin Drum observed, "Until recently my guess was that Petraeus's September report to Congress would be pretty sober" but now it was clear that "Petraeus has been *very* shrewd about providing dog-and-pony shows to as many analysts, pundits, reporters, and members of Congress as he could cram into the military jets crisscrossing the Atlantic to Baghdad on a seemingly daily basis this summer. And those dog-and-pony shows don't seem to have been subtle . . . he's obviously been treating the September report like a military operation, trying to generate as much good press and congressional change of heart as he possibly can in the weeks leading up to 9/11."[9]

Drum's concerns proved prescient. The testimony Petraeus delivered to Congress in September was *highly* misleading. In particular, he put a lot of weight on the so-called Anbar Awakening, an initiative in which Sunni Arab anti-government rebels agreed to stop allying with al-Qaeda in Iraq (AQI) forces against U.S. troops, and to ally instead with the U.S. military against AQI. This "awakening" was not the result of the surge, but the war's proponents—including Petraeus—portrayed it as such. More to the point, when viewed correctly, it vindicated

the doves' longstanding contention that fears of an AQI take-
over in the wake of an American withdrawal were massively
overblown. The Sunni Arabs' embrace of AQI had been purely
an alliance of convenience against foreign occupiers, an alliance that Sunnis reversed as soon as AQI became too powerful.
The military's success in riding this wave of disillusionment il-
lustrated war critics' strategic point about the essentially wrongheaded nature of the belief that AQI was somehow on the verge
of taking over Iraq and was likely to do so unless a very large
number of American soldiers stayed in that country to fight
them. Indeed, during the period of the group's decline, the vast
majority of U.S. troops serving in Iraq were elsewhere on the
unrelated mission of attempting to enhance population security in Baghdad. Before the surge, critics of withdrawal had often
argued that the departure of American forces would set the
stage for a brutal campaign of ethnic cleansing.

Opponents of the war noted that there was no sign the
American military presence was preventing any such turn of
events. And, indeed, large-scale ethnic cleansing appears to
have happened smack in the middle of the surge when civilian casualty rates reached new highs amidst massive refugee
flows. Eventually, the casualty rates began a steady decline
that was claimed as a product of the surge's success, but
one could just as easily see it as evidence of the surge's failure—with the ethnic cleansing complete, violence began to
taper down. Admittedly, it's possible that things would have
been even worse without the surge, but this must remain as
pure speculation.

Democrats expecting a full and honest accounting of
these ins-and-outs were in for a surprise at the hearings, where
Petraeus marshaled facts like an experienced politician, ap-
pearing more in the role of advocate than as neutral analyst.
Realistically, it's hard to know what else one could have expected would result from asking the architect and main im-
plementer of a policy to deliver a report on its progress.

Nevertheless, many administration critics in the press and in Congress appeared not to see this coming. The Democratic congressional leadership could, after all, have simply never scheduled the spectacle of a "Petraeus Report" in the first place had they anticipated that the witness's testimony would be so hostile to their political strategy. But by the time this truth became clear, it was far too late to back out, so Democrats gave grilling him their best shot.

The main focus of the critique was the idea that though "military progress" may have been made, no "political progress" had occurred and, thus, the surge had failed.

Formally speaking, this was entirely accurate. "The objective," Petraeus explained during his confirmation hearings back in January, "will be to achieve sufficient security to provide the space and time for the Iraqi government to come to grips with the tough decisions its members must make to enable Iraq to move forward."[10] This hadn't happened. The national government in Iraq had made no progress on the so-called reconciliation agenda, efforts to reach agreement with Sunni Arab political leaders about sharing political power and revenue. Since the purpose of the surge was to "provide the space and time" for the Iraqi government to adopt such measures, and since no such measures had been adopted, the surge hadn't achieved its goal.

True enough, but Petraeus and the Bush administration had a two-pronged answer at the ready. On the one hand, they argued that tactical operations involving collaboration between the United States military and insurgent groups constituted a form of "bottom-up reconciliation" that could serve as the precursor or catalyst for broader reconciliation. More plausibly, they simply asked for more time, while Bush announced the scheduled end of the surge as if it were an exciting new plan for troop withdrawals. The construction of a dichotomy between "political" and "military" progress helped serve this end because, after all, if a *kind* of progress was occurring that seemed to suggest a strong case for letting the situation continue to play out: time plus progress equals success.

Such arguments were insufficient to dispel the public's generally sour mood about Iraq, but like the original "wait till September" argument, they gave Republican members of Congress the cover they wanted to keep supporting the president. Over the next several months, the post-cleansing decline in casualty figures continued, and though the war remained deeply unpopular, its unpopularity did attenuate somewhat, offering apparent vindication to the GOP strategy. Meanwhile, in a series of special elections—in Massachusetts' Fifth Congressional District, in Virginia's First, and in Ohio's Fifth—Democrats nervous about the politics of the surge largely failed to strongly differentiate their Iraq position from their opponents' views, and all three Democrats went down to a disappointing result.

Lost in all of this was an opportunity to elevate the debate out of the realm of dueling statistics sheets and pleas for more time and into the realm of strategy. After all, these points about "progress" or lack thereof can always be argued both ways. Both parties agreed in late 2006 that the situation in Iraq was very bad and seemingly on a downward trajectory. Democrats concluded that this meant we should begin moving to extricate ourselves from the war. The Bush administration, however, took the view that we needed to escalate our involvement.

And, indeed, this is the general logic of the situation. The public's impression of whether or not things are going well has a substantial impact on the overall public mood, but the "how's it going" issue has no direct bearing on what should be done in the future. Nor does it have a necessary relationship to domestic political outcomes. After all, even back in 2004 the public was aware that the situation in Iraq was much worse than they'd been promised before the war, but they reelected Bush anyway.

The basic reality of Iraq and "the surge" is that behind the pleas to wait a few months to see what happens, is a desire to avoid discussing an unsound and unpopular strategic approach. General Petraeus was, however, at times more honest, telling a BBC reporter that he was envisioning an extremely lengthy engagement. "Northern Ireland, I think, taught you that very well," he said, "my counterparts in your forces really understand this kind of operation . . . it took a long time, decades." Leaving the question of how well the specifics of the analogy hold up, as a recipe for success this is rather chilling. Few people, after all, look at the British experience in Northern Ireland and take the view that a country ought to deliberately put itself in that kind of situation—only in a much larger country. As an active duty military officer, Petraeus is not charged with saying whether or not such an undertaking is worth it. His responsibility to his commander-in-chief and to the soldiers under his command, moreover, is to indicate support for the general policy he's been tasked with undertaking.

It most certainly *is*, however, the role of politicians to ask themselves whether *decades* of intensive engagement with Iraq really makes sense for the United States of America.

The politicians on the Republican Party's side clearly don't want that question asked. That's why they typically insist on slicing the debate up into increments of months, rather than decades. It's also why when George W. Bush feels compelled to concede that he's envisioning a decades-long presence, he prefers to cite models like South Korea that are plainly inapplicable. And from the currently dominant perspective within American conservatism, an engagement of this sort *does* make sense. After all, the Green Lantern Theory says, among other things, that you can never give up on a military adventure no matter how costly or pointless it becomes. Similarly, if you believe that reasserting and redoubling American military hegemony over the Middle East is the appropriate response to 9/11 and the rise of transnational terrorism, a lengthy war in Iraq seems to be as good a way as any to do it. The Iraq theater is, after all, conveniently adjacent to regional adversaries like Syria and Iran. Similarly, there's no better way to ensure that the new regime in Iraq serves as a loyal client state than to have American military personnel directly engaged in keeping it in power. And while simply declaring straight-up an intention to build and maintain permanent military bases in Iraq would be controversial, a war that just continues and continues provides a perfect venue for the construction of bases that are, in fact, permanent even if nobody bothers to say so.[11]

In short, on this view an extremely protracted period of war and occupation, though hardly the preferred result in Iraq, is a small price to pay for transforming a hostile state sitting atop a huge pile of oil into an oil-rich ally dependent on American military support. What's more, from the contemporary right's point of view, the exorbitant financial costs of the war don't count as real costs. They have no intention to pay for them through increased taxes, and no objection to financing them either through increased debt or reduced domestic expenditures.

The internationalist take on this strategy is all rather different. To the liberal, these costs are real costs. What's more, it's not clear that the alleged benefits here are real benefits. Heightening tensions with Iran and Syria and introducing a whole new dimension into our relationship with those countries makes little sense at a time when we ought to be focused on finding compromise solutions to old disputes and ways to work against common foes. And from a liberal perspective, the alleged benefit of a new client state in the Middle East is more likely to prove to be a cost than a benefit. It is precisely the sense among the world's Arabs and Muslims that the United States is trying to dominate their countries and prop up unaccountable and corrupt regimes in order to better

exploit their natural resources that fuels anti-American sentiment around the world. The exigencies of waging counterinsurgency warfare in Iraq, in short, undermine the broader
global counterinsurgency against al-Qaeda and do so at an
enormous price.

The strategic level was the correct place to conduct an argument about the surge and continues to be the correct place
to argue about the continuation of the war. Conventional
thinking suggests that it's always best to have a position closer
to the "center" rather than further from it and, thus, that it
makes sense to slice the salami as thinly as possible. The political problem with arguments about tactics, however, is that
your opponents can always just switch tactics. As, indeed,
Bush did when he turned command over to Petraeus. As a
matter of substance, the problem with the focus on tactics is
even worse: better tactics in pursuit of a flawed strategy won't
ultimately solve anything.

As usual, the shallowness of the Democratic argument was
driven in part by timidity and in part by the basic reality that
despite the rhetoric, some leading Democrats simply didn't
have a particularly deep disagreement with the Bush administration's strategy. After all, there had been a time when the
idea that Iraq needed more troops was a commonplace talking
point among centrist Democrats. On the June 29, 2005, edition of *Good Morning America*, Senator Joe Biden referred to
his Memorial Day trip to Iraq and said, "There's not a single
solitary person I met that said we have enough force on the
ground." Backing away from the implication that this meant
he would support sending more Americans to Iraq, Biden
swiftly clarified that he meant the additional troops should be
provided by "our allies" but he reiterated the point that
"there's not enough force on the ground now to mount a
real counterinsurgency."

And, indeed, there weren't enough troops available for such an undertaking and there never had been in Iraq. And, indeed, such complaints had occasionally featured in John Kerry's presidential campaign and formed the main plank of the "incompetence" argument about the dismal course of the war.

Over time, Democratic Party politicians largely moved away from this talking point, but many elites on the Democratic side continued to share the basic analysis that leaving Iraq would be a mistake and that what was needed instead were better tactics. The clearest example is the thinking that came out of a group called the Center for a New American Security (CNAS), a center-left think tank founded in February 2007 by Kurt Campbell and Michele Flournoy, both of whom had served in relatively junior subcabinet positions during the Clinton administration. Hillary Clinton gave a speech at the CNAS launch event, and the organization swiftly established itself as a go-to source for advocacy of a continued military presence in Iraq from an anti-administration perspective. In a rhetorical twist, this kind of pro-war commentary came to adopt a thin anti-war gloss. The CNAS issue page, for example, described its commentary as aimed at "helping to forge a way forward and, ultimately, out of Iraq." Their signature policy brief on Iraq, however, released in June 2007 and called "Phased Transition: A Responsible Way Forward and Out of Iraq" defined "responsible" as entailing several years' worth of continued military engagement, particularly in the context of a continued mission training and advising local Iraqi security forces. Colin Kahl, a Georgetown professor, a frequent Defense Department consultant, and a CNAS expert emerged in the late summer and fall as a public advocate of the efficacy of the training mission and the broader notion of "bottom-up" reconciliation, and was advising various presidential campaigns and other policymakers.

The logic of these proposals was hotly contested by many (myself included) who followed the lead of Brian Katulis from the Center for American Progress in viewing the security forces in Iraq as part of the problem. "Increasingly," Katulis wrote, "it appears that the United States is training and arming different sides of Iraq's multiple civil wars rather than creating a national army and police force willing and able to protect the nation's fragmented political leadership."[12]

Similarly, Marc Lynch, a political scientist and analyst of Arab politics, observed that "the promotion of alternative elites," an important link between the training mission and the concept of bottom-up reconciliation, "is always a risky business, one which sets up all kinds of problems down the road."[13] In particular, it often leads to unexpected forms of blowback, as when the Islamist groups Israel once backed as an alternative to the Palestinian Liberation Organization (PLO) eventually turned into Hamas. Alternatively, foreign-backed new elites can simply find themselves discredited over time through association with the foreigner—a process that occurred several times at the national level in post-war Iraq and might well be the result of a continuation of decentralizing policies at the local level. Fundamentally, efforts to cultivate relationships with alternative elites are always walking a delicate line between getting out of control and losing their legitimacy by staying too firmly under control.

Undergirding these disagreements was, however, a fair amount of common analytic ground. Both sides agree that a certain form of counterinsurgency tactics that the Bush administration should have adopted years ago and had belatedly come around to in 2007 stood the best chances of securing American objectives in Iraq. Both sides also agreed that the odds remained somewhat dim. According to Kahl, the advocate of continued military engagement, his preferred approach "could work *in theory*—although the probabilities are difficult to assess and are probably not particularly high."[14]

The real disagreement wasn't over the tactics, but the strategy: does it make sense to bear the costs involved in continued military engagement in Iraq in exchange for a dim chance at uncertain benefits? To those who believe that the United States needs to project more power more intensely into and around Iraq, the calculation to continue prosecuting the war makes sense, just as to them it made sense to initiate the war in the first place.

An alternative approach, such as the one outlined by Brian Katulis, Lawrence Korb, and Peter Juul in their 2007 report for the Center for American Progress, would say that just as invading Iraq in the first place reflected a poor setting of priorities, so, too, does the push to continue American involvement under circumstances where even the advocates of involvement concede that the probabilities of success aren't very good. As they argue, "the current Iraq strategy is exactly what al-Qaeda wants," sapping American resources and paralyzing American policy while offering a never-ending recruiting and propaganda tool.[15]

Instead, we should leave Iraq as quickly as is practical, while discharging our moral obligations to Iraqis through more generous treatment of Iraqi refugees (something that should be easier to do politically once the pretext of holding out for success in Iraq is dropped) and related humanitarian matters. More broadly, it would put Iraq in the context of a new approach to America's policy in the region more generally: in particular the urgent need to shift back toward the kind of strategic focus on al-Qaeda that can gain support from around the world and away from a vaguely defined "war on terror" that's done the reverse. In operational military terms, this means the redeployment of American troops (and perhaps equally importantly, the attention of American commanders) out of Iraq and back to Afghanistan where NATO's vital mission is increasingly at risk of failing. In diplomatic terms, it means accepting the recommendation of the

Baker-Hamilton Commission, the American Progress group, the former national security adviser Zbigniew Brzezinski and others for bold, region-wide diplomacy across a broad front: working with Iraq's neighbors on containing the conflict there, working with Iran on a "grand bargain" to secure verifiable disarmament in the context of a broader U.S.-Iranian rapprochement, and working toward a resolution of the Arab-Israeli conflict.

The size of the task appears daunting, but the reality is that the issues are all linked. The Iranians can't reach an accommodation with us on the nuclear issue as long as our troops are at their doorstep and Teheran and Washington have no diplomatic relations. The United States can't reach an accommodation with an Iran that sponsors so much anti-Israeli violence. The Iranians won't want to be seen as "selling out" the Palestinian cause. And most of all, we can ill afford either a Middle East that collapses into chaos or an indefinite and futile effort to endlessly hold it together through direct American military engagement.

Of course, the mere desirability of achieving a broad diplomatic breakthrough doesn't guarantee its possibility. If we try in good faith but fail, we can fall back on what Stephen Walt has characterized as a strategy of "offshore balancing" which would recognize that "the United States does not need to control these areas [like the Persian Gulf] directly; it merely needs to ensure that they do not fall under the control of a hostile great power."[16] This would, at least, put our engagement in the Gulf on a sustainable basis and allow us to focus our energies elsewhere.

For Iraq itself, the main thrust of a diplomacy-centric approach would be to convince all the relevant regional actors that a relatively peaceful Iraq serves their interests better than a relatively bloody act, irrespective of the precise details of who's up and who's down inside the country. Similarly, *within* Iraq, both the United States and partners in the region would endeavor to convince Iraqi factions that the costs of conflict exceed the costs of compromise. Making it clear that different factions won't be able to play external actors off against each other to secure financial or military support should go some of the way to accomplishing that. The point, most broadly construed, would be that a peaceful Iraq is the sort of place that could attract trade and investment to generate vast wealth, making it worth everyone's while to accept a slice of a big pie rather than destructively fight for the whole of a smaller one. It must be conceded that the odds of success here may be dim. But the policy of extended military engagement that Republicans and some Democrats favor might not work either—indeed, its proponents concede in their more honest moments that it *probably won't*. The odds of a diplomacy-focused approach are as good if not better, and the costs much lower. It's only in terms of U.S. domestic politics that a strategic shift appears more difficult.

Since Democrats disagreed with one another about whether the tactics critique or the strategic critique was the correct one, and since there was a hotly contested presidential primary happening at the time, one might have thought this would be a good issue for the candidates to debate. Then the choice of a nominee would also constitute a choice of approach, laying the groundwork for future debates with the Republicans to proceed from a firmer basis. Instead, recapitulating the last-minute flinch away from making such a choice in 2004, the leading Democratic contenders mostly succeeded in blurring the issue. Some second-tier candidates, most notably Bill Richardson and Dennis Kucinich, did make a point of emphasizing their commitment to full and unequivocal withdrawal from Iraq. Richardson's general take on foreign policy, however, was long on emphasis on his personal qualifications to conduct diplomacy and very short on discussion of his basic approach. Kucinich, as during 2004, was admirable in his ability to articulate a clear and coherent theory of foreign affairs, but his approach, centered on a call to "reject war as an instrument of policy" continued—and continues—to be unattractive to the overwhelming majority of Americans.

The front-runners, by contrast, were consistently ambiguous, with all of them promising to end the war, and all of them suggesting openness to a continued American military presence in Iraq for the purposes of training or counterterrorism. Their tendency to emphasize different points to different audiences and leave different people with different impressions of where they're staying frustrated many close observers who sometimes came to believe that the candidates had secret positions on the war that they were unwilling to share with the public.

More realistically, the candidates simply hadn't made up their minds. All of the campaigns took advice and input from a wide variety of people expressing a wide variety of views. Campaigns focus their decision-making energies on campaign decisions, not on policy matters. From a political point of view, it served everyone's interests to be as ambiguous as they could possibly get away with. And since anti-war sentiment, though strong, lacked an organized institutional basis, it turned out that they could get away with a pretty high degree of ambiguity. Thus, the issue of whether Democrats are having a tactical argument with Republicans about the precise modalities of protracted counterinsurgency in Iraq, or a strategic argument about the merits of long-term engagement there remained—and remains—undecided.

And, indeed, from the point of view of a foreign policy watcher, the primary campaign as a whole had a dispiriting feel. While the candidates unveiled more or less detailed plans on health care and global warming and vigorously debated the merits of different approaches to these matters, the foreign policy conversation remained shallow. Iraq was much discussed, but primarily in a somewhat quibbling vein. John Edwards apologized for having voted for the war. Barack Obama bragged that he had criticized the authorizing resolution back in 2002. Hillary Clinton was unapologetic about her vote, but sometimes suggested she had opposed the invasion as such. All this, however, was construed as a debate about who had the character, judgment, and experience to lead. Similarly, a debate between Obama and Clinton about whether or not one should be prepared to meet with the leaders of "enemy" states like Iran or Venezuela without preconditions swiftly became an argument about whether Obama was too green or Clinton too much the prisoner of conventional wisdom.

The big questions of principle and strategy raised by 9/11, by contrast, scarcely played a role. Neither the candidates nor the press showed much interest in arguing about different approaches to non-proliferation policy, or in outlying any ideas about the appropriate long-run strategy for fighting al-Qaeda. Most strikingly, though Iraq as such continued to be the subject of significant interest, the broader Bush doctrine that the ability to wage preventive wars is key to American security in the modern world was scarcely mentioned. Put into this broad context, the failure to debate forward-looking Iraq policy on a strategic rather than tactical level seems more understandable. Evidently, the calculation of the political professionals was that there was more to be risked than to be gained in staking out clear views on national security issues.

Perhaps John Kerry's successful quest for the nomination in 2004 has convinced people that ducking the big questions is a winning strategy in Democratic primaries. But of course Kerry lost in the end, precisely because people could not clearly see where he stood. Strategies of evasion failed in 2002 as well, and even after taking Congress in 2006 Democrats have found it difficult to secure policy gains with merely tactical arguments. At the end of the day, it's the disastrous consequences of the Bush foreign policy strategy that have done more than anything else to create the change in public opinion from when I started this book to when I finished it. But if the opposition political party can't succeed in portraying these consequences as things that flow logically from a flawed strategy—rather than as isolated mistakes, or evidence of personal incompetence—they'll struggle as Bush fades from the scene. Worse, an opposition party that doesn't recognize recent disasters as flowing from a flawed strategy that needs to be replaced runs the risk of not replacing the strategy and merely repeating the disasters.

NOTES

PREFACE. THE ETERNAL RECURRENCE OF TOM FRIEDMAN

1. Thomas Friedman, "The Chant Not Heard," *New York Times*, November 30, 2003.
2. Thomas Friedman, "The Last Mile," *New York Times*, November 28, 2004.
3. Thomas Friedman, "The Endgame in Iraq," *New York Times*, September 28, 2005.
4. Fairness and Accuracy in Reporting, "Tom Friedman's Flexible Deadlines," May 16, 2006.
5. Thomas Friedman, "Tolerable or Awful: The Roads Left in Iraq," *New York Times*, November 8, 2006.
6. Thomas Friedman, "Ten Months or Ten Years," *New York Times*, November 29, 2006.
7. Thomas Friedman, "In or Out," *New York Times*, July 11, 2007.
8. Thomas Friedman, "Seeing Is Believing," *New York Times*, August 19, 2007.
9. Thomas Friedman, "Debating Iraq's Transition," *New York Times*, November 21, 2007.

CHAPTER 1. THE REAL LIBERAL TRADITION

1. Ann Coulter, "This Is War," *National Review*, September 13, 2001.
2. See "Sen. Biden Receives DLC's Truman Award," DLC press release, March 15, 2005.
3. James Chace, "Wise after All," *American Prospect*, June 2004.
4. See Peter Beinart, "A Fighting Faith," *New Republic*, December 2, 2004; and Peter Beinart, *The Good Fight* (New York: Harper-Collins, 2006).
5. See Max Boot, "Truman Acted Alone, Too," *Los Angeles Times*, June 14, 2006; and Noemi Emry, "The Inconvenient Truth about Truman," *Weekly Standard*, July 17, 2006.

6. For the general concept of a reasonably just political order, see John Rawls, "The Justification of Civil Disobedience," in Hugo A. Bedau, ed., *Civil Disobedience: Theory and Practice* (New Haven, Conn.: Yale University Press, 1969), pp. 240–255.

7. John Mearsheimer, "The False Promise of International Institutions," *International Security* (Winter 1994–1995).

8. Ramesh Ponnuru, "The Bystander," *National Review*, October 12, 1998.

9. Bill Clinton, *My Life* (New York: Knopf, 2004), p. 513.

10. Olivier Roy, *Globalized Islam* (New York: Columbia University Press, 2004), p. 12.

11. See Joe Conason, "The President Who Took bin Laden Seriously," *Salon*, July 24, 2004.

12. National Commission on Terrorist Attacks upon the United States, *Final Report* (New York: W.W. Norton & Company, 2004), p. 176.

13. See Richard Clarke, "Strategy for Eliminating the Jihadist Networks of al-Qida: Status and Prospects," National Security Council memo, December 2000.

14. Michael O'Hanlon, "Saving Lives with Force," *New Republic*, July 12, 1999.

15. "Grudge Genocide," *New Republic* (November 29, 1999).

16. Interview with Jim Lehrer, *NewsHour*, June 11, 1999. Transcript available at www.pbs.org/newshour/bb/europe/jan-june 99/clinton_6-11b.html, accessed October 10, 2007.

CHAPTER 2. THE NATIONALIST ALTERNATIVE

1. See Elliot Abrams, "Breaking Ranks: Neoconservative May Have Aided George Bush's Defeat in 1992 Presidential Election," *National Review*, January 18, 1993.

2. See Peter Baker and Michael Fletcher, "Bush Warns against Shrinking Global Role," *Washington Post*, February 1, 2006.

3. Paul Starr, "War, Peace, and the Election," *American Prospect*, November 20, 2000.

4. Charles Pena, "$400 Billion Defense Budget Unnecessary to Fight War on Terrorism," *Cato Policy Analysis*, March 28, 2005.

5. Jonathan Chait, "Underworlds," *New Republic*, August 7, 2000.

6. *The National Defense Strategy of the United States of America*, Department of Defense, March 2005.

7. William Saletan, "Yankee Go Home: Who's Leading the Anti-War Movement? Congressional Republicans," *Slate*, May 7, 1999.

8. *Meet the Press*, May 16, 1999.

9. See the *Final Report* of the United States House of Representatives Select Committee on U.S. National Security and Military/Commercial Concerns with the People's Republic of China.

10. See Walter Russell Meade, *Special Providence: American Foreign Policy and How It Changed the World* (New York: Knopf, 2001).

11. See Eric Shawn, *The U.N. Exposed: How the United Nations Sabotages America's Security and Fails the World* (New York: Sentinel, 2006).

12. Dore Gold, *Tower of Babel: How the United Nations Has Fueled Global Chaos* (New York: Crown Forum, 2004).

13. Bill O'Reilly on *The Radio Factor*, September 14, 2005. Transcript and audio clip available at http://mediamatters.org/items/200509160007, accessed October 10, 2007.

14. Charles Krauthammer, "Democratic Realism: An American Foreign Policy for a Unipolar World," Irving Kristol Lecture, American Enterprise Institute.

15. Ivo Daalder and James Lindsay, *America Unbound: The Bush Revolution in Foreign Policy* (Washington, D.C.: Brookings Institution Press, 2003), pp. 12–13.

16. Peter Beinart, "Tony Award," *New Republic*, June 22, 2006.

17. Jack Anderson and Douglas Cohn, "GOP Returning to Isolationism," *Deseret News*, February 15, 2001.

18. Joe Conason, "Bush's Foreign Policy: Isolate Colin Powell," *New York Observer*, March 19, 2001.

19. Drake Bennett, "Critical Mess," *American Prospect*, July 2, 2003.

CHAPTER 3. A TALE OF TWO WINGS

1. See George Kennan, "The Sources of Soviet Conduct," *Foreign Affairs* (1947).

2. Daniel Chirot and Clark McCauley, *Why Not Kill Them All? The Logic and Prevention of Mass Murder* (Princeton, N.J.: Princeton University Press, 2006), p. 655.

3. See http://www.pollkatz.homestead.com/files/approval-data_files/zzzmainGRAPHICS_14808_image001.gif, accessed October 10, 2007, for a particularly striking visual representation of the discontinuity.

4. Susan Sontag, Talk of the Town, *New Yorker*, September 24, 2001.

5. David Limbaugh, "Speaking with Moral Authority," *Washington Times*, October 8, 2001.

6. Marc Berley, "Peace Movement Blames America," *Seattle Post-Intelligencer*, September 26, 2001.

7. Idiocy Watch, *New Republic*, October 8, 2001.

8. Idiocy Watch, *New Republic*, November 5, 2001.

9. Idiocy Watch, *New Republic*, March 6, 2002.

10. Idiocy Watch, *New Republic*, December 17, 2001.

11. Andrew Sullivan, "A British View of the U.S. Post-September 11," *London Times*, October 15, 2001.

12. See, e.g., Geoff Johns and Dave Gibbons, *Green Lantern Corps: Recharge* (New York: DC Comics, 2006).

13. See Kevin Baker, "Stabbed in the Back! The Past and Future of a Right-Wing Myth," *Harpers*, June 2006.

14. Quoted in Ivan Eland, "Does U.S. Intervention Overseas Breed Terrorism? The Historical Record," Cato Institute Foreign Policy Briefing, December 17, 1998, p. 2.

15. Charles Krauthammer, "Voices of Moral Obtuseness," *Washington Post*, September 21, 2001.

16. Charles Krauthammer, "The War: A Road Map," *Washington Post*, September 28, 2001.

17. Michael Ledeen, "Hot to Lose It," *National Review*, December 7, 2001.

18. Frederick Kagan, *Weekly Standard*, November 19, 2001.

19. R. James Woolsey, "Blood Baath: The Iraq Connection," *New Republic*, September 24, 2001.

20. See Flynt Leverett, "Illusion and Reality," *American Prospect*, September 2006.

21. Seymour Hersh, "The Syrian Bet," *New Yorker*, July 28, 2003.

22. Leverett, "Illusion and Reality."

23. Michael Walzer, "Excusing Terror," *American Prospect*, October 2001.

24. Michael Walzer, "Can There Be a Decent Left?" *Dissent* (Spring 2002).

CHAPTER 4. SEE NO EVIL

1. Jonah Goldberg, "Baghdad Delenda Est, Part Two," *National Review Online*, April 23, 2002.

2. Fred Kaplan, "Another Threatening Storm?" *Washington Post*, November 28, 2004.

3. Kenneth Pollack, *The Threatening Storm* (New York: Random House, 2002), p. xv.

4. See Daniel Byman, Kenneth Pollack, and Gideon Rose, "The Rollback Fantasy" *Foreign Affairs* (January/February 1999).

5. John Judis and Spencer Ackerman, "The First Casualty," *New Republic*, June 19, 2003.

6. Thomas Friedman, "The Iraq Debate Is Upside Down," *New York Times*, September 19, 2002.

7. George Packer, "The Liberal Quandary over Iraq," *New York Times Magazine*, December 8, 2002.

8. Peter Beinart, "A Separate Peace," *New Republic*, March 3, 2003.

9. Bill Keller, "The I-Can't-Believe-I'm-a-Hawk Club," *New York Times*, February 8, 2003.

10. Leon Wieseltier, "Against Innocence," *New Republic*, March 3, 2003.

11. Packer, "The Liberal Quandary over Iraq."

12. Pollack, *The Threatening Storm*, p. 353.

13. Ibid., pp. 397–398.

14. Fred Kaplan, "The Fastest Way to Send a Message," *Slate*, December 2, 2004.

15. Richard Perle, et al., "A Clean Break: A New Strategy for Securing the Realm," available at www.iasps.org/strat1.htm, accessed October 10, 2007.

16. See Fairness and Accuracy in Reporting, "Some Critical Media Voices Face Censorship," April 3, 2003.

17. Paul Waldman, "John Fund Again?" *Washington Monthly*, March 2006.

18. See Ryan Lizza, "Biden Time," *New Republic Online*, November 25, 2003.

19. Tom Daschle, *Like No Other Time* (New York: Crown, 2003), p. 244.

20. See Spencer Ackerman, "A Hawk for All Seasons," *American Prospect Online*, August 14, 2006.

21. "Statement of Senator John D. Rockefeller IV on the Senate Floor on the Iraq Resolution," October 10, 2002.

22. Thomas Ricks, *Fiasco* (New York: Penguin Press, 2006), p. 54.

23. International Atomic Energy Agency, "The Status of Nuclear Inspections in Iraq: An Update," March 7, 2003.

24. Josh Marshall, "There's More than Just U.S. Credibility at Stake in Iraq," *The Hill*, March 5, 2003.

CHAPTER 5. OPPORTUNISM KNOCKS

1. Jonathan Cohn, "Invisible Man," *New Republic*, July 1, 2002.

2. Howard Dean, "Defending American Values, Protecting American Interests," available at www.globalsecurity.org/wmd/library/news/iraq/2003/030217-dean.htm, accessed October 10, 2007.

3. See Will Saletan and Avi Zenilman, "The Worldview of Dennis Kucinich," *Slate*, August 7, 2003.

4. Dennis Kucinich, *A Prayer for America* (New York: Nation Books, 2003), pp. 15–16.

5. See, e.g., "Kucinich Renews Call for the US Withdrawal from Iraq," press release, July 28, 2003. Available at http://kucinich.house.gov/News/DocumentSingle.aspx?DocumentID=28196, accessed October 10, 2007.

6. Ivo Daalder, "Internationalize Post-War Iraq," Brookings Daily War Reports, April 7, 2003.

7. Kenneth Pollack, "With the War Over, the U.S. Faces Hard Challenges," Brookings Iraq Report, April 18, 2003.

8. See Corbin, et al. "A Unified Security Budget for the United States," Center for Defense Information, March 2004, pages 18–20 for one proposal. The Global Policy Forum's "U.N. Standing Force," www.globalpolicy.org/security/peacekpg/reform/standby.htm, accessed October 10, 2007, contains summaries and links to a variety of related proposals.

9. Peter Beinart, "A Fighting Faith," *New Republic*, December 13, 2004.

10. See Joanna Weiss, "Clark Is Cautious When Asked His Stance on Abortion," *Boston Globe*, January 23, 2004.

11. Sean Loughlin, "Rumsfeld on Looting in Iraq: 'Stuff Happens,'" CNN.com, April 12, 2003.

12. Event transcript available at www.aei.org/events/filter.,eventID.274/transcript.asp, accessed October 10, 2007.

13. WashintonPost.com Q&A, November 6, 2003.

14. Jim VandeHei, "Dean Calls for New Controls on Business," *Washington Post*, November 19, 2003.

15. Robert Kuttner, "Dean's Legacy," *Boston Globe*, February 18, 2004.

16. See Franklin Foer, "Beyond Belief," *New Republic*, December 29, 2004.

17. Jonathan Chait, "Wish You Were Here," *Diary of a Dean-o-Phobe*, posting December 17, 2003.

CHAPTER 6. EVASIVE ACTION

1. Laura Blumenfeld, "Former Aide Takes on War on Terror," *Washington Post,* June 16, 2003.
2. *60 Minutes,* March 21, 2004.
3. Ari Berman, "The Strategic Class," *The Nation,* August 29, 2005.
4. Thomas Frank, "What's the Matter with Liberals?" *New York Review of Books,* May 12, 2005.
5. Adam Nagourney, "Domestic Issues Pushed to Front of Campaigns," *New York Times,* October 3, 2004.
6. Mark Penn, "Myth of the Vanishing Swing Voter," *Washington Post,* October 5, 2004.
7. Will Marshall, "Closing the National Security Gap," *Blueprint,* July 2004.
8. Kurt M. Campbell and Michael O'Hanlon, *Hard Power: The New Politics of National Security* (New York: Basic Books, 2006), pp. 6–7.
9. Ibid., pp. 48 and 54.
10. Ibid., pp. 220–221.

CHAPTER 7. THE DEMOCRACY FRAUD

1. Thomas Friedman, "Because We Could," *New York Times,* June 4, 2003.
2. Richard Just, "Moral Imperative," *American Prospect Online,* November 13, 2002.
3. Joshua Micah Marshall, "Practice to Deceive," *Washington Monthly,* April 2003.
4. Gareth Porter, "Burnt Offering: How a 2003 Overture from Iran Might Have Led to a Deal on Iran's Nuclear Capacity—If the Bush Administration Hadn't Rebuffed It," *American Prospect,* June 2006.
5. See Francis Fukuyama, *The End of History and the Last Man* (New York: Harper Perennial, 1992).
6. Most famously, Samuel Huntington in *The Clash of Civilizations* (New York: Simon & Schuster, 1992).
7. Robert Pape, "The Strategic Logic of Suicide Terrorism," *American Political Science Review* 97, no. 3 (August 2003).
8. See "Declassified Key Judgments of the National Intelligence Estimate 'Trends in Global Terrorism: Implications for the United States,'" April 2006, available at www.dni.gov/press_releases/Declassified_NIE_Key_Judgments.pdf, accessed October 17, 2007.

9. Spencer Ackerman, "Save the Date: Withdraw from Iraq This Year," *New Republic*, February 14, 2002.

10. See "Kennedy: Military Fuels Insurgency," Associated Press, January 27, 2005.

11. "Wrong Way," *New Republic*, February 14, 2005.

12. Thomas Friedman, "A Day to Remember," *New York Times*, February 3, 2005.

13. Peter Beinart, "More than Words," *New Republic*, February 28, 2005.

14. *Lou Dobbs Tonight*, October 16, 2006.

15. Douglas Brinkley, "Democratic Enlargement: The Clinton Doctrine," *Foreign Policy* (Spring 1997).

CHAPTER 8. AFTER VICTORY

1. David Kirkpatrick and Anne Kornblut, "G.O.P. Candidates Turn Their Focus to the Economy," *New York Times*, November 3, 2006.

2. Fred Barnes, "How Bad Will It Be?" *Weekly Standard*, October 23, 2006.

3. Jonathan Chait, "The Fat Lady Is Singing," *New Republic Online*, October 16, 2006.

4. Michael Abramowitz, Robin Wright, and Thomas Ricks, "With Iraq Speech, Bush to Pull away from His Generals," *Washington Post*, January 10, 2007.

5. George Packer, "Unrealistic," *New Yorker*, November 27, 2006.

6. See Paul Harris, "Bush Says God Chose Him to Lead His Nation," *The Observer*, November 2, 2003.

7. Ryan Lizza, "Shadow Secretary," *New Republic*, November 13, 2006.

8. Robert Dreyfuss, "A Higher Power," *Washington Monthly*, September 2006.

9. Gary Kamiya, "A Bombshell with a Long Fuse," *Salon*, December 12, 2006.

10. Daniel Levy, "Study Some More," *American Prospect*, December 22, 2006.

11. Sidney Blumenthal, "Shuttle without Diplomacy," *Salon*, January 10, 2007.

12. Alexander Zavis and Greg Miller, "Scant Evidence Found of Iran-Iraq Weapons Link," *Los Angeles Times*, January 23, 2007.

13. Ben Smith, "Schumer Believes Ordinary People, Not War, Will Become '08 Focus," *The Politico*, February 1, 2007.

14. Joseph Cirincione and Andrew Grotto, "Contain and Engage: A New Strategy for Resolving the Nuclear Crisis with Iran," Center for American Progress, February 28, 2007.

CHAPTER 9. IN WITH THE OLD

1. Max Boot, "How Bush Can Ensure No More Iraqs," *Los Angeles Times*, January 31, 2007.
2. See Max Boot, "Washington Needs a Colonial Office," *Financial Times*, July 3, 2003.
3. See Aaron Scholer, "Boots on the Ground: Increasing the Size of the Military to Meet the Missions of the 21st Century," Third Way, May 2005; and Matt Bennett, "Third Way Applauds Bush Comments on Increasing Size of the Military," Third Way, December 20, 2006.
4. See "Iraq/Middle East 2000_1997," The Project for a New American Century, www.newamericancentury.org/iraqmiddleeast2000-1997. htm, accessed October 10, 2007.
5. Francis Fukuyama, "The Neo-Cons Have Learned Nothing from Five Years of Catastrophe," *The Guardian*, January 31, 2007.
6. David Rogers, "Bush Budget Sets Stage for Clashes with Congress," *Wall Street Journal*, February 6, 2007.
7. Robert Wright, "An American Foreign Policy that Both Realists and Idealists Should Fall in Love With," *New York Times*, July 16, 2006.
8. Jeffrey Goldberg, "The Starting Gate," *New Yorker*, January 15, 2006.
9. G. John Ikenberry, "The Security Trap," *Democracy: A Journal of Ideas* (Fall 2006).
10. Suzanne Nossel, "Going Legit," *Democracy: A Journal of Ideas* (Fall 2007).
11. John Mueller, "A False Sense of Insecurity," *Regulation* (Fall 2004).
12. George F. Will, "The Triumph of Unrealism," *Washington Post*, August 15, 2006.
13. Joshua Micah Marshall, "The Orwell Temptation," *Washington Monthly*, May 2003.
14. See Marisa Katz, "Democratease: Rhetoric vs. Reality," *New Republic*, June 6, 2005.
15. Ivo Daalder and James Lindsay, "An Alliance of Democracies," *Washington Post*, May 23, 2004.

16. *Human Security Report* (Vancouver: Liu Center for Global Issues, 2005), p. 3.

17. The Princeton Project on National Security, *Final Report* (Princeton, N.J.: Woodrow Wilson School of Foreign Affairs, 2006), p. 25.

EPILOGUE. SURGE TO NOWHERE

1. Rob Nordland, "Iraq's Repairman," *Newsweek*, July 5, 2004.

2. Lucian Truscott IV, "A Million Miles from the Green Zone to the Front Line," *New York Times*, December 7, 2003.

3. Jacob Heilbrunn, "Eyes Wide Shut," *New York Times*, August 13, 2006.

4. George Packer, "The Lessons of Tal Afar," *New Yorker*, April 10, 2006.

5. Fred Kaplan, "Counterinsurgency by the Book," *Slate*, July 8, 2006.

6. Fred Kaplan, "Mission Impossible: Bush's Smart New General Can't Save Iraq," *Slate*, January 8, 2007.

7. David Stout and Sheryl Gay Stolberg, "Citing 'Rigid' Deadline, Bush Vetoes Iraq Bill," *New York Times*, May 1, 2007.

8. Michael O'Hanlon and Kenneth Pollack, "A War We Just Might Win," *New York Times*, July 30, 2007.

9. Kevin Drum, "The Petraeus Report," *Washington Monthly*, August 28, 2007.

10. See, e.g., Sara Wood, "Petraeus Support Troop Increase in Confirmation Hearing," American Forces Press Service, January 23, 2007.

11. See, for example, Spencer Ackerman "War in Iraq, 2003–???" *American Prospect*, October 22, 2006.

12. Brian Katulis, "Killing the Patient," Center for American Progress, June 11, 2007

13. Marc Lynch, "Kahl-Katulis Debate: My Thoughts," November 12, 2007. Available online at http://abuaardvark.typepad.com/abuaardvark/2007/11/kahl-katulis-de.html.

14. Colin Kahl, "Guest Post on National Reconciliation," November 6, 2007. Available online at http://abuaardvark.typepad.com/abuaardvark/2007/11/iraq-guest-post.html

15. Brian Katulis, Lawrence Korb, and Peter Juul, "Strategic Reset," Center for American Progress, June 25, 2007.

16. Stephen Walt, "In the National Interest," *Boston Review*, February/March 2005.

INDEX

abortion, 94–95
Abrams, Creighton, 40
Ackerman, Spencer, 62, 139
Adelman, Ken, 129
Afghanistan, 224–225
  Beers on, 111
  Kucinich on, 90
  Soviet military action in, 41–43
  U.S. military action in, 45–51,
    58, 135–136, 179–184
  See also Iraq War; Qaeda, al-
Against All Enemies (Clarke),
  111–112
Allawi, Iyad, 136–142, 159
al-Qaeda. *See* Qaeda, al-
American Enterprise Institute,
  43, 97
American Israel Public Affairs
  Committee (AIPAC),
  169, 170
*American Political Science
  Review*, 134
American Prospect, 50
Americans for Democratic
  Action, 90
"Anbar Awakening," 215–216
Anderson, Jack, 31
Anti-Ballistic Missile Treaty, 29
AQI (Iraq forces), 215–216
Arab-Israeli conflict, 49, 51,
  68–70, 202–203

"Arab Spring," 146–147. *See also*
  democracy-promotion
  strategy
Aristide, Jean-Bertrand, 145
Armitage, Richard, 49, 202
Asad, Bashar, 165
Assassins' Gate, The (Packer),
  66–67

Baathist Party, 48–49, 56, 96
Baker, James, 154–155, 160–166
Baker-Hamilton Commission.
  See Iraq Study Group (ISG)
Balkans. *See* Bosnia and
  Herzegovina; Kosovo
Barber, Benjamin, 18
Barnes, Fred, 152
Bayh, Evan, 142, 185
Beers, Rand, 110–111
Beinart, Peter, 2, 65, 93,
    177, 196
  on Bush's democracy-
    promotion strategy, 142–143
  on 2004 presidential election,
    120–121, 123
Berman, Ari, 114
Better War, A (Sorley), 40
Biden, Joseph, 2, 73–75, 120,
    141–142, 156, 221
Biden-Lugar resolution (on Iraq
    War), 73–75